More praise for

CAREER AND FAMILY

"Career & Family is a radical book. It is also brilliantly researched and argued."
—LILY MEYER, *New Republic*

"Goldin weaves together complicated data sets that no one else thought to look at."
—JOAN C. WILLIAMS, *Times Literary Supplement*

"[*Career and Family*] looks at how women have struggled to balance work and home over the decades. Among its many takeaways is the notion that female participation in the workplace changes the very nature of work."
—RANA FOROOHAR, *Financial Times*

"This is no ordinary book. . . . Goldin has written a chatty, readable sequel to [*The Feminine Mystique*]."
—DAVID WARSH, *Economic Principals*

"A must-read for those who care about gender gaps. . . . Goldin does a compelling job of running through the historical data, providing the surrounding cultural context, and explaining how technological and legal changes affected women over the years. . . . Goldin expertly lays out the history of college-grad women's advances in the work force, and she carefully dissects where the remaining gender gap originates."
—ROBERT VERBRUGGEN, Institute for Family Studies

"The COVID-19 pandemic exposed the frustration of mothers who are fed up and exhausted. In a sweeping overview of a century of change in how women work and have families, Claudia Goldin gives this problem a name: greedy work. Her tour de force shows us where we have been and where we must go if women are ever to achieve full equality in their marriages and their jobs."
—BETSEY STEVENSON, University of Michigan

"Now, for the first time in history, women can have families *and* careers. Read Goldin's masterpiece to understand the causes of this twentieth-century transformation and the pathway to gender equality."
—ALICE EVANS, King's College London

"In classic fashion, Claudia Goldin carefully marshals a century's worth of economic data to analyze gender inequity in the household and in the labor market. This sweeping, meticulously researched book is essential reading for those who seek to understand the dimensions and origins of the gender pay gap."

—LISA D. COOK, Michigan State University

"Girls do better than boys in high school, and women are more likely than men to graduate from college, yet men still earn more than women. How come? Claudia Goldin is the expert on this question, and *Career & Family* provides a comprehensive answer in what is the equivalent of a historical novel spanning five generations. The book is concise, thorough, and completely engaging."

—RICHARD H. THALER, coauthor of *Nudge: Improving Decisions about Health, Wealth, and Happiness*

"*Career and Family* provides real answers to a century's worth of questions about the drivers of gender inequality. With the rigor of an economist and the deft touch of a humanist, Goldin combines data with individual life stories, leaving no doubt that the problem lies in the nature of work rather than the nature of women. After reading this book, it is impossible to ignore the unavoidable reliance of the economy on caregiving and the necessity of society-wide solutions."

—ANNE-MARIE SLAUGHTER, author of *Unfinished Business: Women Men Work Family*

CAREER & FAMILY

Career & Family

WOMEN'S CENTURY-LONG JOURNEY
TOWARD EQUITY

CLAUDIA GOLDIN

PRINCETON UNIVERSITY PRESS
PRINCETON & OXFORD

Published by Princeton University Press
41 William Street, Princeton, New Jersey 08540
99 Banbury Road, Oxford OX2 6JX

press.princeton.edu

First paperback printing, 2023
Paperback ISBN 9780691228662

The Library of Congress has cataloged the cloth edition as follows:

Names: Goldin, Claudia Dale, author.
Title: Career and family : women's century-long journey toward equity /
    Claudia Goldin.
Description: Princeton, New Jersey : Princeton University Press, [2021] |
    Includes bibliographical references and index.
Identifiers: LCCN 2021012483 (print) | LCCN 2021012484 (ebook) |
    ISBN 9780691201788 (hardback) | ISBN 9780691226736 (ebook)
Subjects: LCSH: Pay equity—United States. | Wages—Women—United States. |
    Dual-career families—United States. | BISAC: SOCIAL SCIENCE /
    Gender Studies | SOCIAL SCIENCE / Sociology / Marriage & Family
Classification: LCC HD6061.2.U6 G65 2021 (print) | LCC HD6061.2.U6 (ebook) |
    DDC 331.4/21530973—dc23
LC record available at https://lccn.loc.gov/2021012483
LC ebook record available at https://lccn.loc.gov/2021012484

British Library Cataloging-in-Publication Data is available

Editorial: Joe Jackson, Josh Drake
Production: Danielle Amatucci
Publicity: James Schneider, Kate Farquhar-Thomson
Copyeditor: Kelley Blewster

This book has been composed in Arno Pro

CONTENTS

LIST OF FIGURES AND TABLE

Figures

Table

LIST OF ONLINE FIGURES,
TABLES, AND SOURCES

THESE MATERIALS *can be found on the book's PUP webpage or at this link:* https://assets.press.princeton.edu/releases/m30613.pdf

Chapter 2

Chapter 3

Chapter 4

Chapter 5

Chapter 7

Chapter 8

Chapter 9

Chapter 10

Epilogue

1

The New Problem with No Name

NOW, MORE THAN EVER, couples of all stripes are struggling to balance employment and family, their work lives and home lives. As a nation, we are collectively waking up to the importance of caregiving, to its value, for the present and for future generations. We are starting to fully realize its cost in terms of lost income, flattened careers, and trade-offs between couples (heterosexual and same sex), as well as the particularly strenuous demands on single mothers and fathers. These realizations predated the pandemic but have been brought into sharp focus by it.

In 1963, Betty Friedan wrote about college-educated women who were frustrated as stay-at-home moms, noting that their problem "has no name." Almost sixty years later, female college graduates are largely on career tracks, but their earnings and promotions—relative to those of the men they graduated with—continue to make them look like they've been sideswiped. They, too, have a "problem with no name."

But their problem goes by many names: sex discrimination, gender bias, glass ceiling, mommy track, leaning out—take your pick. And the problem seems to have immediate solutions. We should coach women to be more competitive and train them to negotiate better. We need to expose managers' implicit bias. The government should impose gender-parity mandates on corporate boards and enforce the equal-pay-for-equal-work doctrine.

Women in the US and elsewhere are clamoring ever more loudly for such an answer. Their concerns are splattered across national headlines (and book jackets). Do they need more drive? Do they need to lean in? Why aren't women able to advance up the corporate ladder at the speed of their male counterparts? Why aren't they compensated at the level their experience and seniority deserve?

More private doubts haunt many women, doubts that are shared in their intimate partnerships or relegated to private discussions with close friends. Should you date someone whose career is just as time consuming as your own? Should you put off having a family, even if you're sure you want one? Should you freeze your eggs if you aren't partnered by thirty-five? Are you willing to walk away from an ambitious career (maybe one you've been building toward ever since you took your SAT) to raise kids? If you aren't, who will pack the lunches, pick up your child from swim practice, and answer the panic-inducing call from the school nurse?

Women continue to feel shortchanged. They fall behind in their careers while earning less than their husbands and male colleagues. They are told that their problems are of their own doing. They don't compete aggressively enough or negotiate sufficiently; they don't claim a seat at the table, and when they do, they don't ask for enough. But women are also told that their problems are *not* their own doing, even as the problems are their undoing. They are taken advantage of, discriminated against, harassed, and excluded from the boys' club.

All these factors are real. But are they the root of the problem? Do they add up to the major difference between men and women in their salaries and careers? If they were all miraculously fixed, would the world of women and men, the world of couples and young parents, look completely different? Are they collectively the "new problem with no name"?

Although lively public and private discourse has brought these important issues to light, we're often guilty of disregarding the enormous scale and long history of gender disparities. A single company slapped on the wrist, one more woman who makes it to the boardroom, a few progressive tech leaders who go on paternity leave—such solutions are the economic equivalent of tossing a box of Band-Aids to someone with bubonic plague.

These responses haven't worked to erase the differences in the gender pay gap. And they will never provide a complete solution to gender inequality, because they treat only the symptoms. They will never enable women to achieve both career and family to the same degree as men. If we want to eradicate or even narrow the pay gap, we must first plunge deeper toward the root of these setbacks and give the problem a more accurate name: greedy work.

I can only hope that by the time you read this, the pandemic—still raging as I finish this chapter—will have subsided and that we will have benefited from its harsh lessons. The pandemic magnified some issues, accelerated others, and exposed still more that had been festering for a very long time. But the tug between care and work that we are facing preceded this global catastrophe by many decades. Indeed, the journey to attaining, then balancing, career and family has been in motion for more than a century.

For much of the twentieth century, discrimination against women was a major bar to their ability to have a career. Historical documents from the 1930s to the 1950s reveal easily spotted smoking guns—actual evidence of prejudice and discrimination in employment and earnings. In the late 1930s, firm managers told survey agents, "Loan work is not suitable for girls," "People with these jobs [automobile sales] are in contact with the public . . . women wouldn't be acceptable," and "Would not put a woman in [brokerage] sales work." That was at the end of the Great Depression. But even during the tight labor market of the late 1950s, company representatives categorically stated, "Mothers of young children are not hired," "Married women with . . . infants are not encouraged to return to work," and "Pregnancy is cause for a voluntary resignation [although] the company is glad to have the women return when the children are, perhaps, in junior high school."

Marriage bars—laws and company policies that restricted married women's employment—were rampant until the 1940s. They morphed into pregnancy bars and hiring policies that excluded women with infants and small children. Academic institutions and some government agencies had nepotism bars. Countless jobs were restricted by sex, marital status, and, of course, race.

Today, we don't see such explicit smoking guns. Data now show that true pay and employment discrimination, while they matter, are relatively small. This does not mean that many women don't face discrimination and bias, or that sexual harassment and assault do not exist in the workplace. We have not seen a nationwide #MeToo movement for nothing. In the late 1990s, Lilly Ledbetter filed an EEOC sexual harassment case against Goodyear Tire and won the right to sue. That was a real victory for her, but she dropped the charges when she was reinstated as a supervisor. This occurred years before she brought her now-famous case of pay discrimination. Ledbetter received low performance ratings and almost no pay raises because of discriminatory behavior by the men she supervised and by those who were ultimately in command but who ignored the sexism of those beneath them. In Ledbetter's case, 100 percent of the difference between her pay and that of her peers was due to discrimination.

So why *do* earnings differences persist when gender equality at work seems to finally be within our grasp, and at a time when more professions are open to women than ever before? Are women actually receiving *lower* pay for *equal* work? By and large, not so much anymore. Pay discrimination in terms of unequal earnings for the same work accounts for a small fraction of the total earnings gap. Today, the problem is different.

Some attribute the gender earnings gap to "occupational segregation"— the idea that women and men are self-selecting, or being railroaded into, certain professions that are stereotypically gendered (such as nurse versus doctor, teacher versus professor), and that those chosen professions pay differently. The data tell a somewhat different story. For the nearly five hundred occupations listed in the US census, two-thirds of the gender-based difference in earnings comes from factors *within* each occupation. Even if women's occupations followed the male distribution—if women were the doctors and men were the nurses—it would wipe out only, at most, a third of the difference in earnings between men and women.

Thus, we empirically know that the lion's share of the pay gap comes from something else.

Longitudinal data—information that follows the lives and earnings of individuals—allow us to see that right out of college (or out of graduate school), wages for men and women are strikingly similar. In the first few years of employment, the pay gap is modest for recent college graduates and newly minted MBAs, for example, and is largely explained by differences in male and female fields of study and occupational choices. Men and women start out on an almost equal footing. They have very similar opportunities but make somewhat different choices, producing a slight initial wage gap.

It is only further along in their lives, about ten years after college graduation, that large differences in pay for men and women become apparent. They work in different parts of the marketplace, for different firms. Unsurprisingly, these changes typically begin a year or two after a child is born and almost always negatively impact women's careers. But the gap in their income also starts to widen right after marriage.

The advent of women's careers fundamentally changed the relationship between the American family and the economy. We will never get to the bottom of the gender earnings gap until we understand the trajectory of the far larger problem of which it is a symptom. The gender earnings gap is a result of the career gap; the career gap is at the root of couple inequity. To truly grasp what that means, we need to take a voyage through women's role in the American economy and consider how it has transformed across the course of the last century.

Our focus will be mainly on college-graduate women, as they have had the most opportunities to achieve a career, and their numbers have been expanding for some time. As of 2020, almost 45 percent of twenty-five-year-old women have graduated, or will soon graduate, from a four-year college. The level for men is just 36 percent. Women, of course, didn't always outnumber men as college graduates. For a long time, and for many reasons, women were at a great disadvantage in attending and graduating from college. In 1960, there were 1.6 males for every female graduating from a US four-year college or university. But beginning in the late 1960s and early 1970s, things began to change. By 1980, men's advantage had evaporated. Since then, more women than men have graduated from four-year institutions each year.

And they aren't just graduating from colleges and universities in record numbers—they are setting their sights higher and higher. More than ever before, these graduates are aiming for premier postbachelor's degrees and subsequent challenging careers. Just prior to the Great Recession, 23 percent of college-graduate women were earning one of the highest professional degrees, including a JD, a PhD, an MD, or an MBA. That reflects more than a fourfold increase across the previous four decades. For men, that fraction remained around 30 percent during the same forty-year period. Women have increasingly been planning to have long-term, highly remunerative, and fulfilling careers—sustained achievement that becomes embedded as part of an individual's identity.

More of them are also having children—more than at any time since the end of the Baby Boom. Almost 80 percent of college-graduate women who are today in their mid- to late forties have given birth to a child (add 1.5 percentage points to include adoptions to those without a birth). Fifteen years ago, just 73 percent of all college-graduate women in their mid-forties had at least one birth. So college-graduate women born around the early 1970s have a considerably higher birth rate than college-graduate women born in the mid-1950s. There are now more women than ever like Keisha Lance Bottoms, Liz Cheney, Tammy Duckworth, Samantha Power, and Lori Trahan—all of whom have had successful careers plus children and are currently around fifty years old.

College-graduate women no longer accept without question having a career but no family. Those who have children are no longer fully content to have a family but no career. By and large, college-graduate women want success in both arenas. But to do so requires negotiating a slew of time conflicts and making a host of difficult choices.

Time is a great equalizer. We all have the same amount and must make difficult choices in its allocation. The fundamental problem for women trying to attain the balance of a successful career and a joyful family are time conflicts. Investing in a career often means considerable time input early on, precisely during the years one "should" be having children. Enjoying one's family also involves considerable time. Those choices have dynamic consequences, and we have little ability to make amends for bad decisions. Fifty years ago, when advising younger women about career, one female business executive and mother of three said, "It's hard—but do it."

We are always making choices, like partying or studying, taking hard courses or taking easy ones. Some, naturally, are more momentous. Marry early; marry late. Go to graduate school; get a job now. Have a child now; take a big chance that you won't be able to later. Spend time with a client; spend time with a child. Those big, consequential choices regarding time allocation for college-graduate women begin around when they receive their bachelor's degrees.

Not long ago, marriages among college graduates occurred at astoundingly early ages. Until around 1970, the median age at first marriage for a college-graduate woman was about twenty-three years old. The first child was born soon after. Early marriage often precluded further study for women, at least immediately. Newly married couples moved more often for the husbands' career and education than for the wives'. Women didn't always maximize their own future career prospects. Instead, they often sacrificed their careers to optimize the family's well-being.

For women who graduated college from the 1940s to the late 1960s, early marriages occurred because marriage delay was a challenge. Getting pinned, lavaliered, and—the ultimate—engaged soon after starting a serious (and sexual) relationship was an important insurance policy against having a premarital pregnancy. In a world without female-controlled and highly effective contraception, choice was constrained.

By 1961, the Pill had been invented, FDA approved, and procured by large numbers of married women. But state laws and social convention did not allow the Pill to be disseminated among young, single women. Those restrictions began to break down around 1970 for various reasons, most unrelated to contraception. The Pill gave college-graduate women a newfound ability to plan their lives and to obviate the first of the constraints. They could enroll in time-consuming—actually all-consuming—postbachelor's education and training. Marriage and children could be delayed, just long enough for a woman to lay the foundations of a sustaining career.

That's when things began to change, radically. After 1970, the age at first marriage started to increase, and it continued to climb year after year—so that the median age of first marriage for college-graduate women is now around twenty-eight years old.

But even as the time-constraint problem was solved, others cropped up. Postgraduate education began to start later in the lives of college graduates and take longer to complete. The time to first promotion in a host of fields from academia to health, law, accounting, and consulting was increasingly delayed. The additional years mounted, resulting in yet another time conflict that had to be negotiated.

About a decade or more ago, a first promotion occurred in one's early thirties. More recently, it occurs in one's mid- to late thirties. The timing no longer comfortably allows for giving birth to one's first child after one's first promotion to partner, tenure, or other advancement. The first birth often occurs before these career milestones. Children often upend careers. And careers often upend the ability of women to have children.

The timing is brutal. For women who want to have a family, waiting to their mid-thirties to have their first child is stacking the deck against succeeding at the family part and having the children. Yet college-graduate women have managed to beat the odds through various means, including the use of assisted-reproductive technologies. The fraction of women with children has startlingly increased for those who recently turned forty-five years old. The increased birth rate doesn't diminish the frustrations, sadness, and physical pain for those who tried and did not succeed. For those who did succeed, it doesn't mean that they can maintain their careers.

Even with all these difficulties, much has changed historically in a positive direction, bringing us closer to more self-efficacy for women and greater gender equality. Women have better control of their fertility. Marriages are entered into later and, in consequence, last longer. Women are now the overwhelming fraction of college graduates. Multitudes of them enter professional- and graduate-degree programs and graduate at the top of their classes. The best firms, organizations, and departments are hiring them. Then what happens?

If a woman's career has a chance to flourish and she manages to have children, the ultimate time conflict emerges. Children take time. Careers take time. Even the wealthiest of couples can't contract out all care. And why bring children into this world if you aren't going to love and nurture them?

The fundamental time constraint is to negotiate who will be on call at home—that is, who will leave the office and be at home in a pinch. Both parents could be. That couple equity would yield the ultimate fifty-fifty sharing. But how much would that cost the family? A lot—a reality couples are more aware of now than ever before.

As aspirations for both career and family have increased, an important part of most careers has become apparent, visible, and central. Work, for many on the career track, is greedy. The individual who puts in overtime, weekend time, or evening time will earn a lot more—so much more that, even on an hourly basis, the person is earning more.

Greedy Work

The greediness of work means that couples with children or other care responsibilities would gain by doing a bit of specialization. This specialization doesn't mean catapulting back to the world of *Leave It to Beaver*. Women will still pursue demanding careers. But one member of the couple will be on call at home, ready to leave the office or workplace at a moment's notice. That person will have a position with considerable flexibility and will ordinarily not be expected to answer an e-mail or a call at ten p.m. That parent will not have to cancel an appearance at soccer practice for an M&A. The other parent, however, will be on call at work and do just the opposite. The potential impact on promotion, advancement, and earnings is obvious.

The work of professionals and managers has always been greedy. Lawyers have always burned the midnight oil. Academics have always been judged for their cerebral output and are expected not to turn their brains off in the evenings. Most doctors and veterinarians were once on call 24/7.

The value of greedy jobs has greatly increased with rising income inequality, which has soared since the early 1980s. Earnings at the very upper end of the income distribution have ballooned. The worker who jumps the highest gets an ever-bigger reward. The jobs with the greatest demands for long hours and the least flexibility have paid disproportionately more, while earnings in other employments have stagnated. Thus, positions that have been more difficult for women to enter in the first place, such as those in finance, are precisely the ones that have seen the greatest increases in income in the last several decades. The private equity associate who sees the deal through from beginning to end, who did the difficult modeling, and who went to every meeting and late-night dinner, will have maximum chance for a big bonus and the sought-after promotion.

Rising inequality in earnings may be one important reason why the gender pay gap among college graduates has remained flat in the last several decades, despite improvements in women's credentials and positions. It may be the reason why the gender earnings gap for college graduates became larger than that between men and women in the entire population in the late 1980s and early 1990s. Women have been swimming upstream, holding their own but going against a strong current of endemic income inequality.

Greedy work also means that couple equity has been, and will continue to be, jettisoned for increased family income. And when couple equity is thrown out the window, gender equality generally goes with it, except among same-sex unions. Gender norms that we have inherited get reinforced in a host of ways to allot more of the childcare responsibility to mothers, and more of the family care to grown daughters.

Consider a married couple, Isabel and Lucas (modeled after a couple I met several years ago). They both graduated from the same liberal arts college and later earned identical advanced degrees in information technology (IT). They were then hired by the same firm, which we'll call InfoServices.

InfoServices gave each of them a choice between two positions. The first job has standard hours and comes with the possibility of flexibility in start and finish times. The second has unpredictable on-call evening and weekend hours, though the total number of annual hours doesn't necessarily increase by much. The second position pays 20 percent more, to attract talent willing to work with uncertain times and days. It is also the position from which InfoServices selects its managers. It is the "greedy" position, and both Isabel and Lucas initially opted for it. Equally capable and equally free of external obligations, the two spent a few years working at the same level and pay.

In her late twenties, Isabel determined that she needed more flexibility and space in her life, in order to spend more time with her ailing mother. She stayed with InfoServices but opted for the position that, although it required the same number of hours, was more flexible regarding which hours were to be worked. It was less greedy in its demands and less generous in its pay.

We can see their trajectories in figure 1.1. The path on which they both started and where Lucas remained—the greedy, inflexible one—is given by the solid line and has an hourly wage (implicit if the person is salaried, and explicit if the person is paid by the hour) that rises with the number of hours, or perhaps with particular hourly demands. If he works sixty hours a week, he would be paid *more than* one and a half times what he would make if he put in forty hours. Lucas's implicit hourly wage increases with hours worked (or with the inflexibility of hours), which means he could double his weekly earnings even if he didn't work twice the number of hours per week.

Isabel's new role, the more flexible position, is given by the dashed line. Her hourly wage is constant, so it doesn't matter how many hours she works or which hours she works; the wage is the same. If she works sixty hours, she would get one and a half times what she would for working forty hours. A usual week of work puts Lucas, in his greedy position, at the diamond. Equivalently, a usual work week in Isabel's new job places her at the dot.

When the couple decided to have a child, at least one parent needed to be available on call. They could not both work in the position Lucas had, with its inflexible and unpredictable hours. If they did, neither

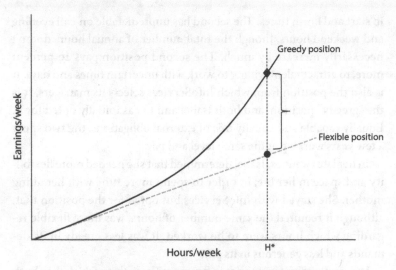

FIGURE 1.1. Gender Inequality and Couple Inequity
Notes: Consider the two positions offered to Isabel and Lucas. One is flexible, and no matter how many hours the employee works per week, the pay per hour is the same. The other position is less flexible (or "greedy"), and the more hours that are worked, the higher the wage per hour. The horizontal axis gives hours worked per week (or a measure indicating that particular hours must be worked). The vertical axis gives the total earnings per week. H* is a usual weekly hours number, such as 40 or 45. The difference between the diamond (the greedy position) and the dot (the flexible position) illustrates the amount of income that a worker gives up each week by not taking the greedy position.

would be available in case the school nurse called or the child's daycare center suddenly closed in the middle of the day. If the position required that they be in the office on Thursdays at precisely eleven a.m., they would have to just hope that their child would not fall off the swing around that hour or that an older family member wouldn't have a doctor's appointment then.

Both of them *could* have worked at Isabel's position. But, especially because they were planning a family, they couldn't afford that decision. Doing so would mean that each would forgo the amount of additional income per week that Lucas brought in. If they wanted to share the childcare fifty-fifty, they needed to weigh that desire against how much that would cost them. It could be a lot—significant enough that they would have to sacrifice couple equity for a higher family income.

As is the case with most heterosexual couples expecting a child, Isabel remained at the flexible position while Lucas stayed at the greedier one. (That would hold true even if we excluded the initial months after delivery and throughout their child's infancy.)

Lucas continued to earn more than Isabel, and the earnings gap only expanded after they had children. He got the promotions; she did not. For other couples in similar positions, the difference in pay might expand even more before having the children, since couples planning for a family often relocate to optimize employment possibilities, especially that of the husband. This is a big part of why the gender gap in pay is still substantial.

For same-sex couples, there will not be a gender earnings gap, but couple equity will likely be jettisoned for precisely the same reasons that motivated Isabel's and Lucas's decisions. In a world of greedy jobs, couple equity is expensive.

If women weren't on call at home, they could take jobs with disproportionately high pay for long hours, unpredictable schedules, on-call evenings, and occasional weekends—and indeed many women do. Choosing long and demanding hours is fine for women right out of college and for those with fewer household responsibilities. But once a baby arrives, priorities change. Primary caregiving is time consuming, and women are suddenly on call at home. To be more available to their families, they must be less available to their employers and clients. As a result, they tend to cut back hours, or they take jobs in areas of the marketplace that offer more flexibility—and earn far less. These responsibilities are reduced as children get older and become more independent, and women's earnings do rise relative to men's at those times. But other family demands often creep in somewhat later in life, replacing the reduced child demands.

Isabel and Lucas's story is not unusual. As college graduates find life partnerships and begin planning families, in the starkest terms they are faced with a choice between a marriage of equals and a marriage with more money.

A Marriage of Equals

Some time ago, I asked the students in my undergraduate seminar what they wanted out of a marriage. One of my students replied in an instant: "I want a man who wants what I want." Her answer struck me as a candid statement of a desire for equity. It has since been repeated by many students and friends of mine, but never as succinctly and clearly. The continuing quandary, however, is that even if that match were made, it will be costly in terms of family equity for both to have demanding careers, or costly in terms of family income for both to have less demanding careers. To maximize the family's potential income, one partner commits to the time-consuming job at the office while the other makes career sacrifices to take on the time-consuming job at home. Regardless of gender, the latter will earn less.

Gender is not a factor that can be ignored, because the person who sacrifices career to be home is—historically and still today—most often a woman. Women aren't lazy or less talented, and they start out on a fairly equal footing with men. Due in part to the entrenched gender norms we'll be exploring, even ambitious, talented women have felt the need to slow down their careers for the greater good of their family. *Men are able to have a family and step up because women step back from their careers to provide more time for the family.* Both are deprived: men forgo time with family; women forgo career.

To the modern reader, the idea of women having careers from which to step back or toward which to step up may seem so normalized as to be unnoteworthy. Women go to school, just like men, and pursue higher education and profitable careers, just like men. But it's worth pausing to reflect on just how new this situation is. In 1900, very few college-graduate women with young children were in the labor force, let alone had anything resembling a career. Those devoted to work generally did not have children and often did not marry. More than a century later, women are not just working; they have meaningful careers that many manage, or intend, to combine with a family in an equitable marriage. In all of world history, this has never happened before.

When more than half the population's economic role changes, it marks a staggering historical shift—one that has had immense ramifications. The lives of college-graduate women have evolved the most radically, but the effects of this profound shift have reverberated throughout American society, affecting the whole social organization of work, schools, and families. When women moved from home to the workplace, they didn't just move from unpaid work to paying work. They moved from domestic responsibilities to positions that required extensive education, that became part of their identities, and that often spanned the course of their lives.

Every generation of women in the twentieth century took another step along this journey, while a host of advances in the home, the firm, the school, and in contraception paved the way for this progress. Each generation expanded its horizons, learning from the successes and failures of the preceding generation and leaving lessons for the next wave of women. Each generation passed a baton from one to the next. The journey has taken us from the stark choice of having a family *or* a career to the possibility of having a career *and* a family. It has also been a journey to greater pay equity and couple equity. It is a complicated and multifaceted progression that is still unfolding.

If this shift across the decades has been overwhelmingly positive, why are we still wrestling with gaping differences between men's and women's earnings, occupations, and positions, and with the yawning disparities between their family responsibilities?

Modern young women, especially during the ongoing COVID crisis, are anxious—and rightly so. Despite their travels along this road that was paved by their great-grandmothers, grandmothers, and mothers (most of whom were anxious, too), they are still caught between devoting themselves to a career and devoting themselves to a family. With technological advances and increases in education, professional degrees, and opportunities, many barriers have been removed and discriminatory roadblocks to women's success have been toppled. As we'll see, throughout the century-long journey, layers of gender differences have been shed, barriers to women's employment have been knocked down, and a host of time constraints have been removed. Clouds have parted. And with better light, the reasons for the final difference have now become apparent.

Collectively, we have arrived at a moment when we can ask how to alter the system to bring about greater gender equality and couple equity. How can we change the basic diagram, that of Lucas's greedy job and Isabel's flexible job, to achieve both? The answer, as we'll discover, is that we must change how work is structured.

We have to make flexible positions more abundant and more productive. Determining whether and how that can be done is where this journey will take us. It will reveal the need for greater support to allow parents and other caregivers to be more productive members of the economy. It will clarify the relationship between the productivity of the economy and the care of preschool and school-aged children—the subject that has been brought home and made so relevant, suddenly and swiftly.

At the moment when we could more clearly see why achieving career and family is so difficult for women—and thereby envisage a solution—we were engulfed in a pandemic of global proportions. A tsunami swept over us. We moved from BCE (Before the Corona Era) to DC (During Corona); from an "old normal" to circumstances that have upended families, sickened millions, killed hundreds of thousands in the US, and erased years of economic growth from the world's nations. It may also have tossed many young mothers off their precarious career ladders as they tried to write briefs, academic papers, and consulting reports, and to care for clients and patients, all while teaching their children addition and subtraction.

We are now moving into an uncharted AC/DC era—a world that is partially After Corona (AC), in the sense that many schools and businesses have opened, but with many of the restrictions and remnants of the DC world. The shift to an AC/DC world has revealed another defect in the American society and economy: caregiving, so critical to the career goals of women and to couple equity, is also crucial to the running of the entire economy. Women cannot be essential workers in two places at the same time. Something has to give.

We will return—many pages from here—to examining the AC/DC world, but to fully grasp how we got here and how we can best use this opportunity to overhaul greedy work, we must return to the beginning. The desire among college-graduate women for career and family has been long in the making. That aspiration has been brewing, changing, emerging, and morphing through several key phases of our history.

At the beginning of our travels, when there were enormous differences between men's and women's education and when running a household required much more time and labor, no one could have realized what the last impediments to a level playing field would have been: the structure of work and our caregiving institutions.

Though we've reached an unprecedented era of equality between men and women economically, in some ways we are still living in the dark ages. Our work and care structures are relics of a past when only men had both careers and families. Our entire economy is trapped in an old way of functioning, hampered by primeval methods of dividing responsibilities.

As more women than ever aspire to have careers, families, and couple equity, and as more couples than ever navigate competing time demands, it is imperative that we understand what the economic gender gap actually reveals about our economy and our society—so that we can work toward solutions that close it and make work and life more equitable for everyone. The data in the chapters that follow will demonstrate the progress made in each generation, how gender norms and workplace structures have evolved for decades, and how the journey must continue.

This book is the story of how the aspirations of career, family, and equity emerged over the past century, and how they can be achieved today. There is no one simple fix, but by finally understanding the problem and calling it by the right name, we will be able to pave a better route forward.

2

Passing the Baton

JEANNETTE PICKERING RANKIN was born in Hellgate Township, Montana Territory, in 1880 and graduated from the University of Montana in 1902. With her initial goal set on social work, she devoted herself to the women's suffrage movement on both coasts, eventually becoming a leader in the national movement after she returned to Montana. In 1916, she won a seat in the House of Representatives, making her the first woman elected to a federal position. She was the only woman empowered to vote for the legislation on which she had worked tirelessly and to send the Nineteenth Amendment—for women's suffrage—to the states for ratification.

An ardent pacifist, Rankin recorded one of the fifty negative votes in Congress in 1917 when war was declared on Germany. She subsequently did not seek reelection in the House and instead sought a Senate seat, unsuccessfully. Many years later, in 1940, she recaptured her House seat, just in time to be the only dissenting vote recorded on December 8, 1941, when the US declared war on Japan. She refused, despite heavy pressure, to make the vote unanimous, insisting, "As a woman I cannot go to war and I refuse to send anyone else."

Although she reached a distinct, singular status in the political realm, she was typical of the college-graduate career woman of her day. She had no children; she never married. Among the twenty-three women of her generation who were elected as US Representatives, more than 30 percent never had children. As high as that figure may seem, it is considerably lower than the fraction of all college-graduate women of that era who would never have (or adopt) a child.

Fast forward to Tammy Duckworth, born in 1968 and a 1989 graduate of the University of Hawaii. She was elected to the House in 2012 and became an Illinois senator in 2016. Her first child was born in 2014, when she was forty-six years old; her second child was born in 2018. Her daughter Maile was the first infant in US history to enter the hallowed halls of a Congress in session. Senator Duckworth has been a pioneer in many ways: she is a decorated veteran, the first disabled woman elected to Congress, and the first Asian American woman elected from Illinois. And, remarkably, she has successfully maintained both a rewarding career and a family.

She's not alone in Congress. New York's current senator Kirsten Gillibrand, born in 1966, has two children. Her second was born in 2008, while she was a member of the House. Representative Jaime Herrera Beutler, from Washington and born in 1978, has had three children since 2013. Ten female members of Congress, from both sides of the aisle, have had children while in office. Other than Yvonne Brathwaite Burke, who in 1973 was the first Congresswoman to have a child while in office, the other nine female members of Congress (the House) who have given birth at least once while in office have all had the births since 1995 at ages that range from thirty-four to forty-six. These women have combined career and family, just as their male colleagues in Congress have always been able to do.

Rankin and Duckworth represent the bookends of five distinct groups of college-graduate women born since the late nineteenth century. Rankin is a member of Group One and Duckworth of Group Five. The women within each of the five groups are more similar to each other than they are to those in other groups.

Although there is a starting point for the groups, there is no end point—just yet. For the purposes of our journey, Group Five's birth year ends around 1980, so that we can observe the trajectories of women into their early forties, to get a fuller understanding of their careers and family histories. In consequence, a woman such as Representative

Alexandria Ocasio-Cortez, born in 1989, will not factor into the data that we'll be exploring.

To get a sense of the journey women have taken, let's briefly get to know each group of women from Group One to Group Five.

The distinctions among the groups are focused on their aspirations, and on the choices that they made, were encouraged to make, and were enabled to make, in the realms of employment and family. Jeannette Rankin's college-graduate group almost always had to choose between employment—sometimes a career, though more often a job—and family. A century later, Duckworth's peers have the desire and expectation to achieve both.

Throughout the century, women faced obstacles in both areas, work and family. There were hiring restrictions, such as bans against the employment of married women as teachers, or limitations in many office positions. There were prohibitions on whether a woman could obtain an advanced degree from an institution. Some of the best law, business, and medical schools were closed to women. Firms offered certain occupations to men only and others to women only. Many were exclusively given to whites, so the barriers to women of color were even higher. The social norms of communities and families provided less official but just as potent injunctions that mothers should not work when their children were young—or ever.

These statutory and procedural barriers that once constrained women's ability to achieve have, for the most part, been dismantled. Social norms have largely changed. But sexism, old-boy networks, and sexual harassment remain. The journey toward the career and family destination has been an arduous one—a long, twisting road trip with ups and downs, blockades and tolls. Though the ambitions of women to achieve career and family began long before, our adventure will start a little more than a century ago, when reliable, trustworthy sources were first recorded, especially in the US census of population.

No definition of family or career will be perfect for everyone, nor will it be all inclusive. But in order to reach a more lucid understanding of the shifts in women's choices, ambitions, and opportunities over the past century, it is necessary to draw distinct lines and create reliable definitions.

For our journey across the century of women, "family" is defined as having a child—including by adoption—but not necessarily a spouse. Families are highly personal entities. I have a husband and a dog, and they are my family. But according to my definition in the pages that follow, they would not constitute a family.

"Career," while less personal, is also tricky to define. The word "career" comes from a Latin word that means to run a race. "Chariot" and "carriage" come from the same root. Career is a "course" or progression through life. It must continue across some period of time. The term "career" does not mean just being employed. A career generally involves advancement and persistence. It involves learning, growing, investing, and reaping the returns. For the women we'll be tracking, a career is defined as long-lasting, sought-after employment for which the type of work—writer, teacher, doctor, accountant—often shapes one's identity. A career needn't begin right after the highest educational degree; it can emerge later in life.

Jobs, on the other hand, generally do not become part of one's identity or life's purpose. They are often solely taken for generating income and generally do not have a clear set of milestones. But "a career," noted a member of Group Two interviewed in the 1970s, "demands full attention—to build and to progress. Otherwise it is not a career but a job."

In practice, careers are an individual's concept of employment, for which pay may not matter. Volunteers and community leaders have bettered the lives of many, even if they earn little or nothing. But despite the important role of saints and saviors, the greatest insights about women's progress can be gleaned by using a definition of career anchored in an individual's employment and earnings across some period of time. The Source Appendix (Ch7), "Career and Family Success," describes the definition of career that I employ.

––––––––––

Sandra Day O'Connor served on the law review of her Stanford law school class in 1952—yet she couldn't land a job in any law firm. Shirley Chisolm broke boundaries as the first Black woman elected to Congress, the first woman to run for the Democratic Party's nomination for president, and the first Black person to do so. She was married twice and had no children. Virginia Apgar, the physician and obstetric anesthesiologist who devised the infant score that bears her name, was born in 1909. She abandoned her quest to become a surgeon after her mentor cautioned her against attempting a surgical residency since, he said, too many women had failed at that endeavor. Instead, he encouraged Apgar to enter the new field of anesthesiology, which had previously been a nursing specialty. Apgar never married, remarking, "It's just that I haven't found a man who can cook."

O'Connor, Chisolm, and Apgar were each thwarted and discouraged in various ways, but they all persevered. They were extraordinary. Few people go to law school only to be denied a job after passing the bar. No one wants to be told that she cannot follow her dreams on account of sex. Most women do not want to pursue a challenging career if they have to sacrifice having children, getting married, or having a meaningful relationship to do so. An unquantifiable load of women's talents that we don't know about has been underutilized.

As fewer women were thwarted from their goals, career and family—which had long been the presumption for most college-graduate men—became twin aspirations of college-graduate women. This remarkable convergence of ambitions of male and female college graduates matters because just about everyone has benefited from this alignment—not merely the women who are leading increasingly satisfying and meaningful lives. The convergence means a whole lot more than just individual gains. The impacts go far beyond greater self-efficacy.

When barriers are lowered, when costs to training are reduced, when acceptance is enhanced, and when discrimination is eliminated, the allocation of talent throughout the economy improves. According to one recent estimate, 20 to 25 percent of economic growth since 1960 has occurred because of reduced barriers to the employment, training, and education of women and minorities in the US. The woman who would have become a legal secretary in a previous era now has the opportunity to be a lawyer; the one who would have become an elementary school science teacher can now be a physicist herself. Individual women gain personally. But the personal is beneficial for all members of society, due to improved allocation of resources and greater economic growth.

The lane for successfully combining career and family for college-graduate women began to be paved as major obstacles to married women's employment were eliminated. It was further smoothed by significant advances in household technologies and modern contraception, as well as in conception. Later generations gradually became aware that, to achieve career and family, the two goals had to be sought concurrently. And, finally, more and more couples in recent decades have come to discover the value of striving for equitable relationships. We can best understand these developments by examining the five groups of college-graduate women, each of whose trajectory was informed by that of the group before it. Collectively, these women's lives trace out one of the most consequential evolutions in social and economic history.

Amazingly, college-graduate women across the last hundred (plus) years divide neatly into five distinct groups (see figure 2.1). Within each group, they are largely unified by the constraints they faced and by the aspirations formed within (or despite) those constraints. Their ages at marriage and when they first gave birth, and the fraction who ever married and who ever had a birth, are also similar within the groups, while they largely differ across groups.

The groups also differ by their combinations of career, job, marriage, and family. One might presume that these divisions were due to the large increase in the numbers of women attending and graduating from college, or to changes in the types of women attending. But for the most part, they are not. As we'll see throughout the book, the shifts in their priorities and accomplishments are symptomatic of fundamental developments in society and the economy. The breaks from one group to the next were due mainly to forces beyond the control of individual agents and not specific to women, let alone college women.

Though the groups are distinct and divided, each one has passed a meaningful baton on to the next. The baton is layered by the imprints of mentors, guides, and advisors who achieved significant gains and progress. The women of Group Five, for example, benefited greatly from the pioneering women in Group Four, who entered various professions,

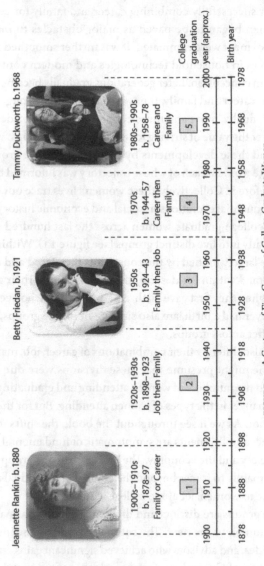

FIGURE 2.1. A Century of Five Groups of College-Graduate Women

Sources: Betty Friedan image © Schlesinger Library, Radcliffe Institute, Harvard University; Tammy Duckworth image © Chip Somodevilla/Getty Images News.

Jeannette Rankin, b.1880
1900s–1910s
b. 1878–97
Family or Career
1

Betty Friedan, b.1921
1920s–1930s
b. 1898–1923
Job then Family
2

1950s
b. 1924–43
Family then Job
3

1970s
b. 1944–57
Career then Family
4

Tammy Duckworth, b.1968
1980s–1990s
b. 1958–78
Career and Family
5

College graduation year (approx.)

Birth year

such as law, management, academia, and medicine, in large numbers. But the baton has also served a cautionary purpose, carrying warnings of various missteps and suggesting alternative routes for the next group of women. Group Five women learned from the experiences of those in Group Four that putting off having children for too long had costs. The women in Group Four learned from the experiences of those in Group Three that labor market reentry is often difficult.

The groups are determined by birth year. The boundaries are of unequal length. The first is twenty years, the second twenty-six, the third twenty, the fourth just fourteen, and the fifth twenty-one, when considering women to when they are at least in their early forties, but still ongoing. The mystery, solved within these pages, is why these women coalesced into these five meaningful groups, what defines the boundaries of each of the five, and what the forthcoming group of women can attempt to adjust, based on the choices and circumstances of those who journeyed on this road before them. Let's briefly meet each of the groups.

Group One: Family or Career

The women of Group One were born from approximately 1878 to 1897 and graduated college around 1900 to 1920. They are the least unified of all the groups in terms of their lifetime realizations. One-half never had (or adopted) a child; one-half did. Among the women who did not have children, the vast majority, and probably almost all, worked at some point in their lives. Few of the other half, who did have children, were ever employed. Almost one-third of the group never married. For the 70 percent who did, weddings for many came late in life.

In broad terms, this inaugural group achieved either a *family or a career*, although many had a series of jobs (not careers). Only a select few could have worked for pay and had a family. There were exceptions, of course. And a small slice among them had a family and a career.

Many of the college-graduate women of this era had successful careers but never married and had no children. The list of those with successful careers, from *Notable American Women*, includes renowned figures such as Edith Abbott, Grace Coyle, Helen Keller, Alice Paul, and

Jeannette Rankin. Also among them are several great female economists (in addition to Edith Abbott) such as Mary van Kleeck, Hazel Kyrk, and Margaret Reid, a research economist at the University of Chicago (and the only senior female economist I encountered during my graduate career).

Group One also includes those who married but never had children, such as Katharine Dexter McCormick, whose late husband's farm-machinery fortune eventually supported the research that produced the birth control pill. Katharine, far more than a wealthy heiress who knew how to use her fortune, was the first woman in the history of MIT to receive an undergraduate degree in biology.

A sliver of this group had accomplished careers, married, and had children. That list, also from *Notable American Women*, is short. On it are Mary Ritter Beard, who wrote *The Rise of American Civilization* with her husband Charles; Jesse Daniel Ames, who is credited with founding the antilynching movement in the US South; Pearl Syndenstriker Buck, who brought Chinese peasants to life in her literature; and Katharine Sargeant Angell White, the fiction editor of the *New Yorker* (and spouse of E. B. White, who charmed the world with *Charlotte's Web*).

Also on that list is Sadie Mossell Alexander, the first Black woman to get a PhD in economics. She is not among the list of noted female economists just mentioned because she left the field when she couldn't get an academic position. She married, earned a JD, had two children, worked for much of her life in her husband's law practice, and then began her own when he became the first Black judge appointed to the Philadelphia Court of Common Pleas.

Of the 237 college-graduate women in Group One in the compilation *Notable American Women*, less than 30 percent had children, and just over half ever married. The women who made it into *Notable* are those who had extraordinarily successful careers. Both the percentage who had children and the percentage who ever married are somewhat higher for all college-graduate women. But these figures were still very low.

The list of notables would have been monumentally longer had the women of Group One been able to marry and have families while still maintaining their intensity of work. They would have faced fewer barriers. They would not have had to make the difficult, life-altering choices that were often forced on them. Taking this even further, and perhaps most importantly, if the list were longer it would have encouraged additional women to invest in further training and to pursue careers, thereby producing higher levels of talent in future generations.

Had that been the case, women who came later, such as those in Group Three, likely would have been less confined to their homes, having had greater precedent to aspire to fulfilling careers. They would have invested more in their education and undertaken majors in college that led to professions. Talent would have been better allocated in society. Productivity would have been higher. The potential upshots are endless.

Many of the women across history who were gay, openly or otherwise, could not have legally married. Some lesbians, even in the early twentieth century, did not hide their relationships, as was the case with Dorothy Wolff Douglas, the Amherst economist. Dorothy had been married to Paul Douglas, a University of Chicago economist and US senator from Illinois, but after they parted ways she lived with Katharine DuPre Lumpkin, a sociologist and writer. Many others were restricted by social and personal norms from expressing themselves, even privately. Rachel Carson, whose *Silent Spring* awakened America to the dangers of DDT, is believed by biographers to have been gay.

It's noteworthy that college-graduate women with greater family resources had the luxury of not marrying, whether they were gay or not. Those from less affluent families often had to marry at an early age to support themselves.

Group One was faced with constraints that made the combination of employment and family nearly impossible. When asked later in their lives why they did not marry, many responded that they did not have to. Even those from less prosperous families could support themselves with the higher pay they garnered as educated workers. Many remained unmarried not because of a higher vocational calling. Rather, they often sought independence to escape the patriarchal norms of their day.

Group Two: Job then Family

Group Two, born from 1898 to 1923 and graduating college from 1920 to 1945, is a transition group. The circumstances of its occupants look like those of Group One at its beginning, with low marriage rates—but at its end they resemble Group Three, with high rates of matrimony, low ages at first marriage, and lots of children.

Because the marriage age for Group Two women was relatively late (as it was for Group One), this transition group is broadly categorized as having achieved *a job and then a family*. Most of the women who eventually married had children, and although the majority would have been employed for some time before marriage, they would not have worked for pay much after.

Many among them had wider aspirations that were squelched by external forces, including the onset of the Great Depression. With the massive economic downturn came the expansion of restrictive policies, including those that barred the employment of married women as clerical workers and expanded similar marriage bars in public-sector jobs, such as teaching.

Group Two, at its start, includes women such as Barbara McClintock, whose work in genetics earned her a Nobel Prize, and Alice Kober, who helped decipher Linear B. Neither married. Also at the start of Group Two are Zora Neale Hurston, a folklorist and writer about the Black experience in America, and Grace Hopper, the pioneering computer scientist and US Navy rear admiral. Both married but had no children. Ada Comstock, actually a late-marrying Group One member, married at sixty-seven after a long and distinguished career as the first president of Radcliffe College. These are not average women, but they are emblematic of the lives of Group Two women at its start.

Bella Savitzky Abzug, the fiery member of Congress, Betty Friedan, the author of *The Feminine Mystique*, and Dinah Shore, the singer and TV personality, were also members of Group Two. All married and all had children. They are characteristic of the collective as it morphed into Group Three. Less celebrated members of Group Two include two courageous public schoolteachers in St. Louis, Missouri: Anita Landy and

Mildred Basden, who challenged the laws that led to their being sacked after getting married. Their case, about which we will learn, put an end to most marriage bars for public schoolteachers.

Group Three: Family then Job

The women of Group Three, born 1924 to 1943, are more like one another than are those in any of the other groups. They expressed similar aspirations and achievements, married young, contained a high fraction who had children, and had similar college majors and first jobs. If the women in Group One divided into two separate paths, one having a family and the other having a job or career, those in Group Three marched in lockstep.

The uniformity of Group Three came about in part because several employment barriers had been lifted. But it was also because Group Three graduated from college from 1946 to 1965, as tides of demographic change were sweeping all Americans into earlier marriages and larger families. Slightly less than 90 percent of college-graduate women in Group Three married, and most married young. And almost all who married had children. Group Three women were largely employed right after graduation and even after marriage. But they left the labor force in droves while they had children and raised them.

Many returned when their children were older, and some used that time to achieve careers. But given their employment interruptions and priorities of family first, most had a tough time getting back into a labor market that had changed radically while they were gone. Many lacked requisite skills. The average woman of Group Three had a *family then a job*.

Yet while home life came first, in terms of timing and importance, that was disrupted for a large portion of this group. Divorce rates soared for those who married in the 1960s. Whereas 12 percent of college-graduate women divorced after twenty years of marriage among those who married in the 1950s, almost 30 percent did among those who married in the 1960s. Some in Group Three must have been caught by surprise as states changed their divorce laws to "unilateral," meaning either member of the couple could dissolve the marriage. Women who had specialized in the home and had scant job experience would have had little bargaining power in their households.

Most of the women in Group Three who left the workforce when they had children later returned in a variety of positions, especially as teachers and office workers. Most are not familiar names, but some who eventually found their métier are. They include Erma Bombeck, Jeane Kirkpatrick, Grace Napolitano, and, ironically, Phyllis Schlafly, who made a career of trying to curtail other women's careers.

There were others, who by necessity or desire, never left the workforce at all. Some had to keep earning after a divorce, especially if they had children. The Nobel Prize–winning writer Toni Morrison apparently took no breaks from her work. After her divorce, she became an editor at Random House, raised her two boys, and wrote her brilliant, haunting novels in early-morning sessions before she served them breakfast.

The aspirations of Group Three women are revealed in the personal imaginings of their futures, which have been encoded in several large surveys. These college women married early and had more children than those who came before or after them. But a large fraction stated that they wanted to be employed while they were married, even when their children were young. Group Three's aspirations were defined for many in Betty Friedan's best seller. But the reality and truth, we will see, were very different. Opportunities had expanded. Jobs for married women after the 1940s were more plentiful with the ending of marriage bars. Aspirations had changed.

Group Four: Career then Family

Group Four, born 1944 to 1957, graduated college from the mid-1960s to the late 1970s. These women had apparently learned from the experiences of their predecessors. The about-turns from Group Three to Four in marriage, children, occupations, and employment are the most extreme in this history of successive groups.

The women of Group Four came of age just as the women's movement was maturing. They knew of the constraints and frustrations about which Betty Friedan wrote in *The Feminine Mystique*. But, as we'll explore, they were less influenced in their educational and career choices by the "noisy" revolution of the 1960s and 1970s than they were by a quieter one. That isn't to say that the raucous movement wasn't a catalyst. But for Group Four, the "Ms." moniker probably had a greater influence than did the founder of the magazine with the same name (and a movement principal), Ms. Gloria Steinem.

As young women, they had witnessed their mothers, aunts, and older sisters of Group Three return to the workforce after the kids had left the nest. Some of these women arrived at their employment without much forethought. Others carefully planned a serial life of motherhood, then a job. But the jobs Group Three women sought and received were not often the lifelong careers to which Group Four aspired. The mothers often saw a different route for their daughters. "I counsel my daughter to have a family and a career. It's expected now," said a highly educated but nonworking member of Group Three about her Group Four offspring.

Group Four women could also see that many in Group Three found themselves unexpectedly divorced, with rusty workplace skills. Group Four women learned at an early age that marketable skills were important not just for their own careers but also for their livelihoods and those of their children. Marriage was no longer forever, if it ever had been. Their Group Two or Three mothers also knew that: "The worst is to be left in middle age, widowed or divorced, without an identity or passionate interest of your own."

Divorce rates of Group Four women were even higher than those of the women from the latter part of Group Three. Of marriages begun in the 1970s, 37 percent of couples did not make it to their twentieth wedding anniversary. Of those begun in the 1960s (mainly Group Three women), 29 percent did not.

Even with that many breakups for Group Four, the element of surprise was not as great as it had been for Group Three. Group Four saw the writing on the wall. They had witnessed it at a young age. The baton that Group Three passed on to Group Four contained a warning about the stability of marriage. It noted the dangers of investing in one's husband's career and not in one's own. Divorce rates started to decline. Those for marriages that began in the 1980s and beyond were about as low as they were for unions from the 1960s. Women began to marry later in life, and those marriages were more stable, despite more permissive divorce laws.

Group Four women thought they could do better than Group Three women. They recognized that Group Three, on the whole, had not prioritized graduate and professional education or long-term careers. Because of their better-informed horizon, the women of Group Four prepared in high school to attend college; then they chose majors, and later graduate school degrees, with durable career goals in mind.

The novel idea of Group Four was to get on the career track first and have the family later. Many surmised that, by the time the career was in place, having kids was not going to derail them. Making a family was the easy part—at least it seemed to be, judging from the high birth rates of Group Three women. Group Four women were also equipped with a special something that prior generations had lacked as young women: the Pill.

Armed with better birth control, they could delay marriage and childbearing with few immediate consequences. Effective, convenient, and female-controlled contraception allowed the women of Group Four to obtain more education and ascend their chosen career ladders without forgoing an active social and sex life along the way. But many delayed for too long, and about 27 percent of all college-graduate women in Group Four never had children. The group aspired to have *a career, then a family*, but aspirations are not necessarily achievements.

Among the better-known members of Group Four are Hillary Clinton and Carol Mosley Braun, the first Black woman elected to the US Senate. Both married, one famously so, and both have children. Others include Condoleezza Rice and Sonia Sotomayor, neither of whom has children.

The women of Group Four were the first to aspire in large numbers to the most highly paid and prestigious professions, such as lawyer, physician, and executive. They wanted what their male colleagues had always sought: to be better off financially, have the respect of their co-workers, and reach the highest possible rung of the ladder within their desired field of work. The men in this group also increased in their own desire for those achievements. Family was important to this group, but it largely rode in the backseat while postgraduate education and career advancement were up in front.

Group Five: Career and Family

Group Five encompasses those born since 1958, who would have graduated college starting around 1980. To allow the members sufficient time to have children and observe their choices after doing so, I will define the birth years of Group Five as ranging from 1958 to 1978, even though the group is still ongoing. The women in this group observed the miscalculations made by Group Four women. That which is deferred is often never accomplished. Group Five avowed that career would no longer eclipse the potential for a family.

Though they have continued the pattern of delaying both marriage and childbearing, and have even extended the delay for both, birth rates have greatly risen for them. Like Group Four, they have received an assist from a host of reproductive technologies, including IVF. In this case the support was to aid in conception, not contraception. This final group has largely aspired toward a *career and a family*.

Boundary Matters

We can now return to the mystery of how these women fit so neatly into five distinct groups. The puzzle can be solved by exploring demographic and economic data on marriages, births, and employment.

Marriage age is an important indicator distinguishing among the various groups (see figure 2.2). Whether a woman marries (or partners) late, early, or not at all has proven to be related to her plans for a career and for having children. The first thing we can observe in the figure is the general U shape to the fraction of college-graduate women who

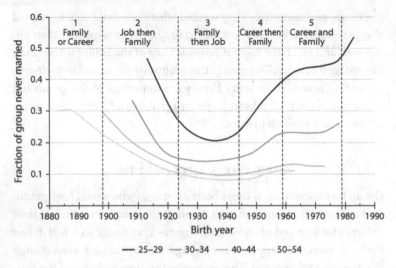

FIGURE 2.2. Fraction of College-Graduate Women Never Married by Age and Birth Group
See Figures and Table Appendix.

remained never married by age, as we traverse from Group One to Group Five. The lowest fraction is reached for Group Three, for which just about 8 percent never married and just 20 percent were not yet married by their late twenties. For Group Five, about half were not yet married by their late twenties.

The use of marriage as a social indicator may seem outdated today. Now, many people have life partners and forgo the institution of marriage altogether. Some couples cohabitate for many years before they marry, and the exact year of marriage may be less meaningful. But even among the most recent groups of college-graduate women, more than 90 percent have been, or are currently, married by the time they have reached their early fifties.

Because the 1940 population census was the first in the US to include information on educational attainment and marital status, information for the entirety of the earliest groups is not available for all ages. In addition, though history is filled with same-sex relationships, data on same-sex unions and marriages are only just beginning to appear. Finally, because of differences in marriage by race and because I need to analyze a closed population, I limit the marriage data here to native-born white women, but I discuss racial differences later. It should be emphasized that all the other data include all racial groups.

Group One college-graduate women had low marriage rates. Even by their early fifties, just 70 percent had ever married. Group Two is not unlike Group One at its start, but by the end of Group Two, just 10 percent had never married by their fifties. The earliest age at marriage and the highest fraction married is found for Group Three, within which almost 80 percent were already married by twenty-five to twenty-nine years old. Nearly all of the women who would ever marry did so before they turned thirty.

Group Four delayed marriage, and that trend has continued with Group Five. But even though marriage for Groups Four and Five was put off, the fraction who would eventually marry is still very high. Their marriage rates in their late twenties and early thirties may look like those of Group One women, born in the late nineteenth century. But the comparison ends there. College-graduate women born since the early 1940s deferred marriage, but few remained single forever.

Another way to measure the timing of marriage is the age at which half a group was ever married. That is, the median age at marriage. For college-graduate women in Group Three, born from the mid-1920s to the early 1940s, half the group married around twenty-three years old. But in just five years during Group Four, for those born from 1950 to 1955, the median age at first marriage rose to twenty-five and continued to increase. For college-graduate women born in 1980, just past the cut-off for Group Five, the age is older than twenty-seven.

An increase in the marriage age from twenty-three to twenty-seven had great consequences. It meant women could pursue advanced degrees and early career training without being concerned with family and without having to move geographically for a husband's education or position.

Women who never attended college have had different marriage rates from those who graduated college. The fraction who attended and who graduated college rises considerably across the groups, and that important distinction will soon be considered. Those without college married young and—for the earliest birth groups—more of them married. The noncollege group did not experience the high nonmarriage rates of Group One. But for the most recent birth groups, those who did not attend college have had a substantial retreat from marriage. Amidst these differences, there is one important exception: marriage occurred early in the lives of all women from the late 1940s to the beginning of the 1960s.

The group boundaries are clear in the marriage data. Group One had low marriage rates, even in their older years. Group Three married early. Groups Four and Five greatly delayed marriage, but eventually married to almost the same degree as those from Group Three. The distinction between Groups Four and Five, as we'll see, emerges in what happens after marriage: children (or lack thereof).

Black college-graduate women share some of the marriage patterns with the white women in figure 2.2. The earliest groups had low rates of marriage, Group Three had the highest rates, and there was considerable delay for Groups Four and Five. The differences for the two most recent groups are that marriage for Black college-graduate women is not just delayed, as it has been for white college-graduate women, but also remains low at older ages.

When women become pregnant soon after college, they are less likely to continue with their schooling. Careers may be put on hold. The opposite occurs when a pregnancy can be delayed. The close relationship that has historically existed between marriage and childbirth has changed in recent times, but the fraction of births to unmarried, unpartnered college-graduate women is still low.

The fraction of college-graduate women who never had a birth is shown in figure 2.3. The wavy lines in the graph look similar to those tracking the fraction of women who never married. The lines for Groups Four and Five contain higher frequency data and, in consequence, are bumpier. Adding adoptions increases the fraction with children by about 1.6 percentage points. (The vertical difference between the lines shows the degree to which births were delayed.)

Although similarities exist between marriage and birth data, the obvious difference is that a marriage does not always produce a birth. That is the key distinction between Groups Four and Five. These two groups

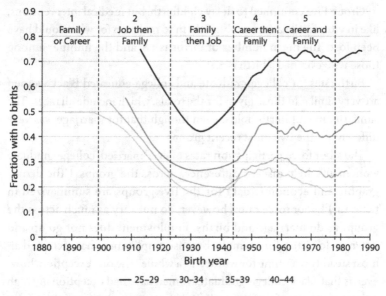

FIGURE 2.3. Fraction of College-Graduate Women with No Births by Age and Birth Group
See Figures and Table Appendix.

married at similar ages and at similar rates, but a greater fraction of Group Five eventually had a child, even though they had their first child at a somewhat older age.

More than half the women in Group One never had children. Group Two, similar to the findings on marriage, is a bridge from the low fertility levels of Group One to the soaring fertility levels of Group Three, who present an entirely different picture. More than 90 percent who married had a child—the highest among the groups considered. By the end of their reproductive lives, just 17 percent never had a birth. Among those who had children, the average at peak fertility was 3.14 births per woman.

Group Four women delayed having children, and the portion of women who would become mothers plummeted. By the end of Group Four, 45 percent had a child by age thirty-five. A delay of that magnitude meant that the fraction who would never give birth to a child topped out at about 28 percent. These facts are for all female college graduates, not just for those pursuing advanced degrees or graduating from a selective institution of higher education.

Group Five continued to delay childbirth, but medical interventions, like in vitro fertilization, enabled them to make up for what could have been lost. The mean number of births is 1.8, and the number among those who ever had a birth is 2.2.

Birth rates for college-graduate and college-educated Black women are very similar to those given for the totals, which include all races. The similarity in childbirth holds, even though that for marriage was very different for the two most recent groups.

The labor force participation rates of ever-married, college-graduate women also help discern differences across the groups. (The demographic and economic data for the five groups are summarized in table 2.1.) Labor force rates, however, do not vary as much across the groups as do marriage and births. Employment does not go up and down as do births, for example, because employment has increased almost steadily over time for women as a whole. The one exception, however, is that Black college-graduate women have had exceptionally high employment rates from the earliest date one can observe women's occupations and employment.

Consider employment rates for the three age groups in figure 2.4 (page 40), from age twenty-five to forty-nine years old. The data begin with Group Two because the 1940 census of population was the first to provide data on education level and employment. The first boundary is between Groups Two and Three. Group Two had low participation when young (and married), but increased its participation later in life. Because of the high percentage with children, Group Three had about equal participation as Group Two early in life but greatly increased their involvement in the labor force as their children entered school, as was the case for some of the better-known women in that group, from Erma Bombeck to Jeane Kirkpatrick and even Phyllis Schlafly.

By the time Group Three women reached their late forties, 75 to 85 percent were in the labor force (88 to 93 percent for the Black women within the group). So Group Three, despite having large families and low involvement in paid employment when young, had reasonably high labor force participation rates when older. In fact, their labor force rates were almost as high as for Groups Four and Five, women who boarded the career track much earlier.

TABLE 2.1. Marriage, Children, and Employment across Five Groups of College-Graduate Women

College years [Birth years] Aspiration/ Achievement	(A) Never married (by age 30)	(B) Never married (by age 50)	(C) No children (by age 44)	(D) Labor force for ever married, ages 25–29	(E) Labor force for ever married, ages 45–49
Group 1: 1900–19 [1878–1897] Family or Career	53%	32%	50%	~20%	30%
Group 2: 1920–45 [1898–1923] Job then Family	38%	19%	36%	28%	58%
Group 3: 1946–65 [1924–1943] Family then Job	16%	9%	18%	35%	73%
Group 4: 1966–79 [1944–1957] Career then Family	21%	9%	27%	76%	85%
Group 5: 1980–2000 [1958–1978] Career and Family	27%	12%	21%	83%	84%

See Figures and Table Appendix.

A few key facts must be noted about the size of our college-graduate groups relative to the population, and the numbers of college males relative to college females. For our journey, college will almost always mean a four-year institution, with graduation generally meaning a bachelor's degree (not an associate's). There are occasions when women who graduated from a two-year teachers' college will be factored in, especially when that was a major route to becoming a teacher.

For men and women alike, being a college graduate was a rarity in 1900. Fewer than one in thirty young people, or 3 percent, would have graduated from college as the twentieth century began. These levels were far lower for Blacks. Leap forward to those born around 1990, and almost one in two females was destined to graduate from college

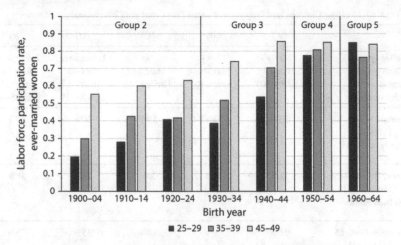

FIGURE 2.4. Labor Force Participation Rates by Age and Birth Group:
Ever-Married College-Graduate Women
See Figures and Table Appendix.

(see figure 2.5 and Online Appendix figure 4A [Ch2]). The levels for Black
women are about two decades or more behind those for white women.

In that span of time, there have been increases and even slight decreases,
at varying rates. Two irregularities are so extreme that they beg for an explanation. Graduation rates for males rose steeply in the mid- to late 1960s
before taking a sharp dip. Both the rise and the decline were due to the
Vietnam War. The enormous increase was a response to the deferments
that allowed males, fortunate enough to have undergraduate status, to avoid
the draft (until they graduated). The aberrant decrease was due to reductions in the draft and the ending of US military involvement in Vietnam.

Another feature that demands mention is the crossover point when
more women than men graduated from college. Males had vastly out-
numbered females as college graduates, especially for graduating classes
from the 1950s to 1960s. But women caught up to men and overtook
them around 1980. Black women overtook Black men about ten years
before that. Women have continued to expand their lead since then.

There are two ways of thinking about the college-graduate series.
One (which we've discussed) considers individuals born around the

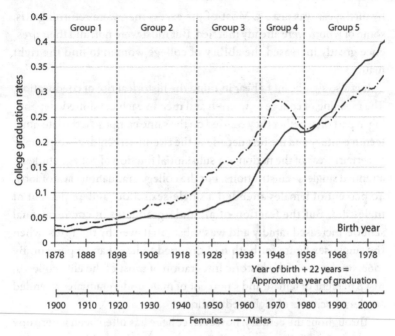

FIGURE 2.5. College Graduation Rates for Males and Females (at Age Thirty)
See Figures and Table Appendix.

same year. But college students vary in age, and it is not uncommon
to encounter a thirty-year-old sitting in a college class alongside
twenty-year-olds. That age mixing has happened throughout history—
especially in the mid-twentieth century, when there were many returning GIs (almost all men).

A related series gives the actual numbers in college by school year
and allows one to better understand social interactions on college campuses and in classrooms. It provides a window on the sex ratio in every
hub of college—in class, the library, dorms, the student center, and the
party scene.

The ratio of males to females (or sex ratio) from that series reveals
that there were far more males than females in college from the mid-
1940s to the mid-1960s. In the late 1940s, for example, the ratio reached
an astounding 2.3 males for every female in college, even when the series

by birth year was just 1.5. Most of the excess men were returning GIs, some of whom were already married. But most were not, and their presence greatly increased the ability of college women to find the right mate.

It is also significant to bear in mind the historical rise of coeducation. The meaning of college to women and men in each era shifted, depending in part on whether they resided on the same campus. In the late nineteenth century and the first decade of the twentieth century—especially in certain areas of the nation—a substantial fraction of college students attended single-sex institutions. For the college graduation class of 1900, 40 percent of females attended a single-sex school and 46 percent of males did. But the fraction of all undergraduates in coeducational schools increased rapidly and was substantial even by the 1930s, when the single-sex figure for both had dropped to less than 30 percent. By 1966, on the eve of the historic integration of most of the elite colleges, just 8 percent of female and 5 percent of male undergraduates attended single-sex schools of higher education.

Throughout the century, however, college has often been where one finds a mate. Single-sex schools were often connected institutionally and had routine bus runs on weekends. Even coeducational schools, especially those with a paucity of female undergraduates, had informal relationships with geographically close single-sex colleges. The bus that linked MIT to Wellesley was colloquially referred to as "the cuddle shuttle."

With the enormous increase in college attendance among the population from the start of the twentieth century, one would think that a shift of the types of people who went to and graduated from college would dominate changes across our groups. After all, women who went to college around 1900 disproportionately came from wealthier families than later in the century. They could afford *not* to marry. Those who went to college in the 1950s may have been drawn from groups who wanted more children. And those who graduated from college recently would presumably differ from the others because they opted for careers. But the changes we've seen in the fraction married and the fraction having children are not primarily due to the type of woman who went to college and the types of families that sent their daughters to college. These changes are more fundamental.

We can confirm this by examining women drawn from the same strata of society who attended the same college, over the course of the century. Even among women who shared similar upbringings and aptitude, we still see considerable change across the five groups that mirrors the aggregate group boundaries. In other words, even when holding the family backgrounds of these women constant, the same shifts in priorities and choices when it comes to marriage, childbearing, and employment remain true for the full group.

Take women who graduated from Radcliffe/Harvard College. Extraordinarily detailed data exist for these women. They have consistently been selected from among the brightest, most capable, most driven young women in the nation.

For much of the period being considered, they were also disproportionately selected from the country's wealthier families. This is significant because admission to an elite private college from 1880 to 1940 was greatly enhanced by attendance at a preparatory school. Standardized tests, which began in the 1940s and diffused rapidly in the 1950s, reduced the need for special preparation in private secondary schools. Even so, the fraction of Radcliffe women who attended a private secondary school was virtually constant at 45 percent, from those graduating in the early 1900s to those graduating in the late 1970s.

Yet even though these women were drawn from the same social class, the propensity of Radcliffe women to be married and have children closely tracks the general trends in the population of groups from around 1900 onward. The fractions never married, by age and birth group, are about the same, and the turning points are almost identical. The similarities in the marriage data are most striking for Group Three. From the late 1940s to the early 1960s, Radcliffe women married early and at high rates. They were no different in that regard from women who graduated from less selective colleges. Similar changes can be seen in the birth data.

Helen Taussig, the pioneering pediatric cardiologist and daughter of Frank Taussig, the Harvard economist, attended Radcliffe around

WWI. Helen never married and was a more typical member of those in Group One who attained careers. Adrienne Rich, the renowned poet, married in 1953, about a year after she graduated from Radcliffe, and had three sons in rapid succession. After her husband's death she began a lifelong relationship with a woman. Rich was a typical (yet atypical) member of Group Three. Linda Greenhouse, the Pulitzer Prize–winning journalist, was in the vanguard of Group Four. She married at thirty-four, about a dozen years after her Radcliffe graduation, and had her first child at thirty-eight.

So Radcliffe women look almost identical to all women in terms of marriage and children. But the reason for the similarity is not that a large fraction of all female college graduates had attended single-sex elite colleges; except for the earliest period, female graduates of single-sex colleges accounted for a small portion of the total. Changes in the selectivity of college-graduate women apparently did not matter much for the extraordinary changes that occurred across the five groups.

Why *did* these monumental changes in career and family occur from Group One to Group Five? The shifts were part of a century-long succession of generations, punctuated by essential changes in the economy and society. Each group took the baton and ran an additional length of road, jumping hurdles and trying to dodge barriers. And each generation has been faced with ever-changing constraints—as well as a host of technological advances, in the household and related to reproduction, that have smoothed the path forward.

Along the way, especially in the late 1960s and early 1970s, discontent with employment, promotions, earnings, and family life bubbled up and exploded in revolutionary ways. Action at the national level filtered down to more local associations and to even more intimate consciousness-raising groups, as they were called, in women's homes and apartments. Each generation set its sights on a better way to achieve its goals and carve out its own legacy.

Throughout the long journey across groups, it wasn't merely women's aspirations that changed course. Men's notions about the qualities and career ambitions of their ideal mates shifted as well. For Group One, college-graduate women were 20 percentage points less likely to ever marry by age fifty than were women with no college at all. For Group Three, they were 5 percentage points less likely. But by Group Five the tables had turned. A college-graduate woman was 5 percentage points more likely to marry than a woman who had no college. This was in part because college-graduate men became more likely to marry college-graduate women.

Increased matching by education level and ambition has meant more high-powered careers for both parents, including for same-sex couples. Achieving a career with on-call hours in the office and managing a family with round-the-clock demands at home is arduous for any one person. The joint marriage decisions of men and women in each of the groups are key to understanding how the current generation can improve on those that have come before. Today, among the greatest challenges, and greatest goals, is to achieve career and family within an equitable relationship. If that is achieved, the question becomes: Where will they take the baton from here? We will first meet each of the groups.

3

A Fork in the Road

WHEN I WAS A GRADUATE student at the University of Chicago in 1971, I often saw a grey-haired woman walking to the computer center carrying a large rectangular box. In the box were hundreds of punch cards, some of them containing just one line of code. All the lines of code, in precise sequence, were needed to perform a single statistical analysis, such as computing means. In winter, the old woman trudged through the snow wearing a long, grey woolen coat and short, black rubber galoshes. I observed that she walked more deliberately in these conditions, taking enormous care—for if the box fell, her code could be scrambled.

The woman was Margaret Gilpin Reid. She was seventy-five years old and had retired as professor of economics a decade earlier. To me and my fellow graduate students, she was "one of the ancients."

On wintry days, I, too, slogged to the computer center carrying a similar, large rectangular box of computer cards. My boots were high, and they were Frye, made of harness leather. My coat was fashionably short, barely covering my miniskirt. I might have been cold. But I was stylish. Margaret and I were separated by more than age, by more than our fashion sense. I had no way of knowing that her work concerned so many ideas that would later occupy my mind and research. More importantly, I had no sense that her life would help inform my understanding of the evolution of women's economic roles.

Still, I was amazed by Margaret Reid. She was determined, and she was still doing research that appeared to be important. But I never spoke a word to her. Instead, I regarded her as an apparition from a bygone era.

As one of the ancients, she provided a plank in a bridge that linked college-graduate women of the past to those whom I teach today. Hers was a narrow lane of women who had succeeded in having a career but did not marry, or married but did not have children. A somewhat wider lane among the members of her Group One contained those who did not have a career. Most of them married, and most of them had children. The lanes on this metaphorical bridge from the past have shifted over time. Some have widened and some have narrowed. Closer to the present, more of those with a career have married, and more of those have had children—in essence, the lanes began to merge.

I wish I had possessed enough foresight to have struck up a conversation with Margaret when I was a graduate student. How naïve I was for not recognizing her importance to the field of economics; how unfortunate that I could not appreciate her contribution to the long journey.

In 1992, Gary Becker was awarded a Nobel Prize for his work on the application of economics to aspects of households and families, such as marriage, divorce, fertility, and time allocation. More than a half century earlier, in 1934, Margaret Reid had published her PhD dissertation, *Economics of Household Production*. Her original dissertation had been used as a text at Iowa State College. Its publication by a major press, with added textbook-like questions, made it accessible to teachers and students at other institutions.

Reid's research was among the first to assess the value of unpaid work in the household and to analyze how married women chose between working in the home and working outside their own homes for pay. When Margaret initiated her studies, married women were just beginning to be employed outside their homes, mainly in a host of white-collar positions, lending her work enormous contemporary relevance.

Margaret's study aimed to put women's unpaid work into calculations of national income. She demonstrated the economic importance of women's labor in the language of national income accounting, just as that arcane field was taking form. We've grown so accustomed to front-page stories that use economists' lingo—GNP, GDP, national income, unemployment rate—that we don't realize just how recently these notions were crafted. The person who played an outsized role in their creation was an immigrant named Simon Kuznets.

Simon Kuznets emigrated from Russia in 1922 and received a PhD from Columbia University in 1926. A year later, he became a staff researcher at the National Bureau of Economic Research (NBER), an institution founded in New York City in 1920 to provide the US with its statistical foundations, something the government began to undertake in the 1930s. Kuznets, the 1971 Nobel Prize laureate, was the thesis advisor of my thesis advisor, the Nobel Prize winner Robert W. Fogel, so I proudly consider him to be my intellectual grandfather.

Early in the 1930s, as the US economy was in freefall into the worst depression in its history, Congress asked the NBER if it could borrow Kuznets to figure out just how much national product had declined. By knowing the damage from the economic downturn, members of Congress believed they could figure out what to do about the catastrophe. In addition, the Department of Commerce needed to come up with a general accounting system to measure the nation's productive capacity, such as its national income, not just for the current extraordinary times but for all time. Kuznets was the person for both jobs.

At the very moment that Reid was espousing the inclusion of women's unpaid labor in estimates of a nation's income, Kuznets was formulating his version of these esoteric, yet critically important, concepts. By the time he had drafted his report to Congress, Margaret Reid had written her PhD dissertation and published a textbook arguing for the addition of household services in estimating what the country produced.

Women and other family members provided labor in their own households to produce goods and services that constituted a significant portion of consumption for nearly every citizen. As the Congressional report and his later writings show, Kuznets agonized over whether to include the labor of unpaid household workers and caregivers in official statistics. He ultimately decided not to.

In his report to Congress, he noted, "It was considered best to omit this large group of services from national income, especially since no reliable basis is available for estimating their value." Reid argued that they should be included, and in the almost ninety years that have followed, many others have echoed her logic.

A central argument is that unpaid caring labor of all types is devalued because it is not remunerated and not included in our national income accounts. At various times, advocacy groups and others, especially those encouraging better treatment of care workers in general and women in particular, have made estimates of the value of unpaid care work in the entire economy. The latest numbers—a full 20 percent of GNP—are staggering. Margaret set forth several methods for doing the calculation. Nonetheless, Kuznets's estimating procedures are very much with us today. And they still exclude unpaid labor in the home and elsewhere.

Margaret's and Simon's intellectual paths crisscrossed in the 1930s. In the mid-1940s, they worked together on an important, controversial commission concerning the cost of living index, known today as the consumer price index (CPI). Margaret Reid moved in high academic and policy circles. In her day, she was important. To me, when I was a graduate student, she was an anomaly, a woman who had long before retired from a department that, by the time I was there, had only men. She was also the only female economist I knew as a graduate student. I didn't realize then how forward-thinking she was about women's work and the contribution made by care work and housework to the income of the entire nation.

By any standard, Margaret Reid led a successful career. She received her PhD from the University of Chicago in 1931 and was appointed as a professor at Iowa State College (later University) in 1934. After a stint in the federal government during World War II that lasted to 1948, she became professor at the University of Illinois, Urbana-Champaign, and later a full professor at the University of Chicago in the departments of economics and home economics in 1951. During her academic career, she published four major books and had articles in the best economics journals.

Was Margaret Reid the Madame Curie of household economics? Perhaps. But there are several others who would also have a claim to this honorific. One was Hazel Kyrk, Margaret's mentor at Chicago.

Hazel Kyrk obtained her PhD from the University of Chicago in 1920, just like Margaret, but eleven years earlier. They both taught at Iowa State and held various positions in government. In 1925, Kyrk obtained a faculty position at the University of Chicago and was promoted to full professor in 1941, almost a half century before I became the first woman tenured in the Harvard economics department. The career similarity between Reid and Kyrk is striking. The personal similarity is as well. Margaret may have been an oddity to me, but, though accomplished, she was not an anomaly in her day for a member of Group One.

Neither Reid nor Kyrk ever married; neither bore a child (although Kyrk raised her cousin's teenage daughter). I have no documentation of their desire for marriage, their marriage prospects, or the possibility of female partners, and I have no statements, expressed earlier in their lives, regarding a desire for children.

Both Reid and Kyrk achieved their careers rather late in their lives. That was true of many others in their group. They were each about thirty-five years old when they received their PhDs, and they became full professors in their mid-fifties. Delayed careers of that magnitude meant that it would have been even more difficult, if not impossible, to have married, let alone had children.

A main reason why they both had late starts is that they each supported themselves in college and did not come from families with much wealth. It is often thought that college women in the early part of the twentieth century came from elite backgrounds. While that might be true of some in the Northeast, it was not necessarily the case for those from the Midwest and West. Reid was from Manitoba, Canada. Kyrk was from Ohio.

Reid and Kyrk lived their lives in a manner similar to those of a select portion of the women who graduated college in the years before World War I and who were born before the twentieth century. They attained careers—not necessarily of the highest stature or renown, but ones in which they were appreciated by students and colleagues, and in which they made contributions to science and to public policy.

Barriers and Constraints

As we've seen, among all women who graduated college around 1910, 30 percent never married and 50 percent never had children. Even among those who married, 29 percent never had a child. These figures are astoundingly high historically. Among college-graduate women born somewhat later, from 1925 to 1975, the fraction who never married by their fifties was less than 12 percent. There was a world of difference between Group One and those who followed.

The marriage and childbearing figures among Group One are for *all* women who graduated college from 1900 to 1919—not just for those from wealthy families or for those who attended the elite single-sex colleges of the Northeast. They do not just apply to women who made important breakthroughs in science, the arts, or literature. As high as these nonmarriage and nonbirth rates were, they were even higher for women deemed to have made "notable" contributions in their lifetimes (such as Margaret Reid and Hazel Kyrk).

These differences are not due to selection—that is, the notion that the women who graduated from college in Group One had different marriage proclivities from those in subsequent groups. The college-graduate women of 1910 were not inherently different from those of 1930 or 1950. The differences in their lives arose because they were faced with different barriers and constraints. Their options were different, not their preferences.

Social norms and hiring regulations often prevented married women from having a job, let alone a career. Two types of regulations were most constraining in the first half of the twentieth century. The first type was regulations of firms and governments that barred married women from being hired and employed in certain positions, such as teaching. These were called marriage bars, which we'll explore in greater depth in the next chapter. Marriage bars help explain why, even though the fraction of Group One who were teachers and academics was high, it was much lower for those who were married, except among Black women.

The other regulations were nepotism rules that prevented wives from occupying positions in the same institution, department, firm, or government agency as their husbands. Anti-nepotism regulations lasted in universities until the 1950s (and in some cases until much later), and are the reason why there is a lower fraction of married notables who were academics in the early groups of women than in later groups. Nepotism rules stopped many women from using their skills and from engaging in the fields about which they felt passionately. They were deprived of their careers in order to remain married.

On the face of it, nepotism rules ended the marriage between economist Dorothy Wolff Douglas and her husband, Paul Douglas, a distinguished economics professor and, later, a US senator from Illinois. After Paul took a position at the University of Chicago and Dorothy could not get appointed at Chicago, she (and their four children) left for Smith College, and Paul for Amherst. Dorothy was not content to just be the wife of a famous economist since she was also an economist. But Amherst wasn't going to be a great place for Paul, and the marriage soon dissolved.

Even without the official and unofficial barriers, having both a career and a family was difficult given the enormous demands of the household. Though most urban households had electricity by 1920, there were no modern refrigerators, clothes washers, vacuum cleaners, dryers, and, of course, no microwaves. Those with sufficient income could often hire domestic servants, but running the household was still a lot of work.

Besides the commonplace aspects of the home, serious life-or-death issues were substantial in the first two decades of the twentieth century. Contraception was rudimentary, yielding families that were generally larger than desired. The demands of family were amplified by high levels of infant and child mortality. In 1900, when the nation's modern urban-sanitation systems were just being completed, one infant in eight died during its first year. In 1915, one in ten did. In the era before antibiotics, both mothers and children died from infection at alarming rates. Wealth, education, and social standing did little to prevent such premature passing.

Among the women in Group One who made notable contributions to science, literature, and the arts, fully 9 percent experienced at least one infant or child death among those who had a birth. In the US as a whole, the babies of farmers experienced lower infant deaths than did those of urbanites, even professors. A mother with a job, let alone a career, had a nontrivial chance of blaming herself for her baby's illness and certainly for its untimely passing.

The Notables

Defining a "career" consistently across the five groups is inherently subjective. Rather than using an individual's earnings, occupation, patents, or honors to measure a superlative contribution, I used the compilations of a host of scholars who have sifted through thousands of possible entries. These experts have created five volumes of the previously referenced *Notable American Women*, providing biographies of American women who made extraordinary accomplishments. Each volume contains information on women who died during a set of years.

Each entry is a biographical statement written by a specialist in the field. Various aspects of the women's lives—birth date, college graduation, marriage year (if ever married), children born or adopted, and career accomplishments—have been coded from these sketches. The latest volume was compiled in 1999, so only Groups One and Two—those born from around 1878 to 1897 and from 1898 to 1923—contain enough entries to be studied, since, as noted, none of the notables were alive at the time the biography was written.

College women in Group One were different from the average woman, and the notables were even more different. Take marriage. For most of the past, the vast majority of American men and women married exceptionally young in absolute terms, especially when compared with their counterparts in England, France, and Germany. American families had substantial incomes compared with those of other nations. Inequality of income (believe it or not) was lower in the US than elsewhere. Ordinary Jacks and Jills could marry and set up their households on America's abundant land. Among all women for most of US history, as well as for the noncollege contemporaries of Group One, fewer than one in ten would never marry. But college-educated women married at much lower rates and the notables at even lower rates.

The nonmarriage rate for the college-graduate women of Group One was 30 percent. Among the notable college-graduate women, that fraction was 44 percent, almost 1.5 times that for all college women.

As great as these differences in marriage rates are, those for childbearing are even greater. Among all women in these years, independent of educational attainment, just 20 percent had no biological or adopted children in their lifetimes. Among all college-graduate women, 50 percent had no children, independent of personal accomplishment and recognition. But the fraction of the Group One notables with no children was almost 70 percent—just three out of every ten notable women had a child. College-graduate women of Group One were clearly different. They were different from their non-college-graduate peers, and they are different from other groups of college-graduate women throughout US history.

Most of the childlessness among the college graduates and the notables was because they were not married. Single women in the early twentieth century, particularly those of financial means, could have adopted infants and children, and some did. In contrast to today, where there is high demand but low supply of domestic infants available for adoption, there was high supply of adoptable babies in the early twentieth century. The birth rate, especially among immigrant women, was substantial, and women who had a pregnancy out of wedlock had little recourse.

There are many examples of married, college-graduate notables who chose to adopt. There are fewer examples of unmarried notables who adopted—but there are some. When Hazel Kyrk taught at Oberlin in the 1920s, she lived with Mary Emily Sinclair, the first woman to obtain a PhD in mathematics from the University of Chicago. Sinclair was a professor at Oberlin and, in her mid-thirties, adopted two infants, a girl and a boy. She was fortunate enough to be able to take a sabbatical leave during their infancy. But not many unmarried career women could adopt a child and maintain an active professional life.

College-graduate women in Group One could apparently create just one type of legacy: children or a career. Out of one hundred college-graduate women in the list of Group One notables, just fifty-six ever married, and only thirty-one ever had children. It was almost impossible for them to combine family and career. Thankfully, it is far easier to accomplish career and family now.

But, again, the notables were a special group. The committee that selected them had considered thousands more who were almost as esteemed. It would be an impossible feat to track all the college-graduate women who achieved some form of career yet were not chosen by the committee as sufficiently "notable."

If we knew the fraction of Group One who had crafted a career, we could determine the fraction of the entire group who had what many women seek today—career and family. We could also establish what percentage had a family but no career, as well as all the other permutations of "career and family." The calculation begins with two percentages we have already established. For all college-graduate women in Group One, 30 percent never married, and a whopping 50 percent never had a child. Those are the data for all college-graduate women, not just those with a career. When we fold in the data from the notables (all of whom attained a career), a bit more than half eventually married, and a bit less than one-third had children.

With the fraction of all college graduates in Group One who attained a career, we have the numbers we need to put the achievements of Group One in perspective. We can reasonably assume that, at a maximum, around 30 percent of the college-graduate women of Group One attained a career by their forties or fifties. Using that assumed figure, just 9 percent of Group One achieved a career and had children by their fifties, and 17 percent had a career and eventually married by their fifties. (The calculation of career and family by age is simpler to do for Groups Three through Five and is set forth in figure 7.1.)

Margaret Reid and Hazel Kyrk, therefore, were not much different from their contemporaries who also managed to launch a career. In fact, had they gone to their twenty-fifth college reunions—around 1935 for Kyrk and 1945 for Reid—they would have encountered a reasonably sized clique with similar life stories. Around 21 percent of their college classmates would have attained a career but not had children, and 13 percent would have had a career but never been married. Only half of their classmates would have been passing around pictures of their children and grandchildren, and 30 percent of their classmates would not have had a husband to drag to the event.

There is evidence that women without children disproportionately attended reunions before the late 1940s. They would have been attending for camaraderie. This would soon change, and the opposite became the norm for those graduating in the 1950s and 1960s. Those with children attended more often than those without. Bragging rights regarding children and grandchildren began to dominate the motivation for attendance, instead of friendship.

The vast majority of college-graduate women in Group One never had a career, even among those who never had children. But that doesn't mean that they weren't employed. Almost all of those who never married were gainfully employed for most of their postschool years. It was this ability of college-graduate women to support themselves that allowed them to retain their independence and not marry.

Notables in Group One were academics, journalists, writers, civic workers, and teachers—in fact, two-thirds fell into these professions. But their occupations differed by marital status and family circumstances. Married notables were less likely to be academics and teachers and more likely to be writers, journalists, lawyers, and artists. Those with children were even more likely to be writers and journalists than any other occupation. The reasons are clear. Professions such as academia and teaching were often restricted to women who were not married. Fields like writing and the arts were unrestricted and easier to mesh with family life.

There is a good reason why romantically inclined female journalists were a staple in mid-twentieth-century movies. *Woman of the Year*, starring Katharine Hepburn and Spencer Tracy, is among the best and is allegedly based on Dorothy Thompson's life.

Dorothy Thompson, a radio personality and an American journalist who covered Nazi Germany, was extraordinary even among the married journalists and writers of her era who were recognized as notables. Others include Pearl Sydenstricker Buck, the Nobel Prize winner who wrote *The Good Earth*, Freda Kirchwey, editor of *The Nation*, Helen

Rogers Reid, president of the *New York Herald Tribune*, and Katharine Sergeant Angell White, fiction editor of the *New Yorker*. These notables achieved the ultimate: they had exceptional careers, but they also married and had children.

Tess Harding and Sam Craig, the protagonists in *Woman of the Year*, like many of the married notables, experienced marital stress. The Hollywood version of the couple eventually reconciled, but the actuality was different. There was a relatively high rate of divorce among the notables in Group One. Although the sample size is small, more than one-quarter of first marriages ended in divorce. The divorces mainly occurred before 1940, prior to the spectacular rise of divorce in America. Thus, the 25 percent rate was exceptionally high for the time.

These notables came of age in the midst of the Progressive Era, when women fought for and earned the right to vote. They explored and acted on the principal social and economic concerns of their day: poverty, inequality, race, and immigration. A century later, these remain among our most daunting issues. Some of the women came from politically active families with fathers and grandfathers who served in state and federal government positions. Others were raised by abolitionists and mothers who fought for women's rights. Several were suffragists themselves.

Most of the early generation of female academics in the US were on the faculties of major universities and published in the most prestigious journals. Yet they were not ivory-tower scholars. They were activists who founded and worked in settlement houses. They were advocates who shifted between academia and policy circles. They were empiricists who collected their own data by interviewing factory workers, prisoners, and immigrants.

Many were acquainted with the great Jane Addams, who founded Hull House in Chicago and was awarded the Nobel Peace Prize in 1931. Several lived and worked at Hull House, including the influential political economist Edith Abbott and her younger sister, Grace, a tireless crusader against child labor and chief of the US Children's Bureau for thirteen years.

Certain institutions played an outsized role in the lives of the notables of this era, including the University of Chicago, Iowa State College,

Columbia, Harvard-Radcliffe, and Wellesley. The Home Economics and Household Administration Department at the University of Chicago (terminated in 1956), together with similar departments at other universities, graduated a large number.

The notables of Group One were an astonishing collection of activists. Probably the best known is Frances Perkins, another social reformer who was influenced by Jane Addams. Perkins married in 1913 and soon had a daughter. But her husband developed an incapacitating mental illness and rapidly deteriorated. His illness both forced and enabled Frances to work. Perkins quickly rose in New York state politics, becoming the state's Industrial Commissioner when FDR was governor.

When FDR was elected president in 1932, he appointed Perkins as his Secretary of Labor, a post she held until 1945 (making her tenure in the position the longest ever). Perkins was involved in the most vital and broad-based social legislation in the twentieth century. She helped craft the nation's Social Security system and its unemployment-insurance laws.

But the only reason that Frances Perkins could be the Secretary of Labor as a married woman with a daughter was because her husband was incapable of supporting her (and had previously lost much of their wealth). Even while her husband was still able to work, Frances kept her maiden name (and fought in the courts to do so), to distance herself from his work in the New York City mayor's office. Such a large part of our nation's resources were wasted when women had to make these difficult tradeoffs just to have a job.

We don't have extensive data on the aspirations of young women at the time, as we do for the post-1960s groups. But we can learn about their dreams and motivations from articles and surveys from the 1890s to the 1920s. Many of these writings were motivated by a concern with the health of college women, starting in the late nineteenth century. Some argued that college physically weakened women, making them unfit for marriage and motherhood. These claims seem fatuous today and were even mocked by many at the time. But marriage rates for college women were so much lower than were those for women who did not attend college that many asked why that was the case.

As psychologist Milicent Shinn maintained, the answer was not because they were having wild and exciting lives. The majority were schoolteachers. The real answer was that college women did not have to settle for the first man who wooed them. They had options.

Unlike those without a college degree, they did not have to get married to be supported financially—instead, they could provide for themselves. "The college woman is more exacting in her standards of marriage, but under less pressure to accept what falls below her standard than the average woman, because she can better support and occupy herself alone." Shinn averred, possibly with little evidence, that "unhappy marriages are virtually unknown among college women." But she further noted that low marriage rates may have also come from the demand side. "Men," she mused, "dislike intellectual women." Still, college women could be pickier than other women. Given the constraints on what married women could do, staying single was a preferred option for many, as soon as it was viable.

Amelia Earhart made this clear to her future husband, publisher George Putnam, when she wrote to him on their wedding day: "You must know again my reluctance to marry, my feeling that I shatter thereby chances in work which means so much to me." He did not shatter her chances to work nor prevent her from taking the flight that led to her unfortunate and mysterious disappearance over the Pacific six years later.

Reinforcing the notion that college women did not marry because they could support themselves are the results of a study published in *Harper's Magazine* in 1928 by Katharine Bement Davis. The information came from a survey of twelve hundred never-married college-graduate women who had received their bachelor's at least five years previously. Most in the sample were in their thirties and older. A clear majority supported themselves financially. When asked why they did not marry, their answers were varied, but the most common response was that they "never met the right man," another way of saying that they could be picky and not settle for someone for financial reasons alone.

The women rarely stated that they remained single to pursue a higher calling. Rather, they did not marry because doing so would have meant that they would have had to forgo their independence. They may not have thought of their employment as a career in the same way it is conceived of today. But they had a life outside their homes, and few would have been able to achieve that had they married.

The study's author, Katharine Bement Davis, was an odd and enigmatic character. Although much of her personal life is obscure, we know that she became, in the words of the *New York Times* (1930), a "noted sociological worker." Her interests were in criminology, particularly the study of prostitutes. She was recruited by John D. Rockefeller Jr. to study the causes of prostitution for the Rockefeller Foundation's Bureau of Social Hygiene, for which she served as general secretary from 1917 to 1928.

It was in doing that research that she was able to explore her interest in human sexuality. Sometime in the 1920s, the Rockefeller Foundation funded extensive research of Davis's that presaged the more clinical work of William Masters and Virginia Johnson. In fact, the survey she used for her article on college women was drawn from *her* survey on sexuality.

There was a dark side to interest in the topic of the low marriage and birth rates among college women. Davis was also a leading eugenicist of her day. Anti-immigration sentiment was building in the 1890s. Eugenicists, worried about the low marriage and birth rates of college women, asked if these women were engaging in a form of "race suicide," causing America to lose its best genes.

Yet another survey, done about the same time as Davis's but far less shadowy, was a canvass of all living alumnae of Radcliffe College to honor the college's semicentennial in 1928. The survey reveals much about the desire of college-graduate women for career and family. Those graduating in the 1910s were not sanguine about combining a job with marriage. But those graduating just ten years later were far more optimistic.

In response to being questioned about whether women could "successfully combine career and marriage," 20 percent of those who graduated in the 1910s and were married "unconditionally agreed" that they could. Ten years later, 35 percent said they could. Married women were becoming far more hopeful that they could pursue a career while they were married. Although these are the responses for those who absolutely agreed that they would be able to combine marriage and career, another group was "hopeful" that such success could be achieved. Including them yields 50 percent in the 1910s (rising to 70 percent in the 1920s) who agreed or were hopeful that women could achieve both.

Although college-graduate women were optimistic that they could combine career and marriage, they were less confident that they could combine career and motherhood. Just 10 percent thought that they could "unconditionally" achieve the goal of having a family and a career. Including those who were "hopeful" increases the group to one-third. The level of optimism holds for those who already had children.

Things were getting better for the college woman who wanted "more." But for most college-graduate women, the realization of an aspiration to have a career and a family would take many more decades.

———

Group One launched our century-long quest for career and family. In many ways, they lived and labored during a magical moment. College-graduate women ran settlement houses and were civic leaders, doctors, prison administrators, and much more. They fought for the right to vote, for the end of sweatshops and child labor, for the minimum wage, work-hours limitations, and birth control. But the only reason that most of them could succeed is because they made a choice, often at a young age, to pursue their passions. They formed groups and were buoyed by one another. They taught women who followed similar pursuits at universities, or provided them shelter. Their stories are so manifold that it is difficult to designate just one as an illustration.

Each generation achieves its own form of success, then passes the baton to the next. Succeeding generations learn from the previous ones. Individuals learn from the decisions of their elders, and in many cases the decisions made were not mistakes. They were appropriate, given the constraints of their time and the ability of participants to peer accurately into the future.

Younger generations coexist with older ones, as I did with Margaret Reid. I observed her in her later years. But I could not see the hindrances that she had faced when young, and the consequent choices she had to make. Most women of her generation had not surmounted the obstacles that she did.

Some of those obstacles had been eliminated. Women no longer had to spend as much time doing household chores. Social lives did not have to be cut back because of rudimentary birth control. Education might not have to be delayed, as it was for Hazel Kyrk, because of insufficient income. A host of technological changes in the household and in people's personal lives released women from drudgery and from vulnerability. Ironically, these were precisely the mechanisms that Reid's research revealed. But many obstacles remained and still endure. Sadie Mossell Alexander, the first Black woman to earn a PhD in economics, couldn't get an academic position due to racial discrimination and became a lawyer instead.

The history of how we got from Group One to today reveals the importance of the larger forces, those we cannot control. They are akin to tectonic shifts moving gigantic plates, adjusting the options for those standing on them. They are the forces that increase general economic growth, shift the income distribution, increase demands for workers in particular sectors, and decrease the demand in others. Ones we think about in our own times include the increase in robots and mechanization, vastly increased trade with nations like China, and the consequent decreased demand for less-skilled labor and increased demand for high-skilled labor.

The fact that I witnessed Margaret Gilpin Reid trudging to the computer center means that we occupied the same moment in time. I admired her perseverance and dedication, yet firmly believed that my life would be different (except for trudging in the snow). I learned from her example that women could have the same commitment to research that my male professors did. What I gained from Margaret was far more than just a role model from a distance. I gained a vision of the possible and a desire to achieve what was lacking. She was an apparition: a reminder of the past, and a hope for the future.

4

The Bridge Group

I FIRST READ Mary McCarthy's semiautobiographical novel, *The Group*, the summer that I turned seventeen. It tells the story of eight young women who graduated Vassar College in the inauspicious year of 1933. Published in 1963, the book instantly soared to the top of the *New York Times* best seller list, where it remained for two years. It was also summarily banned in several nations, for its "frank descriptions of sex, contraception and breast-feeding," according to *The Guardian*.

Though it was tame compared with other banned books at the time, I read *The Group* discreetly, in a cover fashioned from a brown-paper grocery bag, as I commuted on the subway between my parents' apartment in the east Bronx and my summer job in lower Manhattan. I was working as a typist and general gofer in the trade division of MacMillan Publishers off Fifth Avenue near Greenwich Village, not far from St. George's Episcopal Church, the scene of a wedding that begins the novel. My $65 weekly pay provided spending money and enough to buy outfits for my upcoming freshman year at Cornell University. Like the members of the group portrayed in the novel, I, too, explored "quaint MacDougal Avenue and Patchin Place and Washington Mews" with youthful, innocent eyes. (But only during my lunch hour.)

The Group is no ordinary novel. Not only was it a best seller; it forged a new literary style and provided inspiration for, among other works, Candace Bushnell's *Sex in the City*. Over half a century later, it still speaks to many generations about college women's desire for meaning and identity, for career and family.

The eight women left college with aspirations for jobs of some importance, possibly even careers. One aimed to be in publishing, another to be a veterinarian, a third went to graduate school to become a professor of art history. Others took short-term jobs in retail merchandising, social work, public school teaching, or in the exciting New Deal administration. They all wanted to do something—to be productive individuals and worthy citizens.

Each declared that she would work after graduation, at least for a while, and would not succumb to being "languid buds" like their mothers. Almost all were from socially prominent families and were born around 1910—just like Mary McCarthy. They were members of Group Two. Their mothers, born in the 1880s, were members of Group One and had faced the stark choice of picking either a family or a job, possibly aiming for a career. All had taken the "family" route. None of their mothers had a meaningful career, and just two of the eight had ever worked.

The daughters rejected their mothers' lifestyle and agreed that "the worst fate . . . would be to become like Mother and Dad." These eight Vassar graduates "would rather be wildly poor and live on salmon wiggle than be forced to marry one of those dull purplish young men of their own set." They were determined to have lives beyond being just a wife, and they vowed to have acquaintances outside their upper-class social group.

The old order was giving way to the new. A Democrat was in the White House, and all were cheering that "Happy Days Are Here Again." Their parents were Republicans, but change seemed good all around. With newfound optimism that their daughters could accomplish more than they had, even their mothers fostered and encouraged their ambitions.

One can't help but marvel that these eight women, at the peak of the Great Depression, found jobs and kept them for a while, even after they married. In addition to high unemployment, the young graduates faced impediments to married women's work. These barriers, including "marriage bars" and the nepotism prohibitions, had existed before the economic downturn but were greatly expanded with the mounting economic pain.

The women of *The Group* were smack in the middle of a transitional generation of college-graduate women. They bridge Group One, with its low marriage and even lower childbearing rates, and Group Three, with its high rates of both. But an economic disaster—the Great Depression—occurred in the middle. The novel's college graduates planned for something special in life but eventually reconciled themselves to something a bit drearier.

A new set of aspirations for women had emerged in the early twentieth century. College women wanted meaningful jobs, possibly even careers. But they also wanted to marry and have children. Their mothers' generation could envision only one of those twin pillars, and many faced difficult sacrifices and trade-offs. To have a career would mean forgoing a family. To have a family would mean forgoing a career, even a meaningful job. Their daughters grasped at both, in the same way that college women have been doing ever since. Group Two moved the needle in the direction of career and family and away from the harsh Solomonic compromise their mothers had faced.

But the world wasn't yet ready for the college-educated working mother with preschool children. One by one, almost every character in *The Group* married and had babies. Most put aside their career goals, at least for the short time we get to know them. But they had gained an ability to work after marriage largely because of the enormous increase in ordinary white-collar jobs that emerged before the Depression hit.

———

Group Two women were a varied lot. Those born toward the start of the period had lives similar to those of the women of Group One, with low marriage and childbearing rates. Those born toward the end had lives similar to those of Group Three women, with high marriage and childbearing rates. Mary McCarthy was born in 1912, smack in the middle. Like so many of the women in her birth group, as opposed to those in the preceding one, she had a child (plus four husbands, which was far less common).

With such great differences within Group Two, it is useful to separate its women into two parts, assigning the first portion to the birth years

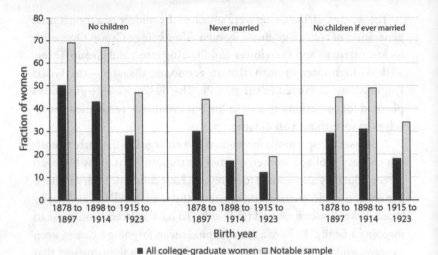

FIGURE 4.1. Marriage and Children among All and Notable College-Graduate Women
See Figures and Table Appendix.

from 1898 to 1914 and the second to those from 1915 to 1923. Doing so allows us to see the large changes in marriage and childbearing among college-graduate women that occurred during those spans. The information on marriage and childbearing for all college graduates and for the notables (the exceptional women we discussed in the previous chapter) is portrayed in figure 4.1, for both Groups One and Two.

The notables all had exceptional careers. It is hard to identify career women in these early groups using other datasets, but the notables were not just women with careers. They were women who made extraordinary contributions. Therefore, it shouldn't be surprising that for Groups One and Two, the notables had far fewer children than did all college-graduate women. In addition, the notables had a higher fraction who never married. What's worth underscoring is that changes over time in marriage and childbearing for the notables and for all college-graduate women are strikingly similar.

In Group One, 44 percent of the notables never married, whereas 30 percent of all college graduates didn't. By the second portion of Group Two, just 19 percent of the notables never married and 12 percent of all college graduates didn't. Although the notables were extraordinary, their marriage rates became nearly identical to those for all college-graduate women, which in turn had become not much different from those for all women, independent of education. College-graduate women were no longer viewed as social misfits, and even the most notable would be seen as less oddball.

Childbearing rates also increased across the two groups. Although just one-half of Group One college-graduate women had children, and even a smaller share of the notables did, by the second part of Group Two, college-graduate women were looking less anomalous. Among those who married, just 18 percent had no children and just one-third of the notables had none. College-graduate and notable women hadn't become as mainstream in terms of childbearing as they did regarding marriage. But their personal and intimate lives had become more similar to those of other women.

By the end of Group Two, women who made exceptional contributions married at much higher levels, and more of those who married had children. Something had shifted that enabled successful women to marry and have children. In fact, many of these women achieved their successes only after they had families. Just like the women in *The Group*, they left college with higher expectations and aspirations for themselves than those who preceded them. They aimed early on for an identity outside their homes and their families, but they intended to have those as well.

Group Two marked a passage from those who had low rates of marriage and childbearing to those with high rates of both, from those who earned women the right to vote to those who were the mothers of the Baby Boom. Changes as dramatic as these beg an explanation. What had shifted to enable college-graduate women to aim for an identity outside the home while also having a family?

A lot. But almost none of the changes had anything directly to do with women and their potential demands for social and economic change. A host of technological advancements appeared in homes and businesses. By the 1920s, most urban dwellings had been electrified, allowing for the diffusion of modern appliances, such as refrigerators, vacuums, and clothes washers. Firms had been largely electrified before households had been, and an abundance of equipment on the job floor and in offices was rapidly put in place.

Firms, consumers, and governments purchased the new goods and adopted the new technologies. In consequence, the economy changed in particular ways and grew. Government regulations did little to expand women's employment and to counter a host of constraining social norms. If anything, local governmental bodies expanded restrictive prohibitions in the form of marriage bars during the 1930s.

As mentioned, among the many technological changes that affected women's roles were a variety of labor-saving devices. The prices of these devices greatly decreased, enabling average families and households to purchase newfangled equipment that substituted for labor. Electrical refrigerators, nonexistent before 1925, were in 70 percent of all homes by the 1940s, when 50 percent had a vacuum and around 60 percent had an electric clothes washer. In the early twentieth century, families began to warm their homes with central heating. They could drink uncontaminated water from their own faucets. They could flush their toilets because cities had constructed urban sewerage systems and flush toilets had become affordable. The time savings from these more mundane and less sensational innovations were enormous, even though they have received far less attention than the horde of household appliances.

All these innovations revolutionized the urban household, reduced the value of women's time in home production, and freed women to be more productive working outside their homes.

But without a separate set of changes in the labor market, the impact of the technological innovations would have been far less. The other labor market changes spectacularly increased the demand for white-collar workers in the early twentieth century and forever altered how women's paid employment was viewed by them, their husbands, and their communities. These changes came about because of a set of technological innovations, albeit somewhat different from those that transformed their homes.

Women had been white-collar professionals of various sorts throughout US history. But what emerged in the early twentieth century was an explosion of demand for workers with more brain than brawn, more flair than flex. In the pre-1900 era, women had been teachers, librarians, journalists, writers, and trained nurses. Some with advanced degrees became government officials, physicians, academics, and lawyers. Office workers, including clerks, typists, and bookkeepers, were of less importance—until the early 1900s. The changes after 1900 were exceptionally rapid. Whereas the number of women in professional service jobs increased by 3.5 times from 1900 to 1930, the number in clerical work increased by more than 8 times.

In 1900, just 17 percent of all working women had white-collar jobs, and a large segment of them—35 percent—were teachers. Most of the teachers at that time were unmarried (think Laura from *Little House on the Prairie*). That was also the case for most other white-collar female workers. Female labor force participants at the dawn of the twentieth century were largely young and unmarried, and that was especially true among the white-collar group. But the dimensions of the female white-collar worker began to change as the attributes of occupations were transformed.

By 1930, about 45 percent of working women were employed in a range of white-collar jobs, including those in offices, agencies, department stores, and as professionals (the group that includes teachers). In fact, teaching increased its share of all working women from 1900. But because of the enormous increase in white-collar work more generally, the share of female white-collar workers who were teachers fell to 18 percent (from 35 percent). In other words, the share just about halved.

Teaching had increased in large part because Americans were expanding secondary education. But all other white-collar employment had increased a lot more. Just about every industry upped its demand for ordinary white-collar workers, including manufacturing, insurance, utilities (especially the telephone company), finance, retail, and catalogue sales (think Sears and Montgomery Ward).

An industrial revolution in the office had vastly driven up the demand for workers, and office jobs proliferated. No longer was there just one "secretary" in each firm who was the keeper of the company's secrets. A massive division of labor changed all of that in the 1910s and 1920s. Firms became monumentally larger, and the role of the secretary was divided into a multitude of tasks. Typists, stenographers, bookkeepers, and operators of all types of machinery, such as comptometers, lithograph machines, and dictating equipment, took over the office. Secretaries remained, but were suddenly accompanied by an army of foot soldiers.

In the mid- to late nineteenth century, US manufacturing was fundamentally altered by mechanization and an intricate division of labor. This was the Industrial Revolution in the US that innovated mass production methods. In the early twentieth century, similar technological shifts occurred in the office, retail sales, and a host of other settings with equally revolutionary impacts.

Not only did the occupations change, but the fraction of women of all ages joining the labor force also increased. Greater demand for office and sales workers led to more jobs with higher pay. Better compensation drew more women into the labor force, since their value in the market began to exceed that in their household and in other activities. The makeover of the office was truly an economic revolution, particularly for women.

Men were also a part of the transformed office, but the effect on their lives was considerably less than for women. Even though 17 percent of all working men had white-collar jobs in 1900—the same figure as for women in that year—and 25 percent did in 1930, the increase was trivial relative to that for women. For men the increase was 8 percentage points; for women it was 28. The forces that increased the demand for white-collar workers had a far greater impact on women than on men.

The economic revolution that vastly increased the demand for office and retail sales workers also boosted the value of literacy and numeracy. The economic returns to years of schooling during that era increased in a manner similar to the rising returns to college in more recent decades, say, in the post-1980s. Jobs in offices required workers who could take dictated gibberish and create comprehensible correspondence. Demand soared for those who could correct spelling errors without a spell-check program, and for those who could construct spreadsheets without access to an Excel program. That took educated smarts.

The consequence of the greater demand for white-collar workers was an increased demand for education beyond that afforded by the common schools of rural America and the eighth-grade classes of the nineteenth-century urban grammar schools. America's response to these new labor market demands was a "high school movement," a moniker given to the increase in secondary education when it took off in much of the nation around 1910. Even though the high school movement began in the very early twentieth century, it was preceded in parts of the nation by an "academy school movement," with tuition paid for by parents. The fact that parents were willing to pay for secondary schooling demonstrates that the high school movement was a truly grassroots crusade.

From 1910 to 1940, high schools mushroomed across much of the nation, and secondary-school education skyrocketed. In 1910, just 10 percent of eighteen-year-olds graduated from high school. But by 1940, the median eighteen-year-old was a high school graduate. The fraction of young people who were high school graduates was greatest outside the US South, which had always lagged the rest of the nation in schooling. It was considerably higher for whites than for Blacks, who largely went to underfunded segregated schools and often resided in school districts where there was no academic high school. High school attendance and graduation rates were also greater in locales away from industrial centers, which enticed youth, mainly the boys, into manufacturing jobs rather than the classroom.

Youths flocked to the new high schools. But in the 1920s girls attended and graduated at greater rates than boys did, in every state in the nation. Females had superior aptitude in high schools and higher graduation rates, just as they have greater college enrollment and graduation rates than do males today. Girls, it seems, do better at school when allowed to excel at it.

The explosion of "good" jobs in offices meant that reasonably educated women could find work that was less physically demanding and safer in many ways than jobs in manufacturing or domestic service, the locus of most previous employments for women. Office jobs were cleaner and in more comfortable settings than those in manufacturing. Everything about them was less dirty, dangerous, and distasteful. Plus, they generally paid more.

When jobs for women are mainly in factories and domestic service, a social stigma often arises concerning women's employment, particularly that of married women. If most of the jobs available to married women are unsafe and unclean, a working wife is a signal to others (say, in the neighborhood or church) that her able-bodied husband is lazy and indolent. He was allowing her to work in a job that not only took her from her children and the care of her home but also was potentially injurious to her health.

A social norm evolved to incentivize men to work in the labor market and support their wives and children. The norm developed when many jobs for men were also rather nasty. It was intended to rebuke husbands and fathers who sought solace in the neighborhood pub and in other wasteful activities. Work was rough and tumble for most, and social standards evolved as ways to protect the vulnerable in society and reduce the burden on other citizens.

But working conditions for most people improved. Jobs in the growing white-collar sector had shorter hours and less harsh work environments. As work became more pleasant and as more women were better educated, the stigma regarding married women's employment decreased, in some places disappearing altogether.

The growth of white-collar employment changed the structure of work for all women—even those with a college degree. These changes enabled even highly educated women to work after they married, not just before marriage and not just later in life. Because the average marriage age for college women remained moderately high until the early 1940s, when it plummeted, employment after marriage meant that jobs could be maintained for several years before the children arrived, if there were any. A college woman could have a job, gain work skills, and then have children. After the kids were older she could return to a position, possibly similar to the one she had left.

Women who graduated college around the dawn of the twentieth century rightly viewed marriage as a loss of independence. But those who graduated a decade or two later, in the 1920s and beyond, saw marriage in a very different light. They did not have to give up their jobs after marriage, at least for a while. The rise of the ordinary white-collar sector was a game changer for almost all women, including the most highly educated.

Mary McCarthy's *The Group* follows the protagonists until 1940, just seven years after their college graduation. We do not know what happened to those eight friends during and after WWII. But as for their real college-graduate counterparts, a large fraction of these women reentered the labor force during the immediate post-WWII era, when they would have been in their late thirties. Twice as many women were employed when they were forty-seven than when they were twenty-seven.

Even though less than 30 percent of ever-married college graduates born around 1910 had jobs in their late twenties, more than 40 percent did when they were in their late thirties. About 60 percent did by their late forties (see figure 2.4; also table 2.1).

The doubling of their employment across that twenty-year period was due to two factors. The first is that many of the twenty-seven-year-olds were moms with young children. Twenty years later, the children had moved out of the house. But there were also important components external to these women's lives, such as rising demand for their skills. Careful analysis demonstrates that around half the total change in women's employment was due to each of these two factors. That is, half of the increase was due to life-cycle changes; the demands of their households, especially those concerning children, decreased. But the other half was due to general economic changes.

The economy went through a series of alterations that increased labor demand in certain sectors, particularly services (such as retail sales), and decreased demand in other sectors (such as agriculture). "Sectoral change," as we saw before, led to a burgeoning of jobs in white-collar employments beginning in the early twentieth century. Women were affected to a greater degree than men, and the impact spilled over even to women with college degrees.

By 1929, when the eight women portrayed in *The Group* entered Vassar as freshmen, they could look forward to obtaining a job upon graduation, getting married a few years later, and retaining their positions for a while before they had children. They would leave for a while and then reenter employment, possibly aiming for a career. Their futures would be very different from those of their mothers and other women in Group One.

But a dark cloud hung over the US in the 1930s that made employment tenuous for almost all Americans. The prospects were especially bleak for married women, even for those with the greatest promise. Unemployment rates in the 1930s were in the double digits, and there were times when the first digit was a two. America had never experienced a national unemployment rate as high and, thankfully, has not since. Unemployment in the era of COVID skyrocketed to almost 15 percent in April 2020, but came down rapidly to around 6 percent by winter 2021.

The lack of jobs was not the only factor. The Great Depression served to turn the clock back for married women's employment. Just when married women, particularly educated married women, were making progress, policies and regulations known as marriage bars were expanded. Prospects for women had been looking up, and there had been support to eliminate marriage bars in teaching. But all that was now a thing of the past.

Marriage Bars

Marriage bars preceded the Great Depression in many occupations, most notably teaching. But they intensified with the enormous rise of unemployment in the early 1930s, long bread lines, and growing economic despair. The decade-long Depression led to an expansion and greater enforcement of existing policies to exclude married women from the best jobs.

Marriage bars were the hiring and firing policies of private firms and governmental agencies, most importantly school districts. The bars were of two types. One governed whether married women were hired. These regulations were called hiring bars. The other concerned whether currently employed women who married while in service would be fired. They were called retention bars.

More school districts in the US had the hire bar than the retention bar. Retention bars denied districts the ability to retain teachers who married, even those who had proven records. Rather, many districts had policies that involved discretion. If the superintendent wanted to fire a teacher, then the excuse of marriage was a good way to do it.

The Depression served to increase the number of school districts and firms with marriage-bar policies, and unemployment was used to justify the enforcement of existing policies. The justification for these policies by both school districts and private companies was that a married woman with an able-bodied husband could be supported by him. Others—single women, widowed women, any man—had greater need. But just prior to the onset of the Depression, there was growing sentiment in various states to overturn existing bars and prevent local school districts from enforcing these rules. The Depression did just the reverse.

Information on the extent of marriage bars is surprisingly scarce given their importance. No systematic data exist across firms. The more than 120,000 separate school districts in the 1920s generally made their own policies with regard to the hiring and firing of their teachers. Fortuitously, school districts were surveyed by the National Education Association at various junctures, and these surveys allow us to pinpoint the fraction of teachers covered by the regulations at four critical moments.

The first moment, in 1928, immediately before the stock market crash, provides a baseline, since no district would have passed regulations in anticipation of a Great Depression. The second date is 1930–1931, at the start of the downturn. The third is in 1942, just after US entry into WWII, and the final survey was done in 1950–1951, during the post-WWII economic upswing.

In 1928, when the economy was still booming, about 60 percent of urban Americans lived in school districts that enforced a marriage bar, and nearly half lived in districts that had the retention version of the bar (see figure 4.2). School districts refused to hire women with impeccable teaching credentials just because they were married. Districts were firing some of their most experienced personnel simply because they had an able-bodied husband.

As unemployment grew during the Depression, the hiring bar on teachers increased, affecting 73 percent of the US urban population. By 1942, when WWII demands had lowered unemployment to almost zero,

FIGURE 4.2. Marriage and Retention Bars for Public Schoolteachers: 1928 to 1951
See Figures and Table Appendix.

an even greater fraction of the urban population (about 80 percent) resided in school districts with marriage bars for hiring teachers. Unemployment had already been subdued. But school districts were slow to recognize that the marriage bar not only was discriminatory but also had begun to harm the goals of teaching.

Less information on marriage bars for office workers is available than for teachers, but it does exist for firms in several large cities at the very start and the end of the Great Depression. These data indicate that as the Depression was winding down, in 1940, about 40 percent of existing female clerical workers were covered by a company policy that barred the hiring of married women. A lower fraction, 25 percent of workers, were covered by a company policy that fired single women when they married. The figures would be considerably higher if discretionary actions of managers could be included. Educated married women found it difficult to obtain an office job during the Depression. But what about before?

Only scant evidence exists for the policy regarding office workers before the downturn. What data are available show that marriage bars, as company policy, existed before the Depression but were greatly expanded as the Depression worsened. So marriage bars were on the books before, during, and after the 1930s, and these regulations seriously restricted the job options of married educated women.

———

College-graduate women of color had very different marriage and employment rates in Groups One and Two than did white women. Black college-graduate women worked, married, and had children—all together. In contrast, white college-graduate women in Group One either worked or they married. Few did both.

Whereas 30 percent of white women in Group One never married, less than 10 percent of Black women did not. Group Two Black women also had less than 10 percent who never married. The figure for white women dropped to 15 percent, half the figure for Group One. Still, Black college women married to a far greater extent than did white college women.

Black college graduates also had far higher labor force participation rates than did their white counterparts. In 1940, among the women in Group Two, about 65 percent of Black ever-married college women were in the labor force, compared with less than 30 percent of white women. The differences exist for these women until they are in their fifties. What explains the disparities in employment and in marriage by race for college-graduate women in Group Two?

Some portion of the difference between the employment of married Black and white college-graduate women was due to the lower family incomes of Black families. Black husbands earned less income than white husbands, for a host of reasons, and their wives pitched in to make ends meet. But that doesn't explain why such a high fraction of the college-educated Black women married. It only explains why, among those who were married, more worked.

Another part of the difference is likely due to the fact that Black women had always worked, in slavery and in freedom, and the social stigma from a wife working in the Black community was far less than in the white community. But that reason, too, goes just so far. Working in agriculture and domestic service might have had less stigma in the Black community. But college-graduate women had far different employment opportunities.

Much of the difference between Black and white college-graduate women's marriage and employment rates is because marriage bars were far less prevalent in the segregated South, where most of the Black population lived in the pre-1940 era. Southern school districts, in general, appear to have had fewer with marriage bars. Alternatively, and with the same outcome, there may have been a lower fraction enforcing the rules that existed.

Information on marriage bars by region, let alone by race, is not available in the surveys previously mentioned. Those surveys provide researchers with the only extant aggregate statistics on the policy, sort of like the Dead Sea Scrolls for marriage bars in teaching. But there are other data that can fill in the missing evidence. Those data concern the fraction of teachers, by race, who were married. The greater the fraction of teachers who were currently married, the less stringent must have been the marriage bars.

In 1920, the fraction married among Black schoolteachers (thirty-five years and older) was 50 percent. That is two to three times what it was for white schoolteachers within the South. It is more than six times the fraction for white schoolteachers in the North. By 1940, it was still the case that about half of Black schoolteachers (thirty-five years and older) were married. The fraction for whites increased, but it was still considerably lower than for Blacks. Black schoolteachers were married to a far greater extent than white schoolteachers—suggesting that marriage bars were less of a constraint on Black, than on white, college-graduate women in Group Two.

The South must have had fewer prohibitions regarding married women teachers, and Black schools in the South likely had even fewer. Part of the reason for the absence of marriage bars for teachers in the South, especially for Black teachers, is that the supply of teachers was smaller there than in other parts of the nation. The South needed as many teachers as it could get, particularly Black ones. For similar reasons elsewhere in the nation, marriage bars would soon be a thing of the past for all teachers.

Anita Landy and Mildred Basden were public schoolteachers in St. Louis with spotless teaching records. Both began teaching immediately after getting their credentials. Landy started teaching middle school English and mathematics in 1929, and Basden began teaching ninth grade English in 1935. They taught every year after their dates of hire—until 1941.

In the summer of 1941, Landy married Arthur Weis, who had once played for the Chicago Cubs. Basden also wed that summer. Their weddings must have been joyous occasions for them. But several months later, each woman received an envelope from the St. Louis Board of Education, and it wasn't a note of congratulations on their nuptials. Rather, it was a notice of dismissal that referred to a regulation that had been on the books, and enforced, since 1897. The regulation stated, "The marriage of any lady in the employ of the Board is considered as a resignation." They both appealed.

In the past, such dismissals went without much notice. But times had changed. Women were working in wartime industries and in civilian jobs vacated by draftees and volunteers. Support increased in many quarters to end the marriage-bar regulations. But there was also resistance to change. In 1944, the two plaintiffs lost their case.

The women immediately filed an appeal with the state supreme court. In 1947, when many school districts in the nation were abolishing their marriage-bar regulations, the Missouri high court ruled in favor of the two defendants. In the intervening six years, Anita Weis had taken a teaching position in a suburban district that did not have a marriage bar. Mildred had left teaching and started a small home-based business. Each woman had given birth to two children. With her reinstatement, Weis, spirited as ever, left her current job and returned to teach in the St. Louis school district, as a "matter of principle."

By 1950–1951, the incidence of the marriage bar for hiring had decreased to covering just under 17 percent of school districts by population, and the incidence of the marriage bar for retaining had decreased to 10 percent. Marriage bars in the nation's school districts would soon be eliminated entirely.

Apart from school districts, many businesses also dropped their bars, although few kept records of personnel changes that have survived. IBM did. On January 10, 1951, IBM's vice president and treasurer signed a brilliantly crafted piece of corporate legalese. "Effective immediately and until further notice: (1) A female employee will not be required to resign from the Company upon marriage. (2) The Company will consider for employment a married female. The above constitutes a temporary modification of the Company's normal policy of non-employment on the regular payroll of married women unless they are the support of their family." The temporary nature of the policy change was, apparently, to protect IBM in case it needed to fire married women again.

Even though marriage bars decreased in teaching and office work after WWII, they persisted in other occupations. One was flight attendants. After 1964, under the Civil Rights Act, employers could not discriminate by sex, but they could discriminate by marital status. A marriage bar that affected both men and women equally was valid. But one that only impacted women was not.

United Airlines, in its drive to make flying more exciting, had hired a cadre of native Hawaiian male attendants on its Honolulu route to provide "local color." These men were not subject to the marriage bar. In 1968, United Airlines was found guilty of violating Title VII of the Civil Rights Act of 1964 and was forced to drop its marriage-bar policy. The "friendly skies" became a little bit friendlier. Several other airlines that hired men as flight attendants under the same marriage-bar rules were able to keep their policies longer.

Why did marriage bars exist prior to the economic downturn, and why did they persist after the Great Depression? In the case of teachers, school districts gained more than they lost from the policy. For much of the period, young female teachers were readily available. Married teachers were older, and while they were more experienced, they also were more expensive and came with baggage—their husbands. School districts and principals wanted a docile labor force, not one that had forceful advocates for the teachers (teacher unions would come later). In addition, most married female teachers at that time would have left the labor force soon after marriage, when they had children.

The reasons for marriage bars in the 1930s varied. Women, according to one firm, "were less efficient after marriage; too much temporary didn't care attitude." In some cases, traditional notions by the person doing the hiring dominated. The manager of a publishing firm in Philadelphia thought "men are too selfish and should have to support their wives," and not surprisingly, the publisher, Presbyterian Board of Christian Education, thought "married women should plan to be in their homes if possible."

But women's work soon began to change. Labor markets became tighter. The demand for labor was outstripping supply. School districts and firms began to lose more than they stood to gain from the discriminatory marriage-bar regulations. The rules were rapidly disbanded, although often replaced by pregnancy bars. Other roadblocks, like anti-nepotism rules, persisted in various employments, such as government and banking, where the rule was considered an important safeguard because of the "possibility of collusion between two members of the bank." Anti-nepotism rules also existed in academia.

Mary Jean Bowman, an economist of education, and C. Arnold Anderson, a sociologist of education, had both been assistant professors at Iowa State, where they met and later married. Together with economist Theodore Schultz (who would later win the Nobel Prize) and several other luminaries who taught at Iowa State, they resigned from the university around 1943 because of what became known as the "oleomargarine controversy." Various professors were asked by dairy-lobbying interests to alter a research statement that oleomargarine was a good substitute for butter. Wartime had greatly reduced dairy supplies, and Americans needed a replacement for butter. (The dairy industry in Iowa appears to have exercised more power in this regard than the corn lobby.) The university president sided with the dairy industry, and the apparent breach of academic freedom led to a wholesale exit of economists from Iowa State. Many of the best moved to the University of Chicago.

But Bowman and Anderson couldn't follow their colleagues to Chicago since the university had an anti-nepotism rule. They decamped to DC to do wartime service in the US government, taught at the University of Kentucky, and had a son. Finally, when the University of Chicago ended its ban in 1958, they became members of the faculty and were reunited with their former colleagues.

Among the notable women, the fraction who were academics (including those listed as research scientists) is considerably higher for Group Two than Group One and is higher still for those born at the end of the Group Two years. One potential reason is that, just as in the case of Bowman and Anderson, the gates of academia opened wider for married academic couples in the 1950s. In addition, relative to Group One, a larger fraction of the academics in Group Two were married. Not only could they be professors and research scientists; they could also be married and retain their professional rank, identity, and life satisfaction.

Serial Lives

Group Two notables who married and had children often had to wait for their moment of career glory. The reason in each case is different, although most involved the care of children and the careers of their husbands. Demographer Irene Barnes Taeuber married Conrad Taeuber, a fellow demographer, and had two children. Irene worked part-time when the kids were young and then followed Conrad to DC in the 1930s. She later made her mark in the field of demography with a path-breaking book, published in 1958, on the demographic history of Japan. She was promoted to senior research demographer in 1961 at the age of fifty-five.

College women from Group Two had serial lives of many types. Their mothers, however, generally had one life: they married and had children. These are the two generations of Mary McCarthy's *The Group*. As we will soon see, the Group Three daughters of the earlier generations intentionally planned serial lives of job, marriage, home life, and then a return to work in their middle years.

Few in the earlier generations of college women managed a serial life better than Ada Comstock. Comstock graduated from Smith College in 1897. She became dean of women at the University of Minnesota, then dean of Smith College and its acting president, and finally, in 1923, at the age of forty-seven, she became the first full-time president of Radcliffe College.

For all its history, Radcliffe had had no faculty of its own. Harvard professors would teach men in Harvard Yard and then walk to the Radcliffe Quad to teach the same class to the women. In a bold move in 1943, when many Harvard men were involved in the war effort and not on campus, Ada worked with the university administration to integrate many classes between Harvard and Radcliffe. Rather than having the professors walk to the Quad, Radcliffe women would walk to the Yard and take their liberal arts classes together with Harvard men. The trip that the women made every day placed them on the same footing as the men. The year 1943 marks the start of a shift to true coeducation at the two institutions. It also marks two important changes in the life of Ada Comstock.

She retired from Radcliffe that year, knowing that she had made a difference in the lives of both men and women for years to come. That chapter in her life was closed, and another would soon open. On June 14, a week after her last official duties at the college, she married Wallace Notestein in Christ Church, Harvard Square. Wallace, who was Sterling Professor of English History at Yale, was an old friend of Ada's from Minnesota. Neither had ever married. She was sixty-seven, and he was sixty-five.

Their wedding was featured in the *New York Times* the following day. Many others were announced on the same page. The grooms were mainly active servicemen. The brides were mainly recent college graduates. One had graduated in 1942 from the Women's College of the University of North Carolina, another was still attending Smith College, and yet another had graduated Sweet Briar College in 1940. Only a few had graduated in the late 1930s. They were the wave of the future. The grooms, thank goodness, would not continue to be active military personnel. But brides had become exceedingly young, almost overnight.

Ada Comstock had lived the life of a career woman in Group One. But she was swept up in the vast sea of demographic and economic changes of the early 1940s, just at the end of Group Two's college years. She married for the first time precisely as female college graduates began to marry, and to have children, at the youngest ages in US history. Her serial life was a harbinger of some of the goals of Group Four. She first had a career and then she married.

Ada is a reminder that lives can be long and encompass many paths. She and Wallace lived in New Haven, Connecticut, and remained married for the next twenty-six years, until he died at age ninety. She lived to be ninety-seven.

5

At the Crossroads with
Betty Friedan

THE HONEYMOONERS, a popular TV sitcom in the mid-1950s, was broadcast live from a set that looked more like a 1930s tenement than post-WWII tract housing. The show was set in the 1950s but looked back in time. Ralph Kramden, a bus driver, and his wife, Alice, struggled to make ends meet. So did Ralph's best friend, Norton, and his wife, Trixie. Neither couple had children. They scraped by from week to week, but neither Alice nor Trixie worked for pay. They could have: there were ample well-paying jobs available for women. But as Ralph announced to Alice when she started looking for a job after he was laid off, "While you are my wife, you will never work. I have my pride." Alice won the argument, as she often did, and took a job as a secretary—for a week.

Lucille Ball, playing her eponymous double in the 1950s staple *I Love Lucy*, didn't have a job, except when she comically strayed from being the stay-at-home wife of bandleader Ricky Ricardo (played by her real-life husband, Desi Arnaz). As far as any real job went for Lucy, Ricky declared, "It's out of the question." *The Honeymooners* was more extreme in its portrayal of the dictatorial husband, but neither show was unique in its depiction of women's roles—and of some married couples.

Other popular TV shows of the 1950s featured children as central characters and more contented couples. In the appropriately named *Father Knows Best*, the Andersons—Margaret, a housewife, and Jim, a salesman—dealt with the everyday problems of their three children, two of whom were in their teens when the show first aired. *Leave It to Beaver* portrayed a model suburban family—June Cleaver, a housewife; Ward Cleaver, a nine-to-five office worker; and their sons, Wally and "the Beaver"—all seen through the perspective of the young Beaver.

Margaret Anderson and June Cleaver were the perfect housewives of the mid-1950s, happy to be in their homes—forever. June cleaned the kitchen wearing a dress and pearls. Chirpy, calm, sensible, and judicious, she and Margaret had no obvious ambitions other than solving the problems of their children.

Before the 1940s, married women, even those without children, were not supposed to work outside their homes. Most became stay-at-home moms after having children; some were stay-at-home wives even before the kids arrived. But after the late 1940s, women's roles began to change. *The Honeymooners* looked to the past for humor about a growing set of tensions. *I Love Lucy* continued the hilarity about gender roles but with a set that reflected 1950s prosperity. *Father Knows Best* and *Leave It to Beaver* were about the new idealized family.

Margaret, June, Alice, and Lucy were fictional characters. What were the circumstances for real women?

Betty Friedan's justly celebrated book *The Feminine Mystique* (1963), which sold millions and is credited with igniting second-wave feminism, told us that, rather than being fictional, these TV mothers represented the reality. According to Friedan, American women had retreated from being the career women of a past generation. College women of the 1950s were taught that "truly feminine women do not want careers, higher education, political rights."

Ironically, Friedan looked to a bygone era to find a better time for women. She viewed the 1950s as a regression, a reversal of what educated women once did—namely, went to college to graduate. But in the 1950s, "60 per cent dropped out of college to marry," and "two out of three girls who entered college were dropping out before they even finished." These women once had career ambitions nurtured by having had paid jobs when they were young. Suddenly, in her view, "Girls were growing up in America without ever having jobs outside the home."

Where they had once flocked to the professions, "Fewer and fewer women were entering professional work."

None of these statements were true—not even close. The past wasn't rosier than the present for most Americans, nor was it any better. In the 1950s, more women were graduating from college—a lot more. Whereas 5.8 percent of those born around 1920 graduated from a four-year college, 12 percent did among women born around 1940. Not only did more women graduate from college; a higher fraction of them continued with their education.

Therefore, it is not the case that "fewer and fewer" of the college women of the group graduating in the 1950s earned professional and advanced degrees relative to the previous group. The fraction of college-graduate women receiving advanced degrees increased from around 30 percent, for college classes graduating in the mid-1940s, to 43 percent, for those graduating in the mid-1960s. The fraction of all women who received an advanced degree expanded by three times.

Women's roles and their ambitions were not regressing; in fact, they were expanding. And their opportunity and capacity to do more were racing ahead.

Friedan was primarily concerned with women who had graduated from the most elite colleges. The core of her message was that women who were of superior ability and high innate determination were trading their dreams for the "feminine mystique." By considering only a select group of undergraduates, Friedan could compare how the ambitions of the crème de la crème changed over time. That would appear to be a fine methodology. But she was wrong.

Among the graduates of Radcliffe College in the 1920s and 1930s, for example, about 7 percent eventually earned a professional or other advanced degree above a master's. Among those who graduated in the early 1950s, 12 percent did, and among those graduating in the late 1950s, 18 percent did. So a greater fraction of elite college-graduate women were awarded premier postgraduate degrees in the era of the "feminine mystique," relative to their predecessors.

What of the notion that these college-going women abandoned their educations as soon as they found Mr. Right? Women did drop out of college more than their male counterparts, until around the mid-1970s. But the dropout rate was nowhere near the fraction claimed by Friedan—who proposed that it was "two out of three." In fact, the dropout rate was actually lower, not higher, for women of this generation compared with the dropout rate of their predecessors.

Friedan often lamented the loss of female talent among those who had entered the elite colleges. But data for those women, measured here using information for Radcliffe entrants and graduates, also indicate that the dropout rate decreased from the 1920s to the early 1960s. The relevant dropout rate here is the fraction of college juniors who did not receive a bachelor's degree, which would roughly measure who left (presumably) after meeting Mr. Right. Whereas this dropout rate hovered around 15 percent during the interwar period, it was about 7 percent in the 1950s and just 3 percent a decade later. By the 1960s, therefore, almost all Radcliffe women who made it to their junior year ended up finishing their undergraduate degrees.

And what about their initial ambitions, as suggested by their employment soon after graduation? About three-quarters of college women in the 1950s held at least one full-time job six months after graduation. That holds even for those who were currently married. College-graduate women in the 1950s, even those who married young, did not lack ambition.

But they did prioritize family. About that, Friedan was spot on. The majority married soon after graduation and had children rapidly thereafter. Most had been employed right after graduation, and almost all of those left the workforce when they had children. But their retreat into domestic life and reemergence after their children were safely in school were well planned. These women were not confined to their homes with an indefinite sentence, as the endless reruns of *Father Knows Best* and *Leave It to Beaver* would have led us to imagine.

The early 1900s weren't better than the 1950s for college-graduate women. The reason is that so many college-graduate women from Groups One and Two didn't marry. Recall that among those graduating in the early 1900s, almost one-third never married, and half of the entire group who graduated from college never had children. Members of

Group Three, graduating in the 1950s—because they did marry in greater numbers and because so many of them did have children—enjoyed more, not fewer, choices than previous groups. They had the choice to have a family first and a job (occasionally a career) second.

But that doesn't mean that the 1950s were perfect. They weren't.

Alice, Trixie, and Lucy weren't college graduates. College-graduate women had better options than their less-educated counterparts. A married woman's employment may have been a signal that a working-class husband was indolent or low paid, but that would not have been the case for the college-graduate husband of a college-graduate woman. That husband would have brought home good money, and the husband's pride would have been less defined by whether his wife worked to supplement his income.

Though their husbands were less opposed to their jobs than Ralph was to Alice's, and generally displayed little opposition to their employment, college-graduate women of the 1950s and early 1960s faced their own doubts about working when their children were young. "The main reason . . . I am not working," a female graduate of 1957 wrote several years later, "is I feel my time is needed with my home and family." Another, who tried to work, noted resignedly, "My own little children seem to be showing the effects of having a babysitter. So I feel that the best thing to do would be to stay home. . . . I shall miss teaching." Only around 30 percent of moms who graduated from college in 1957 or 1961 worked for pay right after they began families and before their children entered school.

Their lack of employment was also due to an inability to find high-quality, affordable childcare services. Then, as now, women with preschool children who did not earn a high salary would see little of their income after paying for childcare and income taxes. As one noted, "Were it easier to obtain a suitable babysitter at a reasonable rate I probably would have worked after my second child. However it is not sensible to work just to pay a babysitter."

But by the time these women reached age forty or so, their labor force participation rates soared. Seven in ten were working for pay, and most were employed full-time. In fact, almost all the women who entered the labor force when their youngest child scampered off to elementary school had, long before, planned their reentry into the job market. Their undergraduate training and skills had been acquired with these expectations.

Whatever barriers college-graduate women faced in the post-1940s, they were slight compared with those blocking earlier generations. The official and legal barriers to their employment had been enormous before the early 1940s, in some ways greater than those facing their less-educated counterparts.

Take public school teaching. By the 1950s, it became the premier occupation for college-graduate women, especially those with school-aged children. When a teacher got off from work, her children were coming home. When her children were home for the summers or vacation, she was too. If she took time off, perhaps to have another child, she could return to her teaching job with little loss of position.

But before the early 1940s, the teaching profession, as noted in the previous chapter, was largely off limits to married women in many US school districts. The same was true of office jobs. Marriage bars were ubiquitous in much white-collar work, including teaching. In fact, they were imposed by school districts in many areas before they were adopted by private firms.

Even in 1928, when the American economy was booming and no one knew they were on the verge of a Great Depression, half of all school districts fired teachers after they married, and six in ten refused to hire married women from the get-go. Prospects dimmed even further for married schoolteachers after the onset of the colossal economic downturn of the 1930s.

Office firms were a bit kinder to married women than were school districts before the Great Depression. But even at the start of the downturn, about one-third of offices fired women who married, and half did not hire married women. Matters only got worse for married women as the downturn continued.

Black college-graduate women in the pre-1940s era were less impacted by marriage bars in teaching than were white women. As discussed in the preceding chapter, the reason may be because fewer

Southern school districts had such bars, or because those that had bars didn't enforce the existing ones.

As noted previously, Dorothy Wolff Douglas, an economist herself and the wife of University of Chicago economist (later US Senator) Paul Douglas, was denied a position at the college because of nepotism rules. She took a position at Smith College, and Paul left his professorship at Chicago and took one, briefly, at Amherst College. Dorothy, it should be mentioned, played an important role in the education of Bettye Goldstein (later Betty Friedan). She taught Bettye economics when she was a Smith undergraduate and introduced her to radical economic ideas and feminist thought.

Opportunities expanded for married college women in the 1940s. With soaring demand for war goods and the decrease in civilian men's labor power due to the draft, the double-digit unemployment of the 1930s became a thing of the past. Suddenly, the discriminatory labor policies that had made sense to many during the Great Depression, and even before, were abruptly ended.

By the 1950s, marriage bars were largely thrown out through various state court rulings. But they ended mainly because the times had changed. Regulations that remained on the books were left unenforced by school districts and firms (most day-to-day rules by private-sector employers had never been written down anyhow). As one large insurance company noted in 1956, "Previously, the personnel department did not favor employing married women . . . but insurance companies have to hire them [now] in order to fill their needs."

Increased demand for female workers during WWII and the postwar era affected all education groups. For young women considering an education beyond high school, it meant that college had become a much better proposition. A college-graduate woman could be employed, she could get married, and she could have children. For those who got married, the college diploma was useful for far more than a wall decoration.

Even if college tuition and fees were low, as they were at state institutions, an education was still expensive. Schooling took valuable time and often involved living away from home with expensive room and board. As a diploma began to guarantee a woman varied jobs even after marriage, college became more worthwhile for women. Attendance began to increase in the 1940s and 1950s, and the gap between male and female graduation rates began its long downward narrowing. (Female graduation rates eventually overtook those of males around 1980, but that is beyond our story for now.)

The benefits of a college degree for women in the 1950s took several forms. Most involved employment at some point. Some were reaped in immediate job offers, but most gains accrued in the future. A college degree, and often a teaching certificate, was an insurance policy against a husband's or a marriage's premature demise. A job was, in addition, something to "fall back on," as it was termed at the time. There was always the chance that something could happen to one's husband. Divorce, disability, and death struck in an apparently random fashion. "An education for the wife," wrote one graduate of the class of 1957, "can be considered a form of insurance." Another noted that education "is security."

But most women of the period were employed at some point, regardless of whether or not one of life's unfortunate events befell their mates. Women worked before and after marriage, but before having children. Employment generally reoccurred after the kids were in grade school, sometimes older.

The college diplomas of the women of this era were not mere adornments, and their educations were not just for contingencies. Nor was their time in college intended only to increase the probability that they would nab a college guy (although college women were, in fact, far better at nabbing college guys). Many accounts, including Friedan's, would have us believe that the woman who had met her match in college and dropped out to get married was the real winner. She wasn't. Not in terms of the eventual education of the man she would marry and not in terms of her career. And not in terms of her general well-being.

Though college women of the 1950s eventually used their educations in the labor market, college was indeed also a great way to meet a man. College women disproportionately marry college men, and a college-graduate man is more financially secure than is one with fewer years of schooling. Furthermore, the number of men attending college in the post-WWII and post–Korean GI Bill eras soared. Whereas there were 1.3 men per woman in college before the WWII draft emptied college campuses of men, there were 2.3 men per woman in college when the GIs returned, and many took advantage of the GI Bill. College-graduate women always stood a higher chance of marrying college-graduate men, but the chances were maximized for those graduating from the 1950s to the 1970s.

Relative to a high school–graduate woman, the woman who graduated college from the mid-1950s to the early 1970s had more than a 60 percentage point edge in terms of marrying a college man. The high school graduate had a 10 percent chance of wedding a college-graduate man, as compared with about 70 percent for the college-graduate woman.

Among married college-graduate women, the fraction with college-graduate husbands increased over time. For the group graduating in the late 1950s, it was 75 percent, whereas for those graduating in the early 1930s, it had been 50 percent. The fraction stayed high for graduating groups from the late 1950s until the early 1970s, when it fell back to 65 percent (the level it had been around the end of WWII).

The women portrayed in *The Feminine Mystique* possessed more agency than female college graduates from previous groups, and more than Friedan gives them credit for. College-graduate women planned their lives. Barriers began to crumble. Married women could finally work in various capacities. But constraints remained. There was still social opprobrium if a woman worked when she had young children.

Tides of Change

As Americans young and old began to readjust to a vibrant post-WWII economy, a host of demographic changes occurred that would alter the face of American society for decades. These changes were so monumental that they continue to affect the US economy and society today. The Baby Boom affected the lives of college-graduate women, just as it affected all others. Though many possibilities have been offered, we still do not know precisely why the marriage age plummeted, why the birth rate soared, and why these changes lasted for as long as they did.

These demographic changes had no precedent in US history. They created a new normal in marriage age and family size. A half century later, we romanticize the post-WWII era as a span of glory. Yet looking at any time series for births and marriages demonstrates what an abnormal time the 1950s and 1960s were. And despite what many claim, standards of living were considerably lower than later in US history. But because the era followed a long economic depression and a world war, it was a breath of fresh air to those living through it.

The first major demographic change in post-WWII America was that the age at marriage plummeted. Marriages had been deferred during the Great Depression, when unemployment was high, often exceeding 20 percent. Economic downturns generally cause an increase in the age at marriage and a decrease in marriages more generally. The downturn of the 1930s lasted almost a decade. Yet the demographic changes during the Great Depression were not so large that the post-WWII era took America back to an "old normal."

The decrease in the age at marriage that occurred beginning in the 1940s more than made up for the increase of the 1930s. It was far greater and more extensive than changes experienced in other post-WWII nations. Whereas the citizens of most other nations married to make up for lost time, Americans married earlier, not just right after V-J Day, but for two decades to come.

Americans became marriage- and family-crazed. Even some women in their older years, who had graduated from college in the early 1900s, got swept up in the marriage boom that occurred at the start of the US entry into WWII. Recall that Ada Comstock, who had enjoyed a highly successful career in university administration, married for the first time in 1943—at sixty-seven years old. Mildred McAfee, who had been the seventh president of Wellesley College and the first director of the WAVES during WWII, married for the first time in 1945. McAfee single-handedly integrated the WAVES. When that was done, she married the dean of the divinity school at Harvard University, when she was forty-five years old.

The second big postwar change is that women's age at first childbearing dropped. American couples were not just having babies sooner in their lives; they were also having more. The well-known boom, which began in the immediate WWII era, was the result. One might have expected such an increase in births; wars cause delays in births while men are off fighting. But just as the lower age at marriage wasn't merely the result of the end of the Great Depression, the increase in births wasn't merely the result of the end of WWII.

The Baby Boom era in the US began in 1946 and lasted until 1964. A mini boom preceded it around 1942, when draft regulations affecting the war effort meant that babies, for a brief time, were draft deferments for fathers. Most important for our journey, the Baby Boom affected the more educated along with everyone else, and led the college-graduate group to have marriage and childbearing rates that were more similar to those of the noncollege group.

Early marriages for women in the 1950s produced young mothers. Almost 60 percent of college-graduate women gave birth to their first child before age thirty. A Women's Bureau survey of female college graduates of 1957 paints a similar picture. In that survey, 64 percent gave birth within seven years after graduation. Just 17 percent of all women who graduated college in the 1950s would not give birth in their lifetime.

College-graduate women had always married later than high school–graduate or college-dropout women, and a lower fraction of college graduates ever married in the first place. College-graduate women in the early 1900s, for example, married later than noncollege women, and about 30 percent of the college group never married. But even they married later and had their children later than those in the 1950s.

The fraction of the 1950s college-graduate group who never married was just 8 percent. Furthermore, those in this group who did marry tied the knot when young. Almost three-quarters married before they turned thirty, with a median age for a first marriage of just twenty-three—meaning that half of these women married within about one year of graduating from college. Survey data of the graduating classes of

1957 show that almost 40 percent had already taken their marriage vows a mere six months following graduation.

———

Given the large fraction of college-graduate women from the 1950s who married soon after receiving their diplomas, many must have met, dated, and been engaged to their future husbands while in college. Many observers, like Friedan, wondered if college had been a serious academic endeavor for women who married so closely on the heels of graduation. We have already seen that the college dropout rate for women was vastly overstated in Friedan's book. Their dedication to planning for a future job was equally understated.

The college academic experience is often gleaned from a student's field of study. A college major usually indicates the job or career path for which the student is preparing. By the 1950s, about four in ten female college graduates majored in education (which included education programs and schools). Nursing, child development, nutrition, library science, and social work were also popular majors for women. All told, about half of all female college graduates in the 1950s majored in a subject or area that directly led to an occupation.

The actual fraction who graduated with training closely related to an occupation was considerably larger, since even those who did not major in education often took education courses, and many graduated with a teaching certificate. According to the class of 1957 survey, more than six in ten female graduates left college that year with a teaching certificate—even though only 33 percent of them had an undergraduate major in education.

So more than half of all female graduates in the 1950s left college prepared to enter low-risk jobs in high-demand fields with hours and days consistent with taking care of one's home and children. Teaching, nursing, social work, and other occupations that attracted so many college women were, and still are, typically female jobs with scant room for advancement and often lower pay relative to other positions requiring a college degree. But they had amenities that made them highly attractive occupations.

Women deliberately majored in these fields with the intention of pursuing paid employment in the future. Many of these jobs would have been off limits to married women in the pre-1940s era, but public schoolteachers in the post-WWII era could work after marriage. The increase in the number of children meant that there was strong demand for teachers. And the increase in fertility meant there would eventually be an increased supply of teachers, from women who wanted to combine family with good employment opportunities.

Why would more than half of all female college graduates major in fields that led directly to a specific occupation unless they wanted to pursue paid work at some point? Why would more than 60 percent have obtained a teaching credential unless there was a nontrivial probability that they would become teachers? Other majors—literature, art history, foreign languages, music—would arguably have been more enjoyable. Yet most college women in the 1950s chose majors that would lead to occupations they could combine with family life. "Teaching," noted a Group Three member with an advanced degree, "is an ideal career for a woman who wants to have a family too. I was able to leave the field for 13 years and return with no penalties."

The college-graduate women of the 1950s generally did not pursue long-term careers—but they did prepare to be in the workforce at some point. And most eventually entered the labor force. The female graduates of the 1950s planned to have a family and then a job. By and large, most did.

A Game Plan

Friedan was correct that from the end of WWII to the mid-1960s, Americans celebrated the home, with the wife as its center. Friedan was also correct that a host of labor-saving devices introduced from the 1920s to the 1950s meant that keeping the home spotless required only a fraction of the time it once had. Product developers indeed had incentives to convince women to use their products. Pledge, a furniture polish, challenged women to shine their dining room table so they could see their own re-flections. Makers of kitchen and bathroom cleaning products encouraged women to sanitize countertops and even toilet bowls as if they were din-ner plates. But Friedan was not correct that the period reversed a prior upward trend in the professional ambitions of college women.

The Feminine Mystique was read by millions. It was the handbook of a revolution. Why were many of Friedan's statements incorrect? One reason is that she was comparing the career accomplishments of women in the 1950s with those of a subset of older college-graduate women who hadn't married and hadn't had children.

Looking backward through this lens meant she didn't observe the full group of college-graduate women in the previous generation and couldn't see the gains they had made. Most of those who attained ca-reers in the previous generation neither married nor had children, whereas those who married and had children generally never had em-ployment. But the college-graduate women in the 1950s gained the abil-ity to have both—serially, in their lifetimes.

The college graduates of the 1950s had considerably more options than those who preceded them. Those graduating in the early 1900s had the lowest levels of marriage and childbearing of any group. They did not make up for that by producing an impressive record of career suc-cess. As they often faced the stark choice of career or family, too many wound up with neither. And looking backward meant Friedan didn't notice the aspirations of the graduates of the 1950s. Her book was pub-lished too early for her to observe their eventual accomplishments, for her to see the fruits of their game plan.

The college-graduate women of the 1950s, by the end of their working lives, achieved a greater level of career success than those of the early 1900s, and a far greater level of success at combining career and family. They lived through many stages. Friedan captured them in their period of confinement. She conveyed the frustrations and lamentations of many. But the members of this group were not frozen in time. Most planned their escape long before Friedan published her book.

We know about their aspirations and achievements from surveys done in the 1950s and 1960s. These surveys are large and extraordinary in their breadth, and are representative of the nation's college graduates of that day. The women (and men, in some) were chosen by the survey design teams to produce nationally representative samples, and each dataset has statistical weights to ensure that. These were not small surveys of one or a few colleges. Rather, they were meant to reflect the range of all bachelor's-granting institutions in the US. There are two major surveys. One covers the women in the college graduating class of 1957. The other includes the men and women in the graduating class of 1961.

Class of 1957

In January 1958, the Women's Bureau of the US Department of Labor surveyed a sample of the June 1957 graduating class of women. A follow-up survey of these women was taken seven years later, motivated by concerns that some college-graduate women who had left the workforce for a time to raise children were finding reentry difficult and might need additional training.

The initial survey of the 1957 class, done six months after their graduation, obtained completed responses for about six thousand graduates. Since eighty-eight thousand women received a bachelor's degree in June 1957, the number of surveys collected was fully 7 percent of the total class. The study was vast for the time, and an impressive, important undertaking of the Women's Bureau.

Each of the women surveyed had attended one of 153 (coeducational or single-sex) colleges and universities. The survey group was distributed regionally and by type and size of institution similar to that of all female college graduates in 1957. So it can be used to learn about all college-graduate women at the time. The follow-up survey done in 1964 had about five thousand respondents.

Both surveys of the class of 1957 clearly show that female college graduates had plans to continue with their education, get a job, and, for some, have a career. They put family first, for sure. But that does not mean they were to be forever confined to their homes.

These women married early, but most were employed before marriage and for some time after. Six months after their June 1957 graduation,

40 percent had married and one in four of the married set already had children. But fully 82 percent of the entire group were employed directly after graduation, and almost all of those were working full-time (including some attending evening school). Six out of ten of the employed group were teachers. Just 7 percent of the entire group, disproportionately those with young children, were not seeking work.

So, how did Friedan ever get the idea that college women of the 1950s had lost the Puritan work ethic? Perhaps part of her thinking is reflected in the reality that, though almost all were employed, just 18 percent of the graduates in 1957 stated that they "planned to have a career." Most responded that they would stop work when they married or had children. And that's precisely what they did. Yet most of those who planned to stop work were confident that they would eventually return—and they did. These were not women who intended to be Margaret Andersons and June Cleavers.

Did they keep their intentions seven years later, when most were married and many had young children? For the most part, they did. Seven years after graduation, 85 percent of the class was married, and 78 percent of that group had children, almost all of whom were preschoolers. Most of the women had young kids when social norms argued against employment for mothers with preschool children, at a time when childcare facilities were rare. Yet even among those with preschoolers, 26 percent were employed.

It cannot be emphasized enough: these were not women lacking in ambition. About half of the college graduates were employed, and almost a fifth of those employed were also attending graduate school. But they often eschewed calling themselves career women. As one put it, "I am a housewife and mother and not a complete career-type of woman [but] I do enjoy teaching school."

That did not mean they wanted to remain at home full-time. Although most claimed that they were working to support their families, 13 percent stated that their current employment was "to have a career," and an additional one-quarter mentioned that they wanted to pursue a career at some later date. Significantly, more than 80 percent in 1964 aspired to be employed in the future (including those currently employed).

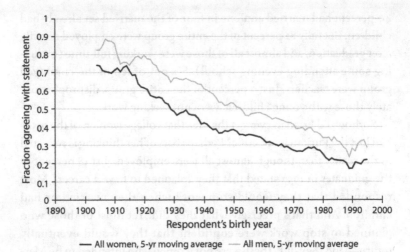

FIGURE 5.1. Fraction of Men or Women (All Education Levels) Who Agree with the Statement "A Preschool Child Is Likely to Suffer if His or Her Mother Works" *Source*: General Social Survey (GSS) micro data from 1977 to 2016. Also see Figures and Table Appendix.

The greatest constraints on these women were the norms of their day that dictated to those with young children that they *should* stay at home and that their children would "suffer" if they worked. The General Social Survey (GSS) has asked a cross section of Americans, ever since 1977, whether they believe that "a preschool child is likely to suffer if his or her mother works." The fraction of women and men who agreed with that statement declines with their year of birth, as can be seen in figure 5.1. For those born in the early part of the twentieth century, about 80 percent of men and 70 percent of women agreed. But for those born toward the end of the century, just 20 percent of the women and 30 percent of the men did. Because these individuals were interviewed at different ages, these data conflate the social norms they acquired in their youth with those they acquired as they aged. Although there is change over time for individuals, the most important factor, by far, in determining agreement with the statement is the year of an individual's birth.

What about the constraints imposed on these women by their husbands? The dictatorial yet comedic husbands of Alice and Lucy (Ralph and Ricky) each opposed their wife's taking a job even though no children had entered the equation at that time. But Alice and Lucy had not gone to college. College-graduate wives in 1964 were better off—83 percent of their husbands were not opposed either to their employment or to their plans for future employment. Even among families with young children, just 21 percent of the husbands were against having their wives work outside the home.

The husbands who opposed their wives' working were mainly those whose wives weren't currently working or seeking work. We can guess that the men's disapproval may not have been the decisive factor in these wives' employment, since likes generally marry likes and perhaps both spouses believed that a woman's place was at home. But, as one woman noted, her husband "considers my role of mother and wife a full-time job, and that ends that."

Notwithstanding such preferences or mores, the class of 1957 had a game plan. Their time at home didn't mean they weren't bored, and it doesn't mean they found a level playing field in the workplace upon reentry. The Women's Bureau surveys in both 1957 and 1964 asked respondents to "add any comments," giving the women a chance to air grievances they may have had. Their tone changed with time, and by 1964 many voiced the variety of protests Friedan had tapped into and provoked.

Six months after graduation, the class of 1957 women were content and chirpy. College had been generally good. Life was just beginning, marriages were new or being planned, and babies imagined. "I plan to be married in June," wrote one, "and believe I am prepared for this in a much broader way than someone not going to college." Said another, "I want a career in social work. If I marry, I would like to return to it when my children are in elementary school."

The majority were in their first jobs, the ones they had prepared for in college. Many praised their liberal arts educations as a once-in-a-lifetime opportunity. "A good job relating to one's major is important but even more so is the personal satisfaction one attains from a liberal arts background." For some, a broad education was also useful for being a good spouse and mother: "Macalester College . . . prepares a woman for an occupation but also requires political, cultural, religious, courses which make for a more informed, community active wife." Others had exactly the opposite sense: "My college training has been invaluable to me in appreciating life and useful in obtaining employment, but almost useless in carrying out my duties as a housewife."

While most reminisced nostalgically about college, some criticized their college education as not providing enough job training, knowledge of the business world, and careers more generally. A surprisingly large number chided their colleges for not requiring clerical skills. "Theatre Art majors should be required to take typing and should be encouraged to take shorthand . . . for beginning a career in the theatre." Those who majored in education often griped about the lack of "practical experience in a classroom rather than hearing an overabundance of lectures." (A common complaint throughout the ages.)

Their responses in 1964, seven years after graduation, are more varied. About one-third wrote additional comments in an open-ended section. These respondents and their comments divide into two obvious groups. The great majority were either actively employed or planned to return to work soon. The others were Junes and Margarets, who considered themselves permanent housewives.

A representative response for the majority group was: "Like most of the women I know, I enjoyed school and working very much, and I am not working now because of the demands of child-rearing. However, once my youngest is in school, I will go back . . . and spend the remaining circa 25 years before retirement in a satisfying job (probably teaching)." About three-quarters of the group were seemingly happy. The less-than-contented quarter voiced disgruntlement about employment discrimination, pay, and, most often, the problems combining motherhood and jobs in a world of expensive and often unavailable childcare. As one noted, "My work experiences with the [mentally] disturbed were a source of constant satisfaction. . . . [But] I had so much difficulty finding competent childcare . . . that I was finally unable to carry the whole load."

The Junes and Margarets, a small proportion of the group, wrote comments like: "As for the present, I am most happily 'employed' by a loving husband and children and am kept very busy with baking, sewing, cleaning, washing, entertaining, reading, and traveling." This group expressed somewhat more contentment than the first, who were either struggling with time constraints or looking forward to returning to work.

Class of 1961

Insights from the class of 1957 are not unique. An even larger and more extensive survey was taken four years later by a private organization and has both male and female respondents. Like the class of 1957, the graduates of 1961 had future plans, although they abided by many of the constraints and social norms of their day.

Findings from the original survey and first follow-up were summarized in several volumes, one appropriately titled *Great Aspirations*. But the survey was too large for the computers of its day. Only a small part of the data was ever analyzed, and the material that was written up mainly concerned male responses. Little was reported about the women. I recently rediscovered this treasure trove of information.

The *Great Aspirations* project was directed at determining whether college graduates, both men and women, planned to continue their studies in graduate and professional schools. It also investigated special issues facing college women. The surveys asked revealing questions about aspirations, achievements, and perceptions of social norms.

Just like information from the class of 1957, the surveys for the class of 1961 demonstrate that these women had ambitions that went well beyond being a housewife. Almost all intended to be employed upon graduation. Most would marry soon after and have children in rapid succession. The majority planned to return to the workplace, and made investments in their education and training to ensure that.

In 1968, when they had been out of college for seven years, just 17 percent of the women considered being a housewife their long-term goal. Although that is higher than the 10 percent who felt that way a year after graduation, it is still low. Even when they were caring full-time for their young children, fully 83 percent did not consider being at home round-the-clock their long-term goal.

Children and the home were, according to 70 percent of the group, these women's top priority for the next decade. But at the same time, an astounding 50 percent also expected that a "career" would be important to them after their first ten years of marriage.

Similar to the class of 1957, they married at high rates soon after graduation: 42 percent of the women were married less than a year out of college. At seven years out, 84 percent were married, and 81 percent of the married group had children.

In the spring of 1961, when they were about to graduate, they reminisced about the ambitions they had possessed when they entered college. A substantial fraction of both the women and the men had thought they would continue in some graduate or professional program in the future. A year after graduation, almost 20 percent of the women and 35 percent of the men were attending graduate or professional schools. At the last survey, seven years after graduation, 30 percent of the women and 40 percent of the men were, or had already done so. According to data on the achievements of all members of the 1961 undergraduate class, 40 percent of the women and 50 percent of the men eventually earned an MA degree or above.

Women with a bachelor's degree today continue their education to about the same extent as do men. They get almost the same number of JDs, PhDs, and MDs (although somewhat fewer MBAs). If the figures for women from the late 1950s and early 1960s seem low by comparison, they are remarkably higher than one would have surmised from descriptions of that era by Friedan and other writers.

But why do we view these college-graduate women as Margaret Andersons and June Cleavers? Because, as we've established, the college graduates of the 1950s put family first. In 1964, 37 percent of the women in the 1961 class who were married and working full-time still referred to themselves as "housewives."

The female respondents expressed views about constraining gender roles. The *Great Aspirations* survey posed statements to the respondents about gender norms, including the one, mentioned previously, that has been asked by the GSS ever since 1977: "A preschool child is likely to suffer if his or her mother works." About 60 percent of the women (and

66 percent of the men) strongly or mildly agreed with the statement. Other questions, probing the relative attachment to the social norms of the day, concerned women's "careers." Three-quarters of the women agreed with the statement "It is more important for a wife to help her husband's career than to have one herself." About the same fraction agreed that "A married woman can't make long-range plans for her own career because they depend on her husband's plans for his."

These were commonly held notions at the time. The belief that harm would be done to a preschool child if the mother wasn't at home full-time is largely what kept many women from working when their children were young. But there were also insufficient daycare facilities. And the facilities were few because the demand for them was not high enough. It was a classic chicken-egg problem. One needed a large enough change in care arrangements to shift the notion that harm would be done to children if their mothers worked.

My mother, who became a highly respected elementary school principal in New York City, repeated that idea to me when I was young and even into my forties, as my nieces, her grandchildren, were raising their children. "Preschool children," she would say, "are better off with their mothers." She did not begin her teaching career until I was safely in school. It was not clear to me whether she really believed that, or whether she was still conforming to the outmoded norms of her day. I recently asked her. At one hundred years old, she insisted that a preschool child, and even an infant, would be perfectly fine in a high-quality daycare facility, perhaps even better taken care of, while the mother works. There was a time when she simply could not imagine that there was an alternative to the stay-at-home mother; later in life she could not imagine there was a time when she would have thought otherwise.

The other two statements, concerning the importance of the husband's career, reflect the relative earnings of the couple. Since the man was presumed to earn far more than the woman, and generally did, deferring to his career objectives would bring more income into the family.

These might seem like antiquated notions that would have been held only by the least ambitious women, but that was not the case. Even the women who expected to attain an advanced degree did not think that employment while their children were young was possible, and given the state of childcare, it might not have been. Family was their priority, but a job and possibly even a career was also on their radar screen. The college-graduate women of the 1950s were constrained, just as June and Margaret were, but they planned to break free. And they eventually emerged from their chrysalises.

The better-known members of this group created a "family then career" path, but most of them arrived at that point in a circuitous fashion. Many reemerged in midlife to reveal their talents and passions.

Erma Bombeck, the humorist writer, was born in 1927. She graduated from the University of Dayton in 1949, the year she married Bill Bombeck, whom she had met in college. She began her writing career while she was adding to her family but put down her pen for ten years while she raised her three children. She then reemerged as a wildly successful syndicated columnist who wrote hilarious tales of suburban family life.

Jeane Kirkpatrick, the first female ambassador to the United Nations, was born in 1926, had three children, and earned her PhD in government two decades after receiving her BA. She became politically active when she was in her forties, and was appointed ambassador in 1981. Grace Napolitano, born in 1936, reared five children with her husband, and beginning at age thirty-five worked at Ford Motor Company for two decades. She first ran for public office (city council) at fifty years old, and at age sixty-seven became a member of the US House of Representatives.

Carrie Meek graduated in 1946 from Florida A&M for Negroes but left the state to obtain an advanced degree since at the time none were offered to Blacks in Florida. She later became an educator and an activist in community affairs in the Miami area. At age fifty-four, she was elected to the Florida state house, and in 1992 she became the first Black congressional representative from Florida since Reconstruction. Upon her retirement, her son Kendrick was elected to her position, succeeding his mother.

Phyllis Schlafly, the well-known conservative, anticommunist, antifeminist woman who sparred with Betty Friedan, provides an exception that proves the rule. Born in 1924, Schlafly wrote an enormously popular book on the presidency, was an activist for conservative causes, and had six children. To advance her antifeminist causes, she earned a law degree at age fifty-four (not entirely with her husband's blessing) and ironically launched a late-stage career in support of the notion that women should be full-time wives and at-home mothers.

The women who reemerged in their older years with a career, as Bombeck, Kirkpatrick, Meek, Napolitano, and Schlafly did, were not a large group. But those who left home for *jobs* when their children had grown were. And this group was joined by an even larger set—those from Group Four who graduated college beginning in the late 1960s and early 1970s. The women in that later group expressed career desires from the outset, rather than later in life.

The reentrance of 1950s college-graduate women into the workforce when they were middle-aged was part of their longer-range plans. But their reappearance as workers coincided with larger changes in society that would usher in the era of career and family.

————

The female college graduates of the 1950s are halfway along our journey. They had far more options than their predecessors did. Those who followed would have even more.

By the early 1950s, married women who were college graduates could become teachers, and they could even work part-time. Surveys of the early 1960s demonstrate that most college-graduate husbands did not oppose their wives' employment—some were delighted with it. College women finally had the option of attaining a family and a job and, for a select few, a career.

They accomplished more than women of previous groups had been able to. A greater fraction of all college-graduate women became professionals, and a greater fraction achieved career and family. They did not drop out of college at higher rates than previous groups, and they certainly did not lack ambition.

But as Erma Bombeck wryly noted, "If life is a bowl of cherries, what am I doing in the pits?" Comments from the 1957 follow-up survey in

1964 exposed a dark side to the progress college women had seen. Some with training in male fields bemoaned, "All the time I was looking for a job [with a BS in chemical engineering] I kept reading . . . how we must encourage our women to take up engineering . . . through the tears, I laughed." Another lamented, "I have experienced some prejudice on the part of employers to hire women in a traditionally man's work. . . . Even under the 'so-called' merit system of Civil Service."

Perhaps the most restrictive constraint facing this group was the widespread notion that young children would be harmed if their mothers were "selfish career women." "Should the intelligent wife who would really like to work do so although her children will suffer somewhat from her absence or should she stifle her own needs for her children's sake?" was the dilemma expressed by many. As one respondent noted, "The cost of having a child cared for while going back to school . . . doesn't leave much in the way of making [employment] worthwhile financially." Deviation from the stay-at-home standard was made even more difficult by the lack of accessible and affordable childcare.

The emptiness and frustration of this generation was the theme of Betty Friedan's celebrated volume, encapsulated by the phrase "Is this all?" But their domesticity had an expiration date. They had mapped out a serial life of *family then job* (with the small subset who eventually achieved *family then career*).

Friedan was right about the role of education in those women's lives, but she was wrong on the aspirations of the group. Friedan's volume was situated in the middle of a varied journey to greater equality for women and greater equity for couples. She looked to the past to find a moment that was better for college women. But the past wasn't better. Change was already underfoot—even the very women about whom she was writing would enjoy some of its benefits. What Friedan did help do, though, was ignite these women's desire for independence, and inspire confidence that they could change the status quo. That fuel would help spur the graduates of the 1960s and 1970s toward a quiet revolution that would alter the face of American life.

6

The Quiet Revolution

MARY RICHARDS, the central character of *The Mary Tyler Moore Show*, was in the vanguard of the Quiet Revolution. In 1970, after breaking up with her boyfriend, Mary moved to Minneapolis and snagged her dream job as associate producer of a local TV station's evening news. She was thirty years old, unmarried, a college graduate, and happily on her own. Her goal was to build her career while maintaining an active social life. She thrived in both areas, armed with raw talent, spunk, charm, and a secret weapon: the Pill.

The show lasted for seven seasons, through more than a dozen boyfriends and two engagements for Mary. Throughout, she remained Midwestern pure, adored by audiences across America. But no TV show had yet to touch on birth control. How did the writers broach the topic of the Pill? Discreetly and humorously, in season two.

Mary's parents are visiting her apartment, and as her mother leaves, she shouts back to Mary's father, "Don't forget to take your pill!"

Mary and her father respond in unison: "I won't."

As an embarrassed Mary tries to conceal her response, her dad looks on, somewhat disapprovingly. The year was 1972—the first time the Pill had been mentioned on a sitcom.

The Pill was approved by the FDA as a contraceptive in 1960 and was released for sale by prescription the following year. Millions of married women began using it, almost immediately. But the laws of many states effectively prohibited the distribution of birth control to unmarried women below the age of majority, without parental consent. And the age of majority was generally twenty-one. In 1969, just seven states had an age of majority younger than twenty years old. Believe it or not, the state laws had been on the books (and often enforced) for a hundred years and were originally sparked by a federal antivice act passed during the Victorian era.

In the late 1960s and 1970s, many states passed legislation that lowered the age of majority, and some even expanded the rights of minors through court action. These legal changes had little to do with sex and contraception, let alone the Pill. The most important change was the Twenty-sixth Amendment to the US Constitution. That gave eighteen-year-olds the right to vote, prompting thirty-six states to lower their age of majority.

By 1972, at least twelve states had loosened restrictions on prescribing the Pill (and other forms of birth control), without parental consent, to unmarried girls sixteen years and younger. By 1974, that number expanded to twenty-seven states, and the age of majority was low enough that college-freshmen women in forty-three states could get the Pill.

The Pill had two mothers and (at least) four fathers. Yet it was an orphan for a long time, as a drug that no one wanted to produce. But once it was produced, everyone wanted to take it, and once it was accepted by consumers, Big Pharma wanted to profit from it.

The notion that a pill could control conception was the dream of Margaret Sanger, birth control pioneer and controversial visionary. In 1916, Sanger opened a birth control clinic in Brooklyn in direct violation of a state law prohibiting the dissemination of contraceptive products. She was swiftly arrested, but remained undeterred, and she worked tirelessly across her long life to help women of all races and ethnicities to prevent pregnancy. She was not entirely noble, however.

Sanger's dream was to create a pill that a woman could take with her morning orange juice. Just one sip and, voilà, the pregnancy risks of sex disappear, as does the dependency on a man to provide such certainty. But only in Sanger's older years could her dream take shape. First off, the biochemical processes of ovulation were not understood until 1937. The science behind synthetic hormones was unknown until the late 1940s. Science wasn't the only barrier. Funding was scarce for research on a project that was expected to be opposed by Catholics and others in still-puritanical America. Even Big Pharma was scared off from this venture, for some time.

In 1949, Sanger convinced Katharine Dexter McCormick to fund research on her visionary pill. McCormick, in essence the second mother, had received a BSc in biology from MIT in 1904 and married the scion of the McCormick agricultural machinery fortune. Her husband died in 1947 and left her an enormous fortune, which she used, in part, to fund Gregory Pincus's work on a contraceptive pill. In the meantime, Carl Djerassi at Syntex produced a synthetic version of progesterone, and Frank Colton at G. D. Searle synthesized a related hormone in 1953. Not long after, researchers Pincus and John Rock conducted tests using synthetic hormones to prevent ovulation. The Pill was, sort of, born. Rock, a practicing Catholic, later came up with the twenty-one-days-on, seven-days-off dosing that mimicked a woman's cycle. (Although some have claimed that Rock hoped this chemically induced rhythm method would pass muster with the Pope, his real reason was to give women assurance that they were not pregnant.)

Even though Mary Richards was unmarried, she was above the age of majority. Still, it took time for Americans to accept the notion of premarital sex on TV. The bedrooms of even married couples, like Lucy and Desi, had twin beds. But by 1972, Mary's lifestyle would not have seemed scandalous to most TV audiences. Viewers were ready for an episode that mentioned the Pill. Furthermore, they were ready for a sitcom that featured a career-oriented woman who asked for her rights and the salary she warranted.

Mary was just one unwitting foot soldier in a movement that would soon sweep the nation: the Quiet Revolution. The movement forever reshaped American society, education, marriage, and family, and did so in a remarkably brief period. Unlike the noisier movements of the late 1960s and early 1970s, featuring women's liberation marches and demonstrations by groups like the National Organization for Women and more radical offshoots and factions, the Quiet Revolution was championed by many who were unaware of their historic significance. Only with hindsight can we trace their role in a grand transformation.

The Quiet Revolution radically changed the happiness formula. The Pill provided part of the liberation that women had been clamoring for in the noisy revolution. It enabled the members of Group Four to enter careers that required large up-front investments of time and money, such as in law, medicine, academia, finance, and management. Such women needed freedom and time. But just like Mary Richards, that didn't mean they were going to retreat from the dating scene or give up intimate relations with the opposite sex.

These young women followed the college graduates of Group Three, who in large measure married soon after graduation and proceeded to have a bevy of children. As we learned, many had plans to reenter the workforce when their kids were older, and most did so. They had majored in subjects that enabled them to take up occupations like teaching.

My mother strongly advised me—many times over—to get a teaching certificate, just like my older sister had done. It was a credential "you could fall back on," she would often say. That was her code for a secure job you could enter after your kids were in school or if your husband left you (by the door or at the coroner). My response, repeated as many times, was: "You fall back on a couch, not a credential." I was a Group Four booster. I didn't want a secure, steady job in a traditionally female occupation. I wanted the excitement, often accompanied by the insecurity, of a PhD in a highly competitive, dynamic field.

Women who graduated college in the early 1970s could not have been more different from those who came a decade, or less, before. But the two groups were intricately bound. Many in the older group, whose children were of school-going age by the 1970s, were just returning to the labor market as those in the younger group were graduating from college. The younger women saw what the older ones had done: graduated from college, entered the labor force, and then left when they had children. Many years later, they reentered the workforce, mainly in female-dominated occupations with low pay.

We, Group Four women, reckoned that we could do a lot better. We had a new vision of the future. By putting career ahead of family, we could increase our chances of obtaining a fulfilling and remunerative profession that would extend over our long lives. Many more of us would enter professions similar to those that men had always occupied, with high status and high pay. That meant investing early in our post-bachelor's educations. For many of us, it meant postponing marriage; it meant delaying childbearing. We could do that. After all, we had something Group Three did not have: the Pill. And we had the ability to obtain it while we were young and could invest in our professional and postgraduate training.

No previous group of college-graduate women had entered career-oriented professions and fields on as grand a scale as did Group Four. A fulfilling career was the pinnacle we imagined attaining as we stood at the trailhead of a new life. We were going to scale the mountain. What Group Three accomplished had been a mere walk in the park, or so we naïvely thought.

We saw that by the early 1970s, 90 percent of the married female college graduates in Group Three already had children. To those in Group Four, family seemed the easy part of life's many goals. Our predecessors, it appeared, had no trouble reproducing. There was little reason for Group Four women to imagine they would not eventually do the same. They just needed time to shore up their careers. *Then* they could add a fulfilling family life.

To understand how much the Pill changed the happiness formula, let's consider why marriages had happened so early in its absence. Putting off marriage in the 1950s and 1960s could have meant forgoing an active life of intimacy with the opposite sex. But that wasn't going to happen. It never had. There was always sex before marriage—and unprotected sex is a game of Russian roulette. Before the Pill (and the IUD), even protected sex (think barrier methods) was a bit of a crapshoot. In the absence of female-controlled, convenient, and highly reliable contraceptives, pregnancy is a real possibility. Earlier marriages were often a consequence of the risk of pregnancy, and a pregnancy almost always led to marriage. In the absence of truly effective contraception, women often tied the knot soon after becoming sexually active.

Just how much premarital sex happened in the distant past can be approximated, as a lower bound, using calculations from clever historians who have matched marriage and birth records. These reveal that from 1700 to 1950—250 years!—around 20 percent of brides were pregnant on their wedding day. That 20 percent is for a period when a premarital conception was widely considered a shameful condition, and one to be concealed.

Pregnancy is simply the tip of the iceberg. If we know that 20 percent, or more, of women were pregnant at their nuptials, then a lot more than 20 percent had engaged in premarital sex but were lucky or skillful in preventing a pregnancy—or they had to terminate one. But when abortion was neither legal nor safe, a pregnancy almost invariably resulted in a so-called shotgun wedding.

For the more recent period, direct information on the age when a woman first had sexual intercourse demonstrates that there was enough premarital sex to keep the age of first marriage low in an era of fallible contraception. In 1960, the median age at which unmarried women first experienced intercourse was around twenty, or when she was a junior in college. (The age is a median—so 50 percent of first sexual encounters occurred earlier than that.)

By 1970, the age at first intercourse decreased to eighteen and a half, or the age of a college sophomore or freshman. In 1980, it was seventeen and a half, and by 1990 it was sixteen and a half. This median fell as better, and female-controlled, contraceptive methods became accessible to young women. Even before the Pill, when the age of first intercourse was still twenty years old, it was sufficiently young that it would have been difficult to put off marriage.

To protect against the risk of getting pregnant in the absence of fairly foolproof and female-controlled methods of contraception, a heap of commitment mechanisms were employed, including the status of "going steady," exchanging rings, getting pinned (a fraternity thing), receiving a lavaliere (another fraternity thing), and the ultimate—becoming engaged with a glitzy ring. Each was a public declaration that a woman was safeguarded, should she get pregnant. Everyone would know who the father was. He had no place to go but to the altar (possibly with a shotgun aimed at his head).

But the safeguards themselves led to earlier marriages, even if the couple wanted to delay tying the knot. Telling the world, especially one's parents, that you were dating raised expectations and made the possible inevitable. A promise to be with someone as a trial run easily morphed into a promise to be together forever.

Contraceptive measures such as the Pill enabled later marriage. Legal and safer abortions did the same. With these improvements, young couples were not enticed into a hasty marriage by the need for pregnancy insurance. Earlier marriages, especially forced ones, had many defects. Many didn't last, especially when legal changes governing state divorce laws allowed them to be dissolved. The enormous increase in divorce in the 1970s was concentrated among those who had married young. Among the Pill's many beneficial effects was that it reduced divorce by increasing the marriage age. Another was that by delaying marriage and postponing childbearing, women were given extra time before marriage and motherhood to pursue advanced degrees and cement their careers.

Women's newfound time to pursue their work empowered them. But no one warned Group Four women about ticking clocks. The medical establishment was not yet jabbering about a precipitous decline in conception after age thirty-five. The potential of birth defects from old eggs hadn't yet made it onto anyone's radar screen. The problem, to Group Four, was *preventing* pregnancy, not getting pregnant. They believed that motherhood could be delayed without much consequence.

Though Group Four women lacked a thorough awareness of the costs of delaying a birth, they knew quite a bit about the price they might pay by not marrying early. Those who didn't marry young wound up with slim pickings. If a woman delayed marriage while most others did not, the probability of never marrying would have increased, and the chance of marrying her perfect mate would have diminished. But as state laws changed and the Pill began to diffuse among young single women, the age at first marriage increased for all.

Armed with the new secret ingredient, the recipe for success became: "Put marriage aside for now. Add gobs of higher education. Blend with career. Let rise for a decade, and live your life fully. Fold in family later." Once this happiness formula was adopted by large numbers of women, the age at first marriage increased, even for college women who did not take the Pill. That reduced the potential long-run cost of marriage delay for any one woman.

For Mary Richards and college-graduate women in the early 1970s, career came first, then marriage, and then, maybe, family. After 168 episodes, Mary was finally promoted to producer of the evening news at WJM-TV, the fictional news station in Minneapolis at which she worked. By age thirty-seven, she had succeeded in establishing her career. We never learn whether she married or had children after the series ended. But if Mary was like others in her group, she stood a fairly high chance—around 30 percent—of ever marrying. But she faced a much lower probability—less than 10 percent—of ever bearing a child.

From the 1950s to 1972, the median college-graduate woman married before the age of twenty-three. To my students today, that is shocking, even terrifying. Women (and men) who married at that tender age must have found their mates when they were still undergraduates. That pursuit weighed heavily on many female college seniors in the 1950s and 1960s who worried that they wouldn't have their coveted "ring by spring."

At least half of Group Three married so young that they would have had little time before getting hitched to begin their careers or continue with their education. Upon receiving their bachelor's degrees, this half mailed their wedding invitations, not their graduate and professional school applications. Making career plans even more remote, a marriage so soon after commencement meant that the college years might have been taken less seriously by many. After all, a spouse would have to be found along the way to a degree.

Being married constrains choice in various ways. Marriage often means solving a joint location problem. Too often, that has meant locating where the husband's job and educational opportunities are the best. And for many in Group Three, marriage was quickly followed by a birth. Neither early marriage nor being a young mom was part of Group Four's new recipe for success.

Around 1972, the median age at first marriage for college-graduate women began to increase. Within five years, the age had risen by more than two years, so that half of the women in the college class of 1977 would marry after they were twenty-five years old. Women could use these extra unmarried years to complete a JD or MBA. The age at first marriage continued to climb, so that by 1982 almost none had their "ring by spring," whereas a decade earlier, half of them did.

My birth year—1946—is right around the start of Group Four, when the median college-graduate woman would have married just under age twenty-three. Did the women in my graduating class marry as young as that? I went back to Cornell University for a reunion event and decided to see if my graduating class had been different. I gave a talk about our class, called "A Pivotal Generation." While preparing, I paged through my twenty-fifth reunion book, remembering the brilliant and talented women from my graduating class. Did they marry just a few years after our graduation? Or did those graduating from institutions that prepared women for meaningful careers marry later in the late 1960s?

I coded the information I could glean from my reunion books and discovered that a third of my class had married within just one year, and half had married within three years of our graduation, around age twenty-four. So the answer was no, they weren't marrying much later than the national average. One of my senior-year roommates married just before graduation, and the other married exactly a year after. I had forgotten. In my mind, I was a central part of Group Four, rather than a forerunner. But my graduating class had one foot in the past and one in the future. Half married young and half married older. Even those who married young became caught up in the trend toward greater career goals. One of my roommates became a professor of child development, and another became a labor arbitrator and a New York State township judge.

Among the college-graduate women born ten years later—in 1956—the median woman married at twenty-five-and-a-half years old, a full 2.5 years later than in my graduating class. Group Four made a clear break with the past. The marriage age in figure 6.1 makes a sharp turn upward just as Group Four begins. But the increase in the marriage age was not only a sharp break with the past. The age at first marriage continued to increase long after; for the most recent college-graduate women, it has increased to around twenty-eight years old. Group Five has continued the trend that Group Four began.

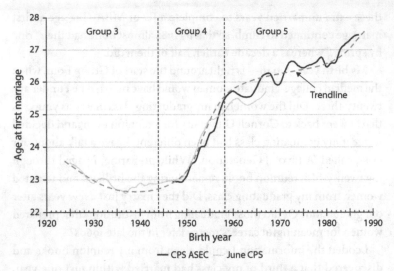

FIGURE 6.1. Median Age at First Marriage for College-Graduate Women by
Birth Year: 1925 to 1988
See Figures and Table Appendix.

The divorce rate also began to increase in the 1960s, as state laws shifted away from those requiring cause to those that allowed divorce by "mutual consent." Some states moved even further and adopted laws that allowed unilateral divorce. (Unilateral divorce means that just one partner can sever the relationship.) Property division is decided separately and determined by state law and, often, by the courts.

The combination of the increase in divorce, particularly earlier divorce, and the later age at first marriage meant that the fraction of a woman's life she would spend married plummeted. Group Three women would remain married for more than 80 percent of the years from age twenty-five to age fifty. But by the end of Group Four, women spent less than 65 percent of those twenty-five years married. These changes altered the identity of women from being family and household centered to being far more involved in the world of work.

Couples in the 1970s reacted to the adoption of unilateral divorce laws by investing less in each other and in their households. Women were less willing to specialize in household production and wanted more portable human capital, in the form of education and job training. They had fewer children, had greater employment, and contributed less to putting their husbands through professional and graduate school. Economic independence became more valuable.

Another very public change appeared in the late 1970s, showing that the women of Group Four had proclaimed their own identity. Not only were they going to put off marriage and have a career, but Group Four women would keep (or try to keep) their so-called maiden names. Throughout history, virtually all married women had taken their husbands' names (except in cultures where family names were more important). The only ones who didn't were movie stars and writers. I remember, as a child, finding it exotic. I would do it too. But how? And what would the DMV, the SSA, and my in-laws say?

The acceptance and diffusion of the appellation "Ms." in the early 1970s enabled women to keep their own last name. Although (according to the *Oxford English Dictionary*) the use of "Ms." dates from 1952, the term did not gain much traction until the appearance of Gloria Steinem's *Ms.* magazine in 1972.

By 1990, about 20 percent of all recently married college-graduate women across the US retained their surnames at marriage. The demand to keep one's family name increased as the age at first marriage soared and as women cemented their careers before marriage. They could "make a name" for themselves professionally before having to choose what their full name would be.

The Quiet Revolution was amazingly swift in its transformation of women's lives. But the transformation didn't come out of nowhere. Its members were in training from the time they were young. They had observed a succession of generations and seen how theirs would be different. They formed more accurate expectations of their future labor force participation and had ambitions that were consistent with it.

The realization of Group Four took root in the 1960s when they, as young women, revised their expectations of their future employment. Since previous generations had greater lifetime employment, Group Four perceived that they would as well. They would have long-run careers, not many short-run jobs. They began to prepare themselves early. They took more science and math courses in high school and increased their scores on standardized tests.

Their path presents a logical progression. Expectations regarding future work, social norms concerning women's family and career, and the determinants of women's life satisfaction each changed in the late 1960s and throughout the 1970s. These factors were the leading signs of change, as a rainbow signals the end of the storm. Group Four, the members of the Quiet Revolution, formulated a new set of goals in the long march of history. To achieve their goals, they needed to delay marriage and they needed to delay motherhood. It is inconceivable that the Quiet Revolution could have occurred without the enabler of delaying both that still allowed for dating, sex, and unchanged marriage prospects when the right time came.

The Power of the Pill

In 1960 the Food and Drug Administration (FDA) approved the use of a product christened Enovid by its manufacturer. Nearly everyone else called it, and its successors, "the Pill." By 1965, more than 40 percent of married women younger than thirty were on it. But few young single women were able to obtain it. Both legal and social factors were at work.

The protagonist of *The Marvelous Mrs. Maisel* quipped, "There's a new thing called a birth control pill. . . . It's just a little pill, and when you take it you can have sex all you want and not worry about getting pregnant. However, only married women are allowed to take it—the ones who don't want to have sex. Who said the Food and Drug Administration doesn't have a sense of humor?" But the culprit was a set of state laws, not the FDA.

Before the late 1960s, it was not legal under the common law in any state for a physician to prescribe the Pill as a contraceptive device to an unmarried woman below the age of majority without consent of her parents. But by 1972, on the heels of the Twenty-sixth Amendment (1971), the "age of majority" had been lowered to eighteen years old in most states, and "mature minors" in many states were enabled, by judicial decision and statute, to obtain contraceptive services. The extension of family-planning services to minors and the changes in local norms regarding appropriate practice had reinforcing effects. Not only was a young, single woman allowed by law to obtain contraception, but she also had a place to go to get contraceptives, family-planning advice, and essential health care services, including testing for STDs.

State laws in the 1960s that directly regulated the sale of contraceptives were an additional impediment. In 1960, thirty states prohibited advertisements regarding birth control, and twenty-two prohibited the sale of contraceptives in some manner. Universities and colleges, fearful of violating state laws, viewed the legal ambiguity regarding the distribution of contraceptives as good reason *not* to provide explicit family-planning services on demand. Even if they offered such services, they were unlikely to advertise their availability. Only after the age of majority was lowered in a state did universities offer family planning to undergraduates.

After the various legal changes, the Pill rapidly diffused among young single women. In 1976, 73 percent of all single eighteen- and nineteen-year-old women who had ever used contraception had taken the Pill. The Pill remained the contraceptive method of choice for a very long time, even as its health concerns mounted.

For the young women of Group Four, the Pill in the late 1960s and early 1970s did not greatly alter their lifetime fertility. Even though it didn't have a substantial impact on the number of births they eventually would have, it did monumentally change the timing of their marriages and the scheduling of their births. And with a larger group of single individuals, others could afford to wait, and an ensuing multiplier effect added to the increased age at first marriage. As the age at first marriage increased, women could be more serious in college, plan for an independent future, and form their identities *before* marriage and family.

Revolutions are generally caused by great events and not by a tiny pill. The empirical argument for the impact of the Pill on the Quiet Revolution relies on the timing of various changes and on econometric analyses of the age at first marriage and career change. Legal changes by states that expanded the rights of minors in the late 1960s and early 1970s facilitated the diffusion of the Pill among young, single women.

We can be confident that the laws *caused* the change, because the timing of those legal changes differed by state. Plus, the states that changed their laws and policies early were neither more liberal nor more conservative. They were random in their politics, religiosity, and social traditions, which suggests that none of these factors played a role.

The legal changes enabled young, unmarried women to obtain the Pill through various routes. College campuses got family-planning clinics that dispensed health care, advice, and contraceptives. Planned Parenthood and OB/GYNs could prescribe it without fear of being shut down. As more women took the Pill and as the marriage age rose, even those who were not on the Pill did not have to be concerned that the pool of eligible men was being drained. With an increase in the age at marriage, more women continued to graduate and professional school without paying as large a personal price (although their tuition remained the same). More began careers that required extensive on-the-job training and progression.

——————

In what ways did the noisy revolution of the late 1960s and early 1970s impact the quiet one? It must have urged it on, if not through legislation, then through greater empowerment and community. "Feminism gave [us] the desire to work, but effective contraception gave [us] the *ability* to work," noted Betty Clark, a petroleum geologist and late-blooming economics enthusiast of Group Four. Betty had, according to Berkeley economics professor Brad DeLong, "accidently stumbled into [his] introductory economics class" the day he was lecturing on my work concerning the Pill's economic and social impact. The discussion compelled Betty to write an e-mail to DeLong about her personal experiences.

Revolutions are often set in motion when a group of preconditions awakens individuals, fires them up, and leads them to believe that life could be different and better. Revolutions are messy affairs, often difficult to dissect. In this case, the origins are reasonably clear. They go back far. This was not a coup d'état. There were several preconditions, none of which would have been sufficient by itself to set the revolution in motion or sustain it. The Pill alone probably would not have sparked it. But it was necessary for the Quiet Revolution to gain traction and continue.

The women of Group Four witnessed social change brewing all around them. As children they passed through the early 1960s and were part of the Cold War mentality. They obeyed the authority of their parents and of the government. But by the late 1960s, when they were young women, many took part in antiwar demonstrations and marched in liberation movements.

Other decades also saw great social change, but those periods did not produce a Quiet Revolution. A distinguishing building block was a large increase in women's labor force participation and in their willingness to be employed, which was due to another set of factors, including the increase in the earnings of all workers.

Consider a sixteen-year-old girl in 1970. Let's say she has an aunt who is thirty-five years old and a college graduate with two children, ages nine and twelve. The aunt has just returned to a teaching job. Many of the aunt's friends are also returning to the labor force as teachers, social workers, dietitians, nurses, editors, and the like, after a hiatus to raise their children. We know from historical evidence that about half those friends would have been employed, mostly full-time.

By 1980, the employment level for the aunt's generation would have increased to 80 percent. They were then about forty-five years old. These women had spent around ten years out of the labor force but, by their mid-forties, had been employed continuously for ten years. Many would continue working until they retired in their sixties or even older. But although they logged many years in the labor force, most were not able to advance much in their occupations, firms, or institutions, because they had not prepared to do so. They'd prepared to have good jobs that they could enter and exit and then enter again. Their earnings were limited by the types of positions they had taken when younger.

Increased female labor force participation for the previous generation (the aunt) served as an important precondition for those of the Quiet Revolution (the niece). Young women in Group Four could see that older college-graduate women from Group Three were employed, but that some of them had not realized early on that they would be in the labor force for as long as they eventually were. Many had not invested appropriately in their further education and training, because they hadn't had the ability to delay marriage and motherhood. Others couldn't return to school after they began their families, and still others discovered it was hard to go back to school when older.

Those in Group Four sensed, as young women, that they could be in the labor force for much of their lives. They prepared themselves for longer and more continuous employment.

But greater labor force participation was not, in fact, a central outcome of the Quiet Revolution. Changes in occupations and a career orientation were the real changes. In fact, there was no great break in the employment trends. The one exception is that the labor force participation for women with infants soared from the early 1970s to the 1990s. Women with young children, even many with infants, worked because they had well-paying careers that rewarded continuity on the job. That was precisely what the Quiet Revolution was about.

Expanded Horizons

Starting around 1970, the women of Group Four began to more accurately anticipate that their future work lives would greatly differ from those of women who came before. As such, they could plan for fulfilling, dynamic careers that would grow with them, rather than taking jobs for the short run that had little room for progress.

Their expectations of future employment when they were in their mid- to late teens can be gleaned from various surveys. Two of the largest and best known are the National Longitudinal Survey of Young Women, which began with a large group of fourteen- to twenty-four-year-olds in 1968, and the National Longitudinal Survey of Youth, which began with the same age group, but in 1979. (I'll refer to both as the NLS.) Each of these surveys asked questions like "What will you be doing when you are thirty-five? Staying home with family or at work?"

When the survey began, in 1968, these young women by and large did not think they would be employed at thirty-five years old. Just 33 percent did. The mothers of these young women had an actual

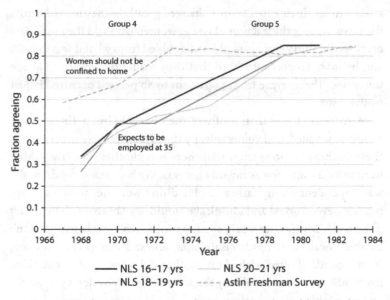

FIGURE 6.2. Employment Expectations and Attitudes of Female Youth by Age and Year
Notes: The NLS data are the response to whether an individual stated that she expected to
be in the paid labor force at age thirty-five and are given here for white women. The NLS
data link the averages for each age group over time. Thus, a fourteen- to fifteen-year-old in
the NLS in 1968 became a sixteen- to seventeen-year-old in 1970 and is linked to the
sixteen- to seventeen-year-old line in 1979 for the NLS. The Astin Freshman Survey data
are the response to whether the individual *disagreed* with the statement "The activities
of married women are best confined to the home and family." The Astin data are for
female college freshman, the vast majority of whom were eighteen years old.
Also see Figures and Table Appendix.

employment rate at the time of about 30 percent. Teens in the late 1960s
were modeling their employment expectations on the labor force participation of their mothers and those in her generation. A fourteen-year-
old in the late 1960s looked to her mother and her mother's friends and
came up with an estimate of her own future employment (and that was
also true for an eighteen-year-old in 1968), as can be seen in figure 6.2.

The fashioning of their future roles as a function of their mothers'
generation is understandable. They were, for a while, looking backward.
But young women began to look forward and to respond to the changes

around them. Their expectations changed greatly as they moved across the 1970s. By 1975 the fraction of young women who said they would be employed at thirty-five years old had doubled from what it was in 1968, and by 1980, 80 percent stated that they would be employed at age thirty-five. The increase from 33 percent to 80 percent occurred in just twelve years.

Many began to see their mothers, members of Group Three, as unhappy, unsatisfied, and vulnerable. By the 1970s, young women such as these freshmen in 1979 knew that there was another way. "I wouldn't want to be as unhappy as my mother was. With so many children, she was dependent on my father. . . . He didn't want her to work." "My mother never worked and I think she would have been much better off if she had." "My mother was home full time when I was [a teen]. I don't think it is healthy. If a mother is unhappy and sacrificing her life for you, it's not good." "I often wished my mother did work. . . . As I got older, my brother and sister would say the same thing: 'Why don't you go out and get a job.'"

All of the NLS respondents, independent of age, revised their expectations upward in each of the subsequent years. This increased anticipation of employment demonstrates that outlooks changed in the 1970s for youth of all ages. Their revised sense of the future was generated by contemporaneous events of the times—not just because these teenagers were growing up and exercising their independence.

By the time the survey respondents were thirty-five, in the early 1980s, their labor force participation rate was about 75 percent. For college-graduate women, it exceeded 80 percent. They were just about spot on with their anticipated 80 percent figure. As young women in 1968, they had been seriously off target with their initial 33 percent estimation.

Young women gained horizon and soon perceived that their lives would greatly differ from those of their elders. These youths in the early 1970s may have been emboldened to make more informed extrapolations because the resurgence of feminism at the time challenged older ways and outmoded norms. The revised expectations of future employment, in turn, may have led youths of the early 1970s to continue with and graduate from college (and there is some evidence that it did).

One of the reasons that young women changed their views of their own employment at age thirty-five is that they became more accepting of women's employment outside the home generally. In 1967, 41 percent of female college freshmen *disagreed* with the statement "The activities of married women are best confined to the home and family." But in 1974, just seven years later, 83 percent *disagreed* with the statement. (Stated another way, and as drawn in figure 6.2, 83 percent by 1974 *agreed* that women should *not* be confined to their home, whereas just 59 percent had in 1967.) "The times they [were] a-changin'," in so many ways, to paraphrase Bob Dylan.

The young women of Group Four didn't just say that they would be more involved in the world of work. They acted on it. With a greater sense that their futures would involve continuous employment and the potential of real careers, girls began to change their academic preparation. Many would be able to attend and graduate from college because of greater preparation as teenagers.

Girls in 1955 were far behind boys in college-preparation courses. They took just 70 percent of the high school math courses that the boys did. But by 1970 they took 80 percent, and around 1990 they logged an identical number. Girls also narrowed the gap with boys in science courses.

Not only did girls take more courses; they also increased their scores in math and reading relative to boys. By about 1990, girls in their senior year of high school had greatly narrowed the gap with boys in math scores and were considerably ahead in reading. With highly competitive math scores, more courses in science, and superior reading scores, female youth could greatly increase their college-going and graduation rates relative to males. Beginning with those born in the late 1940s—the start of Group Four—that is exactly what they did. The increase was so great that the previous male lead in enrollment and graduation was swiftly eliminated and reversed in the early 1980s.

The changes are so dramatic and important that it's valuable to step back and review college graduation rates throughout the journey (as depicted in figure 2.5). For women born from 1877 to the 1910s—Groups One and Two—college attendance rates were fairly equal by sex (in part because women often attended two-year teacher-training schools). Four-year college graduation rates were greater for males, but not by much.

For individuals born in the late 1910s and 1920s, large differences emerged in college-going and graduation rates. Part of the surge in male college going was due to the incentives of the various GI Bills of WWII and the Korean War. Males gained considerably on females, so that by the late 1940s and 1950s (for Group Three) there were almost 2 times as many male as female graduates by birth year. In the 1960s, after the GI Bills, the number of male graduates was 1.5 times that for females.

But just at that moment, an incredible turnaround began. More and more females began to go to college. By the early years of Group Four, male graduates were just 1.3 times the number of female graduates. And by the early 1980s, more females than males graduated from college. A remarkable reversal in the gender gap in higher education occurred just as Group Five was beginning to enter college.

In 1970, the majors of college men and women were vastly different. Half of all women, or half of all men, would have had to switch majors to make them equal. But by 1985, only 30 percent (of either men or women) would have had to switch to obtain equality. That's not equality, but it is a giant step in that direction. Similarly, in 1970, freshmen women and men declared occupational and career preferences that were markedly different. By 1985 the differences were considerably smaller. Their stated career preferences as freshmen would foretell their eventual majors as seniors.

The big change was that Group Four college women began taking courses and majoring in fields that were more career oriented. In 1970, at about the start of Group Four's graduation from college, almost two-thirds of all female graduates majored in a combination of education and the liberal arts (40 percent and 22 percent, respectively). For males, that combined group was just 24 percent. By 1982, both men and women shifted out of education and the liberal arts and into business administration. In 1967, 5 percent of female graduates were business majors. By 1982, 21 percent were. These changes did not occur overnight, but they were rapid.

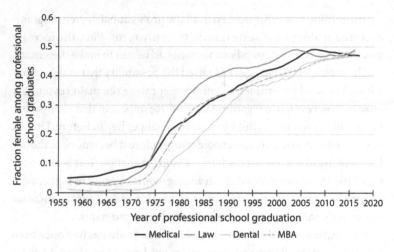

FIGURE 6.3. Fraction Female among Professional School Graduates:
Medical, Law, Dental, and MBA
See Figures and Table Appendix.

Women shifted out of majors that were "consumption-" and job-oriented and into those that were "investment-" and career-related. Group Four women knew what they needed for their futures. They could always read Shakespeare, but they couldn't always learn accounting. They could always get a teaching credential, but they couldn't always become a research scientist or a CPA.

Women also began to further their education in professional and graduate schools around 1970 (see figure 6.3). In the late 1960s, only one in twenty students entering law school was a woman. By 1980, one in three was. By the early 2000s, an almost equal number of males and females had entered (and graduated) from a JD program. A nearly identical trend occurred for medical students. The fraction of female recipients of bachelor's degrees who earned an MD increased by three times from 1970 to 1979. And these are just two of the many advanced-degree programs that Group Four women entered in droves. They vastly increased their numbers in dentistry, business administration, veterinary medicine, optometry, and pharmacy, to mention a few.

The turning points for women in all the professional degree programs occurred at almost the same time in the early 1970s. Plus, the increase was sharp and clear. Group Four women had begun to make their mark.

The timing of the changes has raised the possibility that antidiscrimination laws and governmental enforcement were the main reasons for change. Solid evidence regarding the positive impact of that channel has been difficult to obtain. But because the changes began before Title IX became effective de jure, and considerably before it became operational, laws and mandates are not the likely reason for change. This is not to say that Title IX was ineffectual in advancing women's cause in higher education. But it was not the sole, or even a major, reason for the increase in women's participation in professional degree programs.

Occupations rapidly shifted. Female college graduates had once been teachers, nurses, librarians, secretaries, and social workers. In 1970, 68 percent were among those aged thirty to thirty-four. Just twenty years later, 30 percent were. The exodus from many traditional fields creates a virtual cliff in the graph with Group Four (figure 6.4). The exodus from teaching, however, was relative to all college graduates rather than an absolute decline. So many more women had become college graduates that the numbers going into teaching didn't change much, even as the fraction of college-graduate women who were teachers plummeted. Most of the other fields included in the figure, however, saw absolute decline.

Women left a set of more traditional fields and entered a varied list of professional occupations, including lawyer, manager, physician, professor, and scientist. By 1990, almost 30 percent of all college-graduate women aged thirty to thirty-four were in the newer professions, whereas just 13 percent were in 1970. There was enormous change in the fractions of women in each of the two groups of occupations from 1970 to 1990. But these fractions, for the age group given, have remained approximately as they were in 1990 until today.

Most of the women in Group Four began to perceive that their employment was part of a long-term career. They added their occupation or career as a fundamental aspect of their satisfaction in life and viewed their place of employment as integral to their social milieu. No longer did their employment depend only on how much additional income

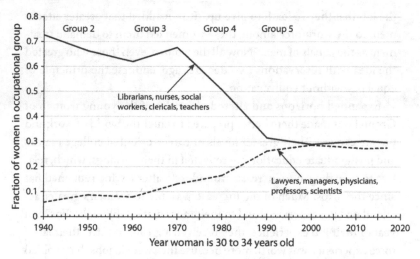

FIGURE 6.4. Occupations of College-Graduate Women, 30 to 34 Years Old: 1940 to 2017
See Figures and Table Appendix.

they would add to the family budget. No longer were they simply topping off their husband's income. Instead, they evaluated their own desires and sense of self when determining whether or not to work.

In consequence, women became more attached to being a part of the labor force. Leaving the workplace involved a loss in identity, just as being unemployed or retired has commonly involved a loss of prestige and social belonging for most men. As Group Four women entered their sixties and seventies in the 2010s, they remained employed far longer than has any previous group of women in that age bracket. They have continued to work even when they have had the means to retire, and even when their husbands or partners have retired. In-depth studies of women in Group Four have shown that they almost doubled their employment rates relative to previous groups in their sixties and beyond, and have not switched to part-time jobs to accomplish this feat. Rather, they have simply extended their existing careers.

There has been a similar increased attachment to jobs among lower-income women. "Universally, the women I interviewed work because they must," reported the renowned ethnographer Lillian Rubin in 1994. "Almost as often they find a level of self-fulfillment and satisfaction on the job that they're loath to give up." Rubin added that greater attachment to the workforce among these women led them to demand treatment as the equals of men. "Now all the women, even those who greeted the idea with reservations two decades ago, endorse the principle of equal pay without equivocation."

Expanded horizons and altered identities of the young women of Group Four made them better prepared to enter the world of work and pursue careers. Their greater levels of career-oriented college majors and postgraduate education are reflected in their earnings, which, relative to men, began to increase around 1980 after having remained flat since the 1950s. Much of the increase was due to women's greater accumulated job experience and to their more marketable skills. For each year of their job experience, they received a greater return. Their labor force experience was worth more because they were in jobs that enabled promotions and more on-the-job learning.

But these gains did not come without costs. Delaying marriage also meant having children later. For many, that meant fewer children. For some, it meant no children. The change from Group Three to Group Four is extremely sharp. For college-graduate women born in 1943—the last of the Group Three women—19 percent were without a birth by their early forties. For those born in 1947, just four years later, 25 percent would not have a birth. For those born in 1955, at the peak of childlessness for this group, 28 percent would not. Not surprisingly, women with graduate and professional degrees had an even higher fraction without a birth—around 33 percent.

The biological clock ran out on many who delayed childbearing. The increased age of marriage and the quest for career meant that family was put off. Members of the group thought they were delaying. Many could not have known that, rather than delaying, they were giving up family as they pursued their other dreams. They realized this after the fact, as did those who followed. "I can't believe it. I forgot to have children!" bemoans the woman in a famed Roy Lichtenstein painting. The pop-art print, completed around 1964, became the iconic poster of many in Group Four. They had declared they would do better than Group Three. In many ways, we did. But many "forgot" to have the children.

Assisting the Revolution

TINA FEY, ACTOR, COMEDIAN, and writer extraordinaire, is a member of Group Five. Like many successful college-graduate women of that group, she had her children late—first baby at age thirty-five and second at forty-one. Motherhood has been a recurrent thread in her sitcom creation, *30 Rock*, and a major part of her starring roles in the films *Baby Mama* (2008) and *Admission* (2013).

As Kate Holbrook, the protagonist of *Baby Mama*, she expressed the angst of her generation: "I did everything I was supposed to do . . . to be the youngest VP at my company. I made a choice. Some women get pregnant, others get promotions." She then added to her first-date dinner soliloquy: "I want a baby now. I'm thirty-seven." Bad topic of conversation, she soon discovers, as the date hightails it in a taxi. After trying artificial insemination and surrogacy, she eventually gets pregnant the old-fashioned way, maintains her career, and marries the alternative-lifestyle-embracing owner of the local juice bar, who is an ex-lawyer. No Tina Fey character does the ordinary.

In her role as Liz Lemon in the acclaimed *30 Rock*, she continued to give voice to the concerns of her group. During the last episodes, when she is forty-two years old, she marries her boyfriend, adopts twin eight-year-olds, and quits her job as head writer for a TV show. But she is miserable as a stay-at-home mom, and her husband, Criss, is equally unhappy as an employed dad. "It's OK to want to work," Criss reassures Liz. "One of us has to. We just got it backwards: You're the dad."

Not everyone is as fortunate as Liz Lemon and Criss Chros, or any of the other fictional and real couples who have created a family later in life when the usual options have failed. But indeed, more college-graduate women have succeeded in having children later in life, often through sheer will and luck and occasionally through costly and emotionally draining procedures. At the height of Group Four childlessness, 28 percent of all college-graduate women did not have a birth by the time they were forty-five years old. For Group Five, that fraction fell to a low of 20 percent. Not only was this an astonishing turnaround, but it was accompanied by a candidness that speaks volumes about the gains that women have made.

When I was an assistant professor in the 1970s, none of the (very few) young faculty women I knew talked about having children, not even in private. Even in the 1980s, when there were many more young female faculty members, I don't recall knowing many who were pregnant, although I knew many faculty members (all men) who had children. Universities rarely had transparent maternity leave policies, and almost no one was asking about them until they needed to make leave arrangements.

In 1980, I had dinner with the chair of my department and an impressive candidate for an assistant professor position. At the time, I was an untenured faculty member. My colleague, who was somewhat socially awkward, asked the candidate if she had any questions about the position (not a question for relaxed dinner conversation). To my amazement, the candidate (a brilliant, gutsy individual who later became the US Commissioner of Labor Statistics) inquired about the university's maternity leave policy. The chair of the department could not offer a single detail.

Today, pregnant assistant professors are not uncommon, and the same goes for associate lawyers, middle-tier managers, accountants, consultants coming up for partnerships, and others on the career track. Parental leave policies are considerably more transparent (and increasingly generous).

The members of Group Five who graduated college from the mid-1980s to the early 1990s were the first to openly express their aspirations to attain both career and family. This new ideal and women's frankness about wanting to attain it was made possible because Group Four had already paved the way in having careers. No prior group had achieved *both* career and family in large numbers. Group Four had sought to focus first on the one—career—that none of the groups had yet attained en masse. Many of their efforts were put into taking the steps needed to achieve that goal.

They gained entry to professional and graduate schools. They grew from being 5 percent of all new JDs in the late 1960s to 35 percent by the early 1980s. They achieved parity with men in college, and then surpassed them in numbers. Ascending the ranks of their given careers took their all.

Group Five could then travel the same road, already cleared of many obstacles. But they had also learned from their Group Four older sisters that the path to career must leave room for family, as deferral could lead to no children.

————

Other changes that enabled Group Five women to be more forthright about their ambitions were the advances in scientific and medical knowledge. Previously, no one knew how fertility changed as women and men aged. The same is true for understanding chromosomal damage and how to select for healthy embryos. To get a handle on how female fertility changes with age, and to determine how that impacts the probability of getting pregnant, one would need to hold constant a large number of factors, such as frequency and timing of intercourse, and the use of contraceptives.

In 1982, a revealing study appeared in the prestigious *New England Journal of Medicine* that was based on a natural experiment. More than two thousand French women married to sterile men had individually requested and were given artificial insemination (AI) from donor sperm at various intervals. Since they differed by age, but not by the procedure, the researchers could determine how their age impacted their ability to conceive. The results were astonishing.

The fertility of these women plummeted from ages thirty-one to thirty-five, a much earlier moment than had previously been believed.

The conventional wisdom had been that fertility declined after thirty-five, but not much before. Successful pregnancies at this fertility clinic dropped from 74 percent at age thirty-one to 61 percent at age thirty-five. Although there have been criticisms of the study and the advice offered by its authors, it remains the most scientific study of human fertility—largely because so many factors determining conception could be controlled.

Most of Group Four's members would have been in the dark regarding the consequences of delaying having children. Group Five not only had better information; they also had superior methods to "beat the clock." They learned from medical evidence why birth deferral could reduce the chance of pregnancy, and they began to have the means to counter it. Many college-graduate women realized that they could successfully go it alone and have children without a husband or partner.

AI is an old technique, first used to impregnate farm animals. The number of births in the US from the procedure was low in the early 1960s, according to a rough estimate. In the mid-1970s, the legality of using the procedure on unmarried women was questioned, and even in 1979, doctors expressed conflict about using the procedure on their unmarried patients due to the legal limbo into which the child would be born. But as more complicated and expensive procedures, such as in vitro fertilization (IVF), were innovated and adopted, the simpler AI gained traction. Plus, it was a procedure one could do oneself, with some success.

When I was almost forty years old, I was buttonholed at a social gathering by a woman my mother's age. She was simply bursting at the seams with joy that her daughter, a woman of my age, was going to have a baby conceived through AI. Her daughter had found a way around the time-consuming process of finding a husband. The elated grandmother-to-be was working hard to win converts to this novel reproductive method.

Popular articles on the fertility consequences of delaying childbirth were rare, even by the 1980s. Scientific evidence on the relationship between age and the probability of conception was inadequate until the aforementioned French study. The subject of "infertility" was infrequently broached in newspapers, scientific literature, or popular books.

Only a tiny fraction of all the articles in medical journals published from the 1950s to the 1970s concerned human female infertility. But that fraction doubled by the 1990s and mushroomed by the early 2000s, to five times the 1990 level. Most of the articles in the 2000s were about infertility procedures such as IVF.

But a run-of-the-mill college woman would not have been reading obscure health journals, and likely was not seeking out medical books about reproduction. She was more likely to read general books, newspapers, and magazines of all sorts. In popular books, the topic of infertility began to skyrocket in the 1980s. A search of the word "infertility" and the procedure "IVF" in Google archives (US published in English) reveals a fivefold increase in just a decade after 1980. The college-age woman may also have noticed that articles about infertility in the *New York Times* greatly increased in the same decade, quadrupling in number in the 1980s. However, after the early 1990s, newspaper articles on the subject of infertility decreased in relative importance—but not because infertility became less of an issue.

Mention of infertility, which had reached a frenzied peak in the late 1980s, subsided as a host of promising medical interventions rapidly spread, providing a potential corrective. Rather than write about the dire consequences of infertility, articles and books were now written about the positive promises of medical advances. The use of the word "infertility" declined, even though it was still the problem to be solved.

All populations contain couples who encounter problems getting pregnant. Exactly what fraction depends on age, the time given for the pregnancy to take, and the number of attempts, among many other factors. Precise estimates for modern times are hard to obtain because of selection issues (only those who can't conceive make that known) and because of contraception (a large fraction of the population is trying to prevent a birth, not advance one). Demographers, using historical evidence when effective contraception did not exist, have found that about 12 percent of even healthy twenty-five-year-old women and men will encounter serious problems getting or remaining pregnant. Infertility for couples has always been a problem and becomes more so as males and females age.

Few women would have consulted their physicians on these issues in the absence of a perceived medical problem. They wouldn't have flipped through magazines for information on how fertility changed with age. Most, however, would have known about an amazing self-help volume about all things female. I still remember the day when my best friend showed me her copy of what would become my personal health bible: *Our Bodies, Ourselves*. Now in its ninth edition, that monumental volume was the go-to book for women in search of health advice (before the internet). Each version since the first in 1970 has charted women's concerns and knowledge about their bodies and making babies.

The inaugural edition was called *Women and Their Bodies: A Course*. It cost 75 cents and consisted of 193 pages stapled together in four sections. It allotted fewer than 4 pages to the issue of infertility and did not mention age as a factor. The 1984 edition, still an oft-used reference on my bookshelf, is 647 pages and weighs in at three pounds (in paperback). It contains a section titled "Infertility and Pregnancy Loss" but has just one brief mention of age as a potential factor in the rise of infertility, noting that women have been "delay[ing] childbearing into their thirties, when fertility decreases slightly."

Even the women's leading reference book for advice on sex, reproduction, and female health had only a meager discussion of infertility, and it omitted the mention of age as a factor in infertility until the 1980s. It is no wonder that even the most forward-looking, intelligent of Group Four women gave little thought to delaying motherhood. Who was going to tell them about the risks they were taking?

When the women of Group Four were first delaying marriage and childbirth, they were not bombarded with articles that would have registered much of an alarm. The warning signs only appeared as they entered their thirties and beyond, when the consequences of the delay became apparent. The cautionary message that delay led to a higher chance of not having a birth reached Group Five just as a mass of medical interventions were being made available to give women an assist. What one puts off today might be obtained tomorrow—but often at a steep monetary, emotional, and physical cost.

With greater knowledge about the costs of delay, the women of Group Five could have made their reproductive lives easier by having children earlier. But they did just the opposite. They increased the delay. Whereas 31 percent of Group Four had a baby by age twenty-six, just 22 percent of Group Five did. That's about a one-third decrease in child-bearing by age twenty-six. Their determination to have children at some point and their faith in the future of fertility technology were apparently stronger than their newfound knowledge of what could go wrong.

By their mid-thirties Group Five had caught up to Group Four in terms of the fraction who had children. And after their mid-thirties Group Five sprinted ahead, greatly surpassing Group Four in starting a family by their forties. The women of Group Five made up for a ton of lost time and had lots of babies in their late thirties and early forties (and even beyond).

The increase in births among Group Five women is yet more amazing since a large fraction have advanced degrees and burgeoning careers, even more so than in Group Four. That increase in births among those with a professional degree or doctorate is striking. Just 70 percent of Group Four women with an advanced degree (above a master's) ever had children, compared with 75 percent for Group Five. Across all college-graduate women, the fraction of Group Five women with a birth by their early forties exceeded that of Group Four by about 3 percentage points, but the difference is 5 percentage points for those with an advanced degree.

Women with advanced degrees in Group Four had motherhood rates that were frighteningly reminiscent of the exceptionally low rates that existed for Groups One and Two. For the Group Four women born from 1949 to 1953 who achieved the highest advanced professional and graduate degrees, almost 40 percent did not have a child by their forties. But recent data for Group Five show that motherhood rates of those with advanced degrees are now almost identical to those for women with just a bachelor's.

We all know women who have had their first child later in life, certainly far later than was common in prior generations. We know so many that we are no longer amazed. Having even a first child later in life shouldn't be that incredible since women live longer and are (often) in better shape than they were in the mid- to late twentieth century. Furthermore, late-reproducing couples generally have more financial resources. Still, it is wondrous that Group Five has engineered such a remarkable change.

Medical advances in infertility treatments (such as IVF, gamete intra-fallopian transfer or GIFT, egg freezing, and chromosomal screening) have enabled many to have children who could not otherwise. But these are expensive procedures for which health insurance coverage matters. Group Five's strides have arisen not only from medical advances in reproductive technologies and their demand for them, but also from new state mandates requiring that private health insurance plans cover the procedures.

How important were both medical advances and the added health insurance coverage to the increase in births from Group Four to Group Five? It's not an easy answer. For one thing, until recently, no one was asking women how they got pregnant. But ever since 2011, the Centers for Disease Control and Prevention (CDC) has released data in a consistent form and with useful age groupings on whether a birth occurred because of an infertility treatment of any type.

Using CDC micro data, we know that 26 percent of college-graduate women forty years and older in 2018 had their first child because of at least one form of infertility treatment, and the same is true for 11 percent of those age thirty-five to thirty-nine. These are big segments of the female population, and the women (and their partners) who had a baby in these older age groups were greatly affected.

But only 13 percent of all first births to college-graduate women occur to those thirty-five years and older, and just 3 percent do to those forty years and older. In other words, a large change occurred for a group that produces a small fraction of births. Yet the effect was substantial (and was obviously of great consequence to the affected couples).

What part of the gains in childbearing was due to the newfangled methods and the ability of women and couples to take advantage of them? As we have learned, the rate of childlessness decreased from a high of 28 percent for college-graduate women born around 1955 to a low of 20 percent for those born around 1975. Almost all of the decrease occurred for women older than thirty-five. Between 37 percent and 50 percent of the increase in first births among the college-graduate population can be accounted for by advances in reproductive technologies and the greater ability of women and couples to pay for them with the aid of health insurance. Therefore, even though about 4 percent of all first births to college-graduate women in 2018 were assisted in any manner, that was enough to greatly increase births for the women and couples of Group Five.

How to Define Success

Women who graduated college in this millennium have accomplished something never seen before. Group Five college-graduate women who are now in their forties have rates of motherhood that are about as high as they were for baby boom college-graduate mothers at the end of Group Three, when they were in their forties. The turnaround has been extraordinary. Group Five hasn't produced a second baby boom, but they have produced a bumper crop. And they have done so with enormous delay—even greater than that experienced by Group Four—and with a personal commitment to having both a career and a family.

Nonetheless, there are many who would disagree and point to the ways women, especially mothers, are consistently robbed of their careers, pushed off ladders, and sideswiped by male colleagues. Many speak about a "failed revolution." Although individuals may feel as much on a case-by-case basis, and endemic misogyny continues to present roadblocks, we know that this certainly isn't true for the group as a whole. To regard the journey women have been on for the past century as failed suggests an extremely limited vision.

A paltry 6 percent of the earlier portion of Group Three that could be analyzed, born 1931–1937, achieved both career and family by the time they were in their late thirties. Most had aspirations focused on having a family first and then, perhaps, a good job. And indeed, 84 percent had children by their late thirties—the highest ever for college-graduate women. These were the core baby boomer moms, few of whom attempted to achieve a career, and many were not employed until they were much older. The bulk of these women never intended to achieve both a career and a family, and yet the fraction who did more than doubled across their lives, making their strides noteworthy. Careers started to move along for the latter half of Group Three, born 1938–1944. For them, 21 percent had achieved both career and family by the time their kids were beginning high school or had left the nest to go to college or elsewhere.

We saw how much career success lurched upward with Group Four. Their family success waned, but they did a bang-up job with their careers. Among college-graduate women born 1951–1957, 14 percent of those in their late thirties attained both career and family, and 27 percent of those in their early fifties did. Finally, Group Five starts off with 22 percent achieving career and family by their late thirties and winds up with 31 percent crossing the career and family finish line by their fifties.

That's a lot of numbers to digest. (They are depicted in figure 7.1.) In addition, the definition and computation of "career" is a rather complicated matter. In brief, to have a career, a woman (or man) had to have an annual income that exceeded a particular level for a number of consecutive years. The income level it had to exceed is that of a comparable man (same education, same age) at the twenty-fifth percentile of the male income distribution. "Family," as mentioned in an earlier chapter, is defined as having at least one child, by birth or adoption.

Much of what we see is far from lamentable, and in no way failed. Career and family success increased enough from Group Three to Group Five to give us cause to feel hopeful for our future, even in the face of the pandemic. In fact, it is conceivable that working from home during the pandemic will decrease the costs of workplace flexibility for the future.

The most intriguing increases are those found *within* the later groups of women as they aged. It wouldn't be that surprising if the fraction who achieved careers increased across these groups, with the latest having the most success. The increase *within* each Group is not due to having more family as they aged from their thirties to their fifties. Rather, the careers of those with family flower as they age. Those without children

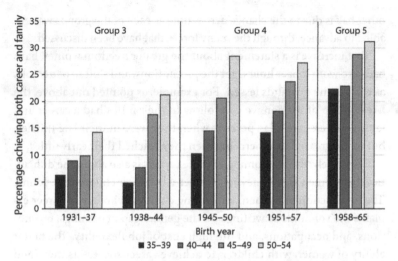

FIGURE 7.1. Career and Family Success for Four Age Groups: 1931 to 1965
See Figures and Table Appendix. For the definition and calculation of "career" for these birth
groups, see Source Appendix (Ch7), "Career and Family Success." "Family" is defined as
having a child by birth or adoption.

in Group Five show fairly high success in their careers early on, and that level of success remains high. In terms of their career success as they age, their numbers look more like men's, albeit with a somewhat lower rate of career attainment. Tellingly, the success rate for men doesn't change much with age, whereas it greatly increases for women. Women's time is freed as their children age, and with fewer fetters they fly higher.

For the most recent of the groups, those born 1958–1965, women thirty-five to thirty-nine years old had a career and family success rate that was 40 percent that of men. Those fifty to fifty-four years old had a rate that was almost 60 percent that of men. This means that women narrow the success gap with men across the course of their lives. For an earlier group, those born 1945–1950, women had a success rate around 20 percent that of men when in their thirties, but 50 percent by their fifties.

By and large, the increase in career and family across these groups of women can be divided two ways, and it turns out that they are two equal parts. One half is due to the change across an individual's life cycle, beginning in a woman's late thirties and continuing to her early fifties. The other half is due to the change across time as each of the groups was enabled to advance, through the many forces that have been discussed.

That increase is a statement about the greater freedom women have had—to work longer hours, get the promotions, and shift to better jobs as their home demands lessen. For example, as pointed out above, the latest group of women we can follow to their fifties had a career and family success rate of 22 percent when they were in their late thirties, but that increased to 31 percent when they reached their early fifties.

Conversely, the blossoming of these careers is also about the difficulties that women face achieving a career when their children are young. The low fraction of women with young children who have a career explains the voluminous writings on the gender gap in earnings, promotions, and occupations, and the high cost of job flexibility. The better ability of women with children to achieve career success as they (and their children) age speaks to what life was like for young women in the past—and is for many younger women right now.

The change across the groups demonstrates general advancement of women's professional education and gains in the labor market. But the drag on their careers that is evident in the difference between younger and older women with children and the difference between women with children and those without is the real problem of the gender gap in earnings and advancement.

More recent longitudinal survey data for those born 1980 to 1984 allow us to analyze career and family success at an early age for the most recent Group Five women and men that can be studied. These women are currently too young to learn much about their long-run futures. But we can perform the same type of calculation with these data, to see whether they have achieved more than their predecessors at the same age.

They have indeed advanced relative to their predecessors, but they are not a major break. By the time they reach their late thirties, just more than a quarter have achieved career and family, and about 40 percent have career, independent of family. That's a slight improvement over the latest group depicted in figure 7.1. Change has been slow and steady. But in comparing the men's career success rates to those of women, there is too little change early in the lives of talented women. The gains for women as they age is proof that they were held back when young, by themselves or others, by the competing demands of family and their occupations, whereas men with families do not appear, from these data, to have been held back.

Do we see similar changes among the women elected to Congress from Groups Three to Five? It would be fitting to begin the analysis with Jeannette Rankin, but the numbers of women elected from Groups One and Two are too low for a statistical analysis.

All the women elected to Congress clearly achieved a career. Until recently, most were elected later in their lives. The median age (also the mean age) at the first Congressional election for Group Three women is fifty-three. That doesn't necessarily mean that they did not have a career before their election. Most would have previously been involved in local politics or community action groups. Few get to Congress by accident. But those from Group Three were truly late bloomers, and their elections to Congress were more often than not the start of their real careers.

Many from Group Three married right after college and, like many of their less political counterparts, remained out of the labor force when their children were young. Others were schoolteachers, nurses, and community volunteers. That was the case for Darlene Olson Hooley (D, OR), born in 1939, who was a high school teacher before becoming involved in local and state politics in her forties. She eventually served in Congress for six terms, beginning when she was fifty-eight. Similarly, Connie Morella (R, MD), born in 1931, taught high school and college classes while caring for her three children and six of her deceased sister's. She served eight terms in Congress starting in 1987, when she was fifty-six years old.

For some, the route to Congress zigzagged, as was the case of Eva McPherson Clayton (D, NC), born in 1934. She had intended to pursue a degree in medicine but was energized by the civil rights movement to enter law school. Nevertheless, she "left to be a mom" after the birth of her fourth child. Despite the support of her lawyer husband, she advises her younger colleagues to assert themselves early: "I think I would ... demand more of my husband." As she noted, "I wasn't super enough to be a supermom." Yet she was super enough to serve in Congress for five terms beginning in 1992, when she was fifty-eight. A year after she entered Congress and many years after her children had grown, Clayton remarked, "It's amazing, I think he [her husband] is aware of my demands. I don't think he was as sensitive then."

Group Four women were also elected to Congress when they were around fifty-three. But few were late bloomers. They were different from their Group Three sisters and ascended to their lofty ranks in Congress from grander initial places. Group Four women often had JDs, PhDs, and other advanced degrees, and often began in high-earning careers before being elected to Congress.

Michele Bachman (R, MN), born in 1956, worked for the IRS as a lawyer, then earned her LLM (master of laws) in tax law and was employed by the IRS until she had her fourth child. She was elected to the House in 2007 at age fifty-one and served four terms. Similarly, Maggie Wood Hassan (D, NH), born in 1958, was a lawyer and a health care executive with two children, one with a severe disability. She served in the New Hampshire state senate, served as governor, and in 2016 was elected to the US Senate when she was fifty-nine. Madeleine Dean (D, PA) ran a law firm but switched to teaching college English to mesh with caring for her three children. At sixty years old, she joined the 2019 congressional class.

Those in Group Five were younger when elected; on average they were forty-six. But there is a mechanical reason why Group Five women would be younger when elected: simply, Group Five women were born closer to the present. If one limited the years of Group Four women to be the same number as Group Five has had to become elected, the mean age at election would not be much different. The mean age is higher for Group Four because more older women could be elected.

Today's women in Congress born after 1978—the upper limit imposed on Group Five to enable observing them to at least age forty— are, as a group, the youngest ever, with a mean age of just thirty-five. They also include the largest group of women, thus far, elected to Congress in one election: thirty-four elected in 2018 and twenty-six in 2020. Plus, the group contains the youngest women ever elected to Congress:

Alexandria Ocasio-Cortez was sworn in at twenty-nine, Abby Finke-nauer, recently defeated, at thirty, and Sarah Jacobs at thirty-one. But, once again, even though they are exceptionally young, the entire assemblage is the youngest primarily by construction. Given the constraint that all were born after 1978, none could have been elected much older.

The newest groups have been active in politics or in grassroots organizing from early on in their postcollege lives. They, like those beginning with Group Four, have been the early-blooming varieties.

Time Binds

Just as Group Four women were resolute that they would do better than their mothers' generation, Group Five women have sought to "have it all." Group Four may have had the Pill, but Group Five had a host of newfangled ways to beat the odds. They would have a career and a family without compromising.

They continued to delay marriage and childbearing, even more than Group Four. Their overall career success rate improved relative to that for previous groups by age, and they achieved even more success than the others did across the life cycle. But their economic success as younger women remained low. The reason is that even the most educated and talented women—the lawyers, doctors, and PhDs—with children work part-time to a great degree. And many who work part-time when young find ramping up later in their lives to be difficult.

How do we know this, when most longitudinal datasets do not have a large number of observations on college graduates (let alone for those with advanced degrees)? I was part of a project that studied the Group Four and Five members of Harvard College classes that graduated around 1970, 1980, and 1990. We called the project Harvard and Beyond. Information we gathered helps illuminate why even the most advantaged and educated women have been challenged in achieving career and family. We chose to anchor their answers fifteen years after their college graduation, since most who eventually had a child would have done so by then. In addition, that is also the moment when many would have already come up for tenure, partnership, or a major promotion.

The vast majority of college-graduate women—even those with young children—were employed fifteen years after their bachelor's graduation. Only 10 percent were not employed at all. It doesn't appear that college-graduate women with children were opting out and slowing down, even for brief periods.

But the data reveal something else. When we explore deeper, we see that about one-third of the women who were employed fifteen years after receiving their bachelor's stated that they worked part-time. Some considered themselves to be part-timers even though they logged in considerably more than thirty-five hours a week, the usual cutoff for defining part-time work. The reason is that they were comparing their work hours to the standard in their professions or firms.

Of the women working part-time, 80 percent had young children, and 90 percent of those not in the labor force also did. Almost none of the men in these graduating classes worked less than full-time, and most probably worked many more hours than the usual forty.

At fifteen years out, independent of whether these women graduated college around 1970, 1980, or 1990, about 30 percent were working full-time *and* had children. Let's deem those who are working full-time as the career group. This means that a tad under one-third had something resembling career and family when they were in their late thirties. About 50 percent were in the labor force, though not necessarily working full-time, and had children. For men, the figures are about 65 percent for working full-time and having children or being in the labor force and having children.

The 30 percent figure is higher than the career and family success rate given in figure 7.1 for the nationally representative populations. Arraying the data by advanced degrees shows why. A whopping 65 percent of these women obtained either a JD, an MBA, an MD, or a PhD (and some had more than one of these special achievements). Employment and parenthood differ among the educational elite by the type of advanced degree. The greater the training, as seen in figure 7.2, the greater is the fraction who are working full-time at fifteen years out and have children.

Those with a professional or graduate degree have higher employment and full-time status than those with no further education. The

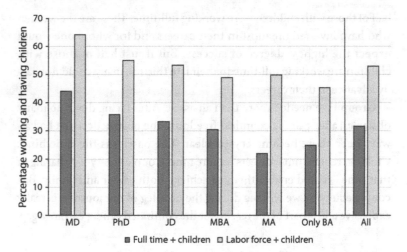

FIGURE 7.2. Career and Family by Advanced Degree, Harvard and Beyond
Fifteen Years after College
See Figures and Table Appendix.

largest fraction of those who achieved career and family fifteen years after graduation are the physicians. Next are those with doctorates, then lawyers, and finally those with MBA degrees. Those with MAs and no additional advanced degrees have the lowest rates of full-time employment and children. Their rates are more comparable to those from the nationally representative samples for the same groups.

MBAs have among the worst records for working full-time while having children. The findings from the Harvard and Beyond Project are echoed in another project, to be discussed, that dives deeper into the world of work in the corporate and financial sectors. These sectors have among the least flexible work and impose the greatest penalties for short hours and brief leaves of absence.

The educationally elite were our best hope of finding a group of college-graduate women who would be sufficiently prepared academically, have the most contacts and resources, and be persistent and demanding enough of themselves and those around them to achieve a career and family. Their rate of professional and advanced degree completion is extremely high. Yet fifteen years after college graduation, only half of those with children were working full-time. These are the women who have invested the most in their careers and for whom one would expect the highest degree of success. But if just half of those with children are working full-time in their late thirties, many could not easily advance in their careers.

Group Five needed more than an assist. After facing down so many obstacles, after gaining countless freedoms, the obstruction that had always been there became crystal clear. The barrier is the time bind. Children require time; careers require time. Couple equity—a sharing of that time—could enable them to achieve both career and family. But couple equity, as we will see during the next leg of our journey, is really expensive and is part of the reason for the continued gender earnings gap.

8

Mind the Gap

AS A YOUNG GIRL in Possum Trot, Alabama, Lilly McDaniel aspired to be a lawyer. She never realized that dream. But she did get a law named after her: the Lilly Ledbetter Fair Pay Restoration Act. How that came about is a case study of sexism, as reflected in the workplace and on the pay stub.

Lilly married when she was only seventeen and had two children soon after. Ten years later, when her family was low on funds, she took an H&R Block course and became a tax preparer. She loved her new-found financial independence and the personal rewards it brought, and she was so capable that, over time, she advanced to managing fourteen offices. But the children were heading off to college, and the family needed even more money. In 1979, when she was forty-one, Lilly learned that Goodyear Tire, the local high-wage firm, was seeking female managers for the first time in its history. She applied and was hired.

Almost immediately, Lilly experienced resentment among the men on the shop floor. She endured insults, harassment, and offers of higher ratings in exchange for sex. She won the right to file an Equal Employment Opportunity Commission (EEOC) sexual harassment lawsuit against Goodyear, but dropped the charges when she was reinstated as a supervisor. That only added to her misery—resulting in daily taunts, a vandalized car, and a job transfer.

She remained with Goodyear because the pay was good and there were many in the plant who appreciated her competence. In 1998, an anonymous ally left her a scrap of paper with key information that would soon lead to the second, and more famous, EEOC case. The paper contained the salaries of the other managers. She hadn't known how low her pay was by comparison, having always been told that she was just below the middle of the pack. "Everything at Goodyear was top secret," she wrote years later in an autobiography. She and the male managers hired in the same year began at the same salary. Twenty years later, she was making 15 to 40 percent less.

Her EEOC claim fell under three separate statutes: the Equal Pay Act of 1963; Title VII of the Civil Rights Act of 1964; and the Age Discrimination in Employment Act. Under the first, she claimed to have been paid less than men doing identical work. Under the second, she argued that she was denied promotions, transfers, and raises due to her sex. Under the third, she asserted that she was discriminated against on the basis of age and replaced by a younger employee. She suffered a hostile and abusive work environment that deleteriously affected her physical and mental health. Goodyear mounted an attack, but the jury awarded Lilly $3.8 million in back pay and punitive damages.

Lilly never received any of that money. According to the Eleventh Circuit Court of Appeals, the Title VII case should have been brought within 180 days of the original discriminatory paycheck, almost two decades before Lilly knew it was discriminatory. The 2007 US Supreme Court verdict in *Ledbetter vs. Goodyear Tire & Rubber Co.* (550 U.S. 618) upheld that interpretation of the statute of limitations. Lilly had lost, and American women had as well.

The US Supreme Court's interpretation of the Civil Rights Act of 1964 overturned precedent and twisted the original intent of the act. Ruth Bader Ginsburg's dissent, delivered from the bench, reminded all that "this is not the first time the Court has ordered a cramped interpretation of Title VII, incompatible with the statute's broad remedial purpose." "Once again," she noted, "the ball is in Congress' court." Two years later, it was successfully played out.

The Lilly Ledbetter Fair Pay Restoration Act, which passed both the House and the Senate in 2009—as the first important act signed into law by President Obama—made certain that workers would be protected *every* time they received a discriminatory paycheck, not just the first time.

The culprits in the Lilly Ledbetter story are many. Those she directly supervised were noncompliant and caused her to receive poor ratings as a manager. Those low ratings led her supervisors to deny her merit pay increases. But under the doctrine of "cat's paw," her supervisors were also guilty of discrimination, because they did not discipline their subordinates. As in the fable for which it is named, an unwitting cat does the dirty work of the monkey who wants a chestnut from the fire. The cat is the guilty actor (and burns its paw).

In addition to a variety of bad actors, Lilly was hampered by other factors that disproportionately affect women. She did not bargain effectively, for several reasons. She didn't know how low her salary was because of the lack of pay transparency, and she could not easily ask her fellow managers their salaries. Plus, she didn't have many other employment options in and around Gadsden, Alabama. She was tethered to the place because of her husband's job, their children, her elderly mother, and their home.

But are discrimination by managers and fellow employees and the presumed inadequacy of women's negotiation skills largely responsible for the gender gap in earnings today? Without depreciating those who indeed have been discriminated against and paid less simply because they are women, or because they are women of color, the answer is, emphatically, no. Only a small part of today's gender earnings gap (for full-time workers, around 20 cents on the male dollar) is due to these factors.

So what is the gender earnings gap, and how has it changed across the past half century, covering our last three Groups? Though the phrase is used widely, the gender earnings gap is not a single statistic, as it is usually depicted. Rather, it is dynamic. It widens as men and women age, get married, and have children. It also differs considerably by occupation, especially among college graduates.

These complexities don't muddy the gender inequality waters. On the contrary, they clear the waters to reveal the real issues that inhibit women who are seeking both a fulfilling career and an equitable family life.

The "gap" is generally expressed as a ratio: the earnings of women relative to those of men. The ratio conveniently captures and conveys a relative difference.

Among the most egregious (and publicized) cases of gender pay discrimination in recent memory is that of actress Michelle Williams. Williams was paid $100,000 for reshooting scenes in a movie for which actor Mark Wahlberg was paid a whopping $1.5 million, even though she was the lead actress and he was a supporting actor. The movie, *All the Money in the World* (a fitting title for one that didn't offer enough to its female stars), had to be reshot after Christopher Plummer replaced Kevin Spacey, who had been accused of sexual harassment.

I was a participant in a similar discrepancy many years ago (minus the glitter, the coverage, and the high stakes). I was asked to review an internal report of a prominent international agency. The agency needed three reviewers; two distinguished, older male economists were asked to review the report as well. Each of them regularly served as consultants, for which they charged a (substantial) daily rate. I did not. The agency, in consequence, paid me its standard rate. As a result, the two male economists were each paid double what I received for our review. The inequity was later discovered by the agency's chief economist, and I was recompensed at the higher level. The review, ironically, concerned gender discrimination at the agency.

Stories like these abound. But even if we eliminated all cases of discriminatory treatment and all instances in which women have been taken advantage of, the gender earnings gap would not narrow by much. The amount that women earn would not rise substantially.

The gender earnings gap—not just for movie stars and PhD economists—has been front and center in news and in policy outlets. But where does the blame lie? As in a canonical "whodunit," countless potential culprits are lurking. And given the large number of conceivable culprits, there are many more self-appointed detectives who have proposed theories on who did the deed and how to solve the case.

Many believe that the gender earnings gap is caused by biased and discriminatory individuals who take advantage of good-natured female workers. According to a 2017 survey, 42 percent of women (and 22 percent of men) claim that they have experienced "gender discrimination" at work. The most frequently cited form of discrimination is being paid less: 25 percent of the women, but only 5 percent of the men, claim to have received less in pay than a member of the opposite sex when doing the same job. So one potential culprit is explicit or implicit bias.

Purging the labor market of bias is among the many quick fixes that have been proposed to rid the workplace of gender inequality. Some have proposed debiasing individual supervisors and managers through diversity training. Others have pointed to the limited success of retraining individuals and have espoused debiasing entire organizations. Starbucks famously closed all its eight thousand stores for one day in August 2018 to provide antibias training for all its personnel. Although the cause was a racial incident, similar techniques are used to try to tamp down gender bias.

Another one of the most cited examples of a quick fix regarding hiring comes from my own research on orchestras and the use of screens in auditions. The screen hides the identity of the player. Though the use of blind auditions has enabled far more women to gain entry to the nation's most prestigious orchestras, debiasing organizations so that women are hired in the best jobs, while a noble endeavor, is still not going to get rid of gender earnings differences.

Then there are those who like to point the finger at women's capabilities. Women have been accused of lacking the negotiation skills of comparable men. The mayor's office of the city of Boston, together with the American Association of University Women, has offered free salary-negotiation workshops for women (not men) who live or work in Boston. Relatedly, women have been charged with competing less than men and being overly risk averse in their choice of jobs. Entire industries concerned with making managers aware of their unconscious bias and advising firms how to read applications and interview candidates in a less biased fashion have emerged from each of these quick-fix notions.

Other fixes have involved legislative actions by states and the federal government. In July 2018, Massachusetts passed an Equal Pay Act that prohibits firms from requiring new hires or applicants to disclose their prior earnings, and from retaliating against employees who share salary information. In 2017, New York State passed similar legislation, and in 2015 California extended its previous equal-pay legislation with a Fair

Pay Act to protect employees who discuss coworkers' wages. The intent of the California, New York, and Massachusetts laws was to level the playing field through greater pay transparency.

Still others, and probably a majority of writers on the topic, see occupational differences between genders as a major, if not primary, cause. College-graduate women are more often in professions such as teacher, nurse, and accountant, whereas college-graduate men are more often in occupations such as manager, civil engineer, and sales representative. Women are also in lower-paying firms, even if they have the same occupational title as men. The phenomenon is generally termed "occupational segregation," making it sound like legal barriers and firm policies exist that deliberately segregate—such as the marriage bars that we saw with Groups Two and Three.

As we've seen, at one point in our history many firms had strict policies that limited the occupations women and men could enter, although it did not follow that women were restricted to only lowly jobs and men were barred from them. Newspaper ads once clearly noted which jobs were open to each gender (and race, for that matter). Such practices, of course, are now all illegal.

But men and women are in different occupations, and it is worth asking how much of the difference in earnings between them is due to differences in their employments.

Consider a thought experiment that equalizes occupations by gender simply by moving enough women (or enough men) across occupations to create a world in which the fraction of women and men in each occupation is the same. That is, if 5 percent of all workers are truck drivers, then 5 percent of employed men are truck drivers and 5 percent of employed women are as well. We won't worry about how this could be done. It is a thought experiment.

Earnings by gender and occupation are the ones that previously existed. The thought experiment allows us to imagine how the elimination of sex segregation would impact earnings by gender and the gender earnings gap. The main assumption is that actual earnings by gender and occupation remain the same and the only part of the apparatus that changes is the share of an occupation that is female or male.

To see how the thought experiment works, assume that there are an equal number of males and females in the workforce, and that 30 percent of women are teachers but just 10 percent of men are, and that the opposite is true for engineers. The remaining occupations are equally distributed by gender. One would have to move 20 percent of all women (or all men) to even things out. A magic wand would take two-thirds of the teachers (20/30) and make them into engineers. The thought experiment shifts the workers but holds the earnings of the teachers and the engineers constant by sex.

Reassigning workers to get equal occupational representation by sex might appear to be one way to eliminate the gender gap in earnings. And it would, in fact, eliminate some part of the gap. But it eliminates a surprisingly small part of it.

For college-graduate workers, 40 percent (either male or female) would have to shift occupations to achieve equality. For all workers, 50 percent (either male or female) would have to shift to attain gender equality by occupation. That's a lot of people to move around and all the more challenging given the different skills and preferences of the workers. But let's wave an empirical thought-experiment wand to see what might happen if we tried.

Even if one could accomplish the daunting task of rejiggering occupations to create equality, only around one-third of all gender earnings inequality would be eliminated. Occupational segregation isn't the main issue. It isn't even half of it, although many have claimed that it is the main offender. The reason that one can't eliminate more of the gender earnings gap is because it exists within just about every occupation. Furthermore, earnings gaps within occupations are larger for the more highly educated.

———

In 1968, the older members of Group Three and the younger members of Group Four waved protest signs about women's unequal pay that read, "59 cents on the [male] dollar." Fifty years later, similar signs held by members of Groups Four and Five read, "81 cents on the dollar." How were these figures computed? We hear these statistics so often that it is important to know what they mean.

The standard measure is constructed by taking all full-time, year-round workers (those who work thirty-five hours or more per week and fifty weeks or more per year), and computing the median annual earnings of females and males. The median measures the earnings of individuals at the middle of the distribution. The ratio of the median for women to that for men is the standard gender earnings gap measure.

Note that the gender gap measure that gets all the attention is for all workers, not just for the college graduates whose journey we have been following, and not just for Blacks or Hispanics or any other group.

The standard measure has many virtues. It is just one number. And by including only those who work full-time, it omits individuals who work sporadically. By using the median, it is less affected by the fact that there are more men than women with very high earnings.

But the measure isn't perfect. Although it uses full-time workers, it doesn't adjust for the fact that the average full-time male employee works longer hours than the average full-time female employee. It doesn't account for the fact that relatively more men than women work on-call and irregular hours, even if they work the same hours. Another shortcoming is that it is calculated for all workers, whereas—for our purposes—we're most interested in evaluating college graduates.

Because of its virtues, the measure has been calculated and reported by the Bureau of Labor Statistics (BLS) since 1960. Any piece of data that appears regularly on the front pages of our newspapers and is a topic for bloggers and opinion writers deserves some scrutiny. The series, shown in figure 8.1 as a solid line, reveals that the gap decreased from 1960 to 2017. So the difference between female and male earnings narrowed substantially. But the figure tells us a lot more.

Starting with the earliest year, the ratio of female earnings was stuck for two decades at almost 60 cents on the male dollar. We can now see why the "59 cents" mantra was so potent. But the ratio then began to rise. By 1990 women earned 70 cents on the male dollar, and by 2000 they earned 75 cents (once again, for full-time workers at the median). The figure is now 81 cents. The steepest increase occurred in the 1980s.

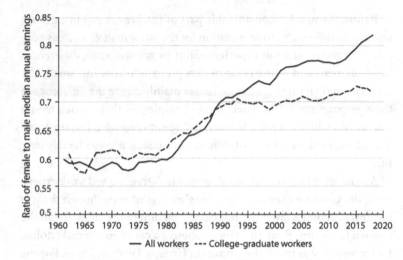

FIGURE 8.1. Female to Male Median Annual Earnings Ratio, Full-Time,
Year-Round Workers: 1960 to 2018
See Figures and Table Appendix.

The dotted line in figure 8.1 provides the series for college graduates. Although the standard series and the college-graduate series overlap for much of the period, a different path is followed by the college graduates after 1990. The standard series continues to increase, but that for college graduates flattens out. The divergence of the two is partly because earnings inequality greatly expanded in the post-1980s. College graduates began to win big, but college-graduate men were the biggest winners of all. We'll soon discuss why men are disproportionately in the upper portion of the earnings distribution.

Returning to the standard series, although it has continued to rise, there was slower progress in the 2010s. On Equal Pay Day of 2018, headlines read "Gender Gap Stuck" and "Equal Pay Day: Not Exactly Cause for Celebration."

Most agree, and I concur, that the narrowing in the 1980s was largely because women, relative to men, improved their labor market skills and their education, and, in consequence, had greater continuity in the labor force.

Before the 1980s, a considerable part of the gender gap in earnings was due to differences in preparation for the labor market, such as education, training, and job experience. But by around 2000, differences between men's and women's job market preparation became small. The disparity in their earnings was no longer mainly due to the difference in their preparation or the expectation of employers that women would not remain with their firm. Women still spent somewhat less time employed than did men. But that difference also shrank considerably over time.

As a result of the enhancements in women's training and work experience, the gender gap in earnings also shrank. But even though the gap narrowed significantly, it did not close. The difference today, for all the women in Groups Four and Five, is about 20 cents on the male dollar, half of what it was for all the women in Groups Two and Three. For the college-graduate women in Groups Four and Five, it is more—around 27 cents on the male dollar.

The difference in their earnings was once due to factors that were easy to measure, such as education, job experience, and a host of job-related skills. Now that many of these attribute differences have been eliminated, the remaining disparity in earnings is more worrisome. Because it isn't due to observable traits, many have blamed it on how the labor market treats women: the biases of those who hire and set wages. Others have attributed it to the possibility that women have inferior bargaining skills and a lack of competitiveness. This misunderstanding of the blame has led to the quick fixes discussed earlier. But the real reasons must be sought elsewhere.

The gender earnings gap is complicated. For one thing, it is more than just one number for each year. Male and female earnings change over time and with various life events, with women usually taking a big earnings hit when they have children. Men don't. Women also take an earnings hit after marriage or meaningful cohabitation, as it often leads to the couple relocating to optimize the two careers, often by maximizing the gain to one of them. Preference is more often than not given to the male's. So the ratio of female to male earnings tends to change after schooling ends and even after the first job.

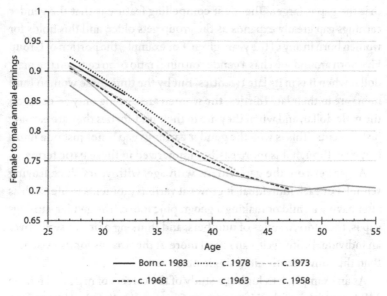

FIGURE 8.2. Relative Annual Earnings of College-Graduate Men and Women:
Group Five, Born 1958 to 1983
Notes: Earnings ratios correct for hours and weeks worked and education beyond
college graduate. Also see Figures and Table Appendix.

When male and female college graduates take their first jobs, their
earnings are reasonably similar. But sometime after the first job, their
earnings begin to diverge. The divergence can be seen using data from
the US Census and American Community Survey, as is done in figure 8.2. The gender earnings gap (or ratio) is graphed for those in Group
Five, who aspired to have career and family, not just one or the other.

Consider the ratio of female to male earnings for college graduates
in their late twenties, members of Group Five born around 1978 (the
top line in the figure). These women were doing fairly well relative to
men. They earned 92 cents on the male dollar and were probably doing
even better when they were just out of college or some postgraduate
school.

The rest of the lines in the figure refer to portions of Group Five. The
initial ratio given is somewhat smaller for those born earlier, meaning

that the gap is larger. The most compelling feature is that the gender earnings gap greatly expands as the group gets older, and this holds for women born in any of the years given. For example, the portion of Group Five born around 1963 has a gender earnings ratio of 90 cents on the male dollar when it is in its late twenties. But by the time these women (and men) are in their late thirties, the women are earning only 76 cents on the male dollar, and when they are in their mid-forties they are earning just 70 cents. This is why the gender earnings gap is not just one number, even though it is more easily summarized in those basic terms.

As we've seen, the gap widens with age, with years since leaving school. For each individual, it grows at various moments in life, such as after having a child or making a geographic move. The gender earnings gap is, therefore, a series of numbers, and thinking of it as a series over an individual's life cycle can reveal more of the reasons for its existence than the conveniently cited single number.

As an example, let's look at a study of the careers of male and female MBA graduates of the University of Chicago Booth School from 1990 to 2006. Because all participants have the same top degree and graduated from the same business school, many confounding factors are already held constant. The earliest graduates in the sample received their MBAs ten to sixteen years earlier, so we can use the shorthand of thirteen years in discussing their experiences.

Directly after the new crop of MBAs leaves the university and accepts their first jobs, women earn 95 cents on the male MBA dollar. But with each passing year, the difference in their earnings widens. By year thirteen it has dropped to an astounding low level of 64 cents on the male dollar. These differences are given, by year since MBA completion, by the dark bars in figure 8.3.

The key to why the drop-off occurs can be found by looking at the light bars, which give the ratio of female to male earnings for women who did not have a child relative to all men in the sample. Those bars are generally higher than the dark bars, especially so three years after MBA receipt, and the differences in the dark and light bars are greater with time since MBA. Although there is variance in the light bars—they go up and they go down (and then up again) in part because of the small

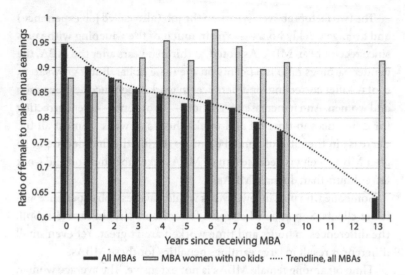

FIGURE 8.3. Ratio of Female to Male MBA Annual Earnings by Years since MBA Receipt
See Figures and Table Appendix.

sample—there is little trend. To the contrary, there is a clear downward trend in the dark bars. Women who never had a child (and never took a leave of more than six months) are almost at parity relative to all men, although they still earn less, whereas those who have had a child keep on doing worse.

We know from an in-depth analysis of these MBA histories that the growing gap in earnings doesn't appear randomly. Rather, it emerges largely with the arrival of children. Because the group that we analyzed were all graduates of the same (highly ranked) business school, and because we have administrative data on when they were students, we can control almost perfectly for their ability, training, and education.

Two factors take primary responsibility for the large gender gap in earnings that emerges among these MBAs: career interruptions and average weekly work hours. Female MBAs in the sample have longer career interruptions within their first thirteen years than do male MBAs. In addition, during the first thirteen years out, weekly work hours for female MBAs decrease relative to men's.

The two factors above—years on the job (also called job experience) and average weekly hours—explain much of the widening with years since receipt of an MBA. As noted, at thirteen years after the MBA, the gender earnings ratio is 64 cents on the male dollar. But it grows to 73 cents—after correcting for differences in work experience between men and women. And it increases even more—to 91 cents—after correcting for differences in time off and weekly hours of work. Almost all the decrease in the ratio of annual earnings during the first decade or so after MBA receipt is because female MBAs take more time off and work fewer hours than do male MBAs.

Someone who puts in fewer years would have less job experience and fewer clients. Someone who works fewer hours should earn less. Still, the differences in hours and time worked aren't great. Yet even small differences result in large earnings penalties for these MBAs.

Time off among female MBAs is not extensive. The average woman employed seven years after receiving her MBA had taken 0.37 of a year off—just more than four months. The average man had taken just 0.075 of a year off—less than one month. By around thirteen years out, the average woman had accumulated time off of about a year, the average man a mere six weeks. Time off the job for women isn't extensive, but it is a lot greater than for men.

Hours of work are long for both male and female MBAs. During their first few years after their MBA, the average work week is around sixty hours for both men and women. Thirteen years after graduation, the work week for women declines to forty-nine hours, compared with fifty-seven for men.

Much of the difference in average hours between male and female MBAs is because some women work part-time. In fact, about 18 percent of the women work part-time thirteen years after graduation. (Part-time for these MBAs, it should be noted, means working around thirty hours per week.) Tellingly, the majority of the MBA women working part-time were self-employed. Jobs in the corporate and financial sectors are rarely part-time. To work part-time, many MBA women employ themselves.

Another important fact is that by thirteen years out, 17 percent of the MBA women were not employed at all. That figure is higher than that experienced by other college-graduate women who have attained a prestigious advanced degree—higher than that for JDs, PhDs, and MDs.

But the fraction of these MBAs who considered themselves "not currently employed" was considerably less than one would have expected given the buzz regarding "opting out" among college-graduate women with children, especially among those with MBAs. The employment breaks for the MBAs were often temporary. College-graduate women generally don't opt out of the labor force for good. Some just take employment pauses.

Women's earnings relative to men's decrease with time after receiving an MBA. But this is not mainly due to large disruptions in their employment, extensive periods of absence, and shifts into low-hour positions. Rather, female MBAs earn considerably less than their male counterparts because the high-paying corporate and financial sector positions heavily penalize employees who have even brief career disruptions and those who do not work exceptionally long and grueling hours.

The arrival of children and the ensuing caregiving responsibilities are the main contributors to the lesser job experience, greater career discontinuity, and shorter work hours for female relative to male MBAs. In addition, some MBA moms in our sample took a break from the labor market within a few years following their first birth.

MBA mothers do not reduce their hours of work immediately after coming back from maternity leave. Rather, they return to their jobs and continue working the arduous hours. After about a year or two some start cutting back. Others change course by engaging in self-employment. The largest changes occur at three to four years after the first birth. At that point, women's earnings, on average, drop to 74 percent of their prebirth levels.

Some MBA women with young children find that the hours and intensity of work in the corporate and financial sectors are too much after a birth. And the wake-up call occurs even in the absence of a second child. The data speak volumes about a group of women who want to put their careers back on track. Career and family are each trying to occupy the same space, and something has to give.

MBA women without children, whether they have been married or not, have a different trajectory than do MBA women with children. Although the earnings of the MBA women who do not have children (and who have no career disruptions) are still lower than are those of the MBA men (with and without children), they are only about 9 cents lower on the MBA male dollar at thirteen years after graduation. That figure, while not zero, is phenomenally lower than the 36-cent gap on the male MBA dollar that exists for the entire group.

———

Women choose to cut back at their jobs for a host of reasons after giving birth, even several years after. But there is also the possibility that they do not leave or slow down by their own volition. Women with children may be pushed out of the workplace in various direct and subtle ways. Well-intentioned paternalism by supervisors (both male and female) could be at work. Women with young children might be protected from more demanding clients by their supervisors and passed over for challenging projects. They could also be denied access to the richer clients and to promotions by managers who are uncertain about their long-run future with the company.

But there is compelling evidence from the MBA study that choice, rather than paternalism or bias, is the major factor. The evidence concerns what we see in the data on how a husband's income impacts an MBA mother's hours of work. The largest change in hours of work, and thus the largest change in annual earnings, occurs for women whose husbands earned above the median salary for MBA men (let's call them the top-earning husbands). In addition, the largest reduction in employment is also for those with top-earning husbands. In the first two years after the birth, a woman whose spouse was in the top-earning group was 22 percent less likely to be working than if her husband was not. After five years, she was 32 percent less likely to be working.

But the mere fact of having a "rich" husband is not the critical determinant of years of experience, hours of work, and employment. Women who have high-earning husbands but no children put in as many years of employment and hours of work as do those with less prosperous spouses. A clear interaction exists between having children and having a high-earning spouse in determining which MBA women are employed and the hours they put in at the office.

Most parents cannot (and do not want to) contract away all care for their children. Having a husband who is hopping across continents means he cannot be home every day and possibly not every week. Having a home in the suburbs means that both working parents would have to commute. Something has to give. And with one really high income, the second income is less crucial.

Such evidence suggests that most of the effect of children on an MBA mom's employment is due to choice, not bias, either well-intentioned or not. Of course, the choices of MBA mothers are highly circumscribed by the relative inflexibility of work schedules in much of the corporate and financial sectors.

One study, no matter how well done, cannot provide incontrovertible evidence on as complex and enduring an issue as the gender earnings gap. However, a large number of studies can point the way. Other research, mine included, has confirmed the findings from the MBA project. Using extensive firm-level and census data on US employers and their employees, my coauthors and I discovered that the earnings of college-graduate women decreased relative to those of college-graduate men during their first seven years of employment, and that the decrease was greater for those who were married. Women shift into lower-paying firms, and within firms they receive lower increases in their salaries.

Additional evidence comes from research on the impact of childbirth on the incomes of each parent. Among the most convincing and startling of these studies are those that use data from several Nordic countries. These studies provide "cradle to grave" evidence and are startling because the conclusions are similar to those of the MBA study, even though they are for nations that have among the most generous family-centered policies in the world, including subsidized childcare and extensive paid leave for both parents.

Their data allow for precise estimates of the role of births on mothers' and fathers' earnings, which they look at several years before and many years after an event—here a birth. Various teams of researchers have produced such studies using extraordinary administrative data from Sweden and Denmark. The Swedish study observes earnings for the father and the mother of the baby sometime from 1990 to 2002, and estimates how the birth impacts the couple's earnings differences. The Danish study does a similar analysis but compares the impact of birth on women relative to comparable male workers.

As expected, a substantial earnings penalty occurs to women after a birth. But even fifteen years after the birth, the income gap between the husband and the wife remains wider than it had been before the birth. The differences are large. If the two parents had made the same amount before the birth, the husband earns 32 percent more than his wife when the child is fifteen years old. Much of that widening, according to the Swedish study, is due to a reduction in the wife's hours of work, but about a third of it is from a reduction in the hourly rate of pay.

An identical calculation for the US, which lags the entire world in family-friendly policies, would be almost impossible to produce because of the absence of the type of administrative records that exist for Sweden (and some other nations) that link earnings information to birth data. But there is no reason to believe that the results would be smaller here, and there are many reasons to believe they would be larger.

All these findings—that the gender earnings gap widens with family formation, that women shift into lower-paying firms, and that they do not advance as much as men do within firms—beg an examination of earnings gaps by occupation for the college-graduate group. There are large differences in the gender pay gap across occupations. Are some more conducive to gender equality and couple equity? What are the occupational characteristics that render occupations more or less friendly to women (and to couples more generally)?

Consider those who have been awarded among the most prestigious advanced degrees: JD, MBA, MD, and PhD. These degrees enable their recipients to enter the most lucrative fields, which are also the ones with the greatest income inequality and enormous benefits to those who put in the hours, days, and weeks. Women who hold one of these degrees, especially if they have children, will generally do less well than their male counterparts. Women naturally take off more time from employment and often scale back their hours when their children are young. They will pay a price for that in terms of their careers, as we just saw in the case of the MBAs. How great a price depends on the type of work they are doing.

Fathers also pay a hefty price. Almost half of all fathers surveyed in a Pew Research Center study about whether they spend enough time with their children said that they spend too little. It is time that cannot easily be made up later in life. Many older men relish their time as grandparents because they missed out on time with their own children as toddlers. The costs to each parent who specializes in one realm or the other—career or family—add up to the loss of couple equity.

The previously mentioned Harvard and Beyond Project, among Harvard College graduates from the late 1960s to the early 1990s, together with related data, allows us to measure the career penalty associated with breaks in employment. The penalty for time out is substantial for each of the career paths that recipients of these degrees usually take—lawyers, managers, physicians, and academics. It exists for both males and females, but it is experienced more by women, because they take more time off and reduce their hours more.

The annual earnings penalty for taking time out varies by degree, and the differences are large. The earnings penalty measured at fifteen years since leaving college with a BA is lowest for MDs and highest for MBAs. Those with a JD or a PhD are somewhere in between. The penalty for MBAs is 1.4 times that for MDs, and the penalty for JDs and PhDs is 1.2 times that for MDs. What causes the penalties for career breaks and for reductions in hours of work to vary by degree and, thus, occupation?

To answer these questions, I used a huge dataset from the American Community Survey containing information on several million college-graduate men and women, twenty-five to sixty-four years old. Although around 500 occupations are enumerated in the US census, 115 occupations are represented here, because the sample is limited to college graduates working full-time. The occupations range from some of the most prestigious to many that are less exalted, such as sales representative, budget analyst, and health care technician.

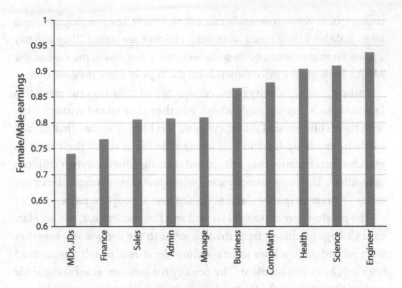

FIGURE 8.4. Gender Earnings Ratio for College Graduates by Occupational Sector
Notes: Earnings are adjusted for age, hours and weeks worked, and education
above a bachelor's degree. Data used aggregate the ACS for 2009 to 2016.
Also see Figures and Table Appendix.

Some of these occupational groups have extremely large gender earnings gaps, whereas others are closer to parity. The gender earnings ratios are arrayed from lowest to highest in figure 8.4, after correcting for usual hours and weeks worked, the age of the worker, and education above a bachelor's degree.

The lowest ratios of female to male earnings—that is, the largest gaps—are found in professional occupations with considerable self-ownership, such as law firms, as well as those dealing with finance, sales, administration, management, and business operations. The highest ratios, and thus the lowest gaps, are in math and computer science, health care (excluding physicians), science, and engineering. The occupations, therefore, divide into two groups. Women in tech earn 94 cents on the male tech dollar, but women in finance earn 77 cents on the male finance dollar.

Is there something particularly bigoted and chauvinistic about those in the finance sector but not in the tech sector? Are there lots of biased and opportunistic bosses in finance, but not in tech? There are unprincipled managers and bosses in each sector. Seeking the underlying reasons for gender earnings differences by sector or industry requires that we know what people do in each of these occupations and the demands of each, especially regarding time.

It would be a herculean task to ferret out this information for each occupation. Fortunately, a huge team has already put together a standard group of characteristics for all census occupations. The database is O*NET—Occupational Information Network—maintained by the US Department of Labor.

Before revealing their findings, we should consider some general notions about why women—especially mothers—prefer some jobs to others, and gravitate to them, even if the positions pay less. This logic is predicated on the fact that women traditionally take more responsibility for their children and for other family members. That doesn't mean that men don't spend considerable time with their children, and it doesn't mean that our current household division of labor is correct. But women are more often the "on-call-at-home" parent (as well as the "on-call" offspring).

Because of differences between men and women in their responsibilities at home, occupations that have shorter hours, fewer on-call hours, more predictable schedules, and more control over hours should be preferred by women. By extension, jobs for which there are teams of workers who can easily substitute for one another and for which there are standardized services or products should also be preferred by women.

But workers are not often perfect substitutes for one another, and clients generally prefer to see a professional with whom they have a relationship. Staff members may have to work evening and weekend hours to meet with clients, and that often means paying workers more to compensate them for missing time with their family. Men generally opt for the jobs that have greater time demands but pay more. Relative to women, they generally care less about the time flexibility and more about the earnings advantage. Women with children, however, don't often have the ability to do that.

Remember Isabel and Lucas, the couple from chapter 1 who both work for InfoServices? The company needed someone to be on call at work and was willing to pay more for it. Let's say that the premium for that position was $20,000 per year, enough to entice Lucas to take the job. Isabel did not, since both of them could not be on call at work because she was initially taking care of her parents and later of their young child.

Lucas and Isabel would have preferred to be "on call at home" together, rather than have one be "on call at the office." That would have ensured greater couple equity. But the $20,000 premium was too high for them as a couple to pass up. The more the firm has to pay for the on-call-at-work employee, the greater the gender earnings gap—if women remain the ones who are generally at home. But even if there are no gender differences regarding who takes the on-call-at-work job, there will be couple equity issues.

So, returning to what we should expect to see in the actual data, smaller gender earnings gaps should be found in occupations for which longer hours aren't worth that much more, for which firms can put together teams of substitute workers, and for which services and products are more standardized. Larger gaps should be found in occupations for which on-call and irregular hours are worth a considerable amount, for which rich clients demand specific professionals, for which teams are made up of those who do different, complementary tasks, and for which services and products are idiosyncratic.

O*NET provides hundreds of characteristics for each occupation. Some concern the physical attributes of a job, but our interest here is less in the physical demands of the job and more in the time demands of the workplace, interactions among workers, and relationships with clients. All census occupations offer information on six relevant characteristics:

1) Contact with others: How much contact with others (by telephone, face-to-face, or otherwise) is required to perform your current job?

2) Frequency of decision making: In your current job, how often do your decisions affect other people or the image or reputation or financial resources of your employer?

3) Time pressure: How often does this job require the worker to meet strict deadlines?

4) Structured versus unstructured work: To what extent is this job structured for the worker, rather than allowing the worker to determine tasks, priorities, and goals?

5) Establishing and maintaining interpersonal relationships: What is the importance of developing constructive and cooperative working relationships with others and maintaining them over time?

6) Level of competition: How competitive is your current job?

The first five characteristics measure time demands on the job. If women are less able to give as much time as men, or if they are less willing to be at work during particular hours or days, they may be paid less on an hourly basis, even if they have the same job title. Isabel and Lucas have the same job titles; they work the same number of hours. But Lucas is paid $20,000 more per year because he is on call at the office. Since she is paid $100,000 per year, Isabel makes 83 cents on Lucas's dollar because she has a more predictable schedule, allowing her to be on call at home.

Occupations in the engineering, science, and computer-math fields all show that the first five characteristics have low time demands and limited personal interactions. In these fields, employees often work at separate tasks, rarely have client relationships, have somewhat flexible deadlines, make decisions that are similar from day to day, and engage in tasks that are often left up to the independent researcher. These occupations also have low gender earnings gaps.

The occupations at the high end of gender inequality are those in management, administration, and sales, as well as those with significant self-employment, such as doctors, dentists, and lawyers. These occupations are also at the high end for the first five characteristics. In these fields, people have clients, must meet strict deadlines, and make decisions that vary from day to day.

The only anomalies in the large group of occupations are those in the health field and in financial operations. Health occupations (such as physical therapists and dietitians) generally have highly specific tasks.

They have low levels of gender inequality, but also higher-than-average time demands. On the other end, occupations in financial operations (such as financial advisors and loan officers) have high gender inequality but lower-than-average time demands.

Although these occupations do not fit the framework using the five characteristics concerning time demands, they are strongly related to the sixth characteristic: competition. Health occupations have among the lowest degree of competition. Finance occupations have among the highest.

An average of the six characteristics (the five measuring time demands and the sixth, assessing competition) goes a long way to "explaining" the gender earnings gap by occupation. Those with high time demands and/or considerable competition have larger gender earnings gaps. Alternatively, occupations with low time demands and/or low levels of competition have smaller gender earnings gaps. Women incur penalties in certain occupations because they require more controllable hours.

Another important feature of these occupations concerns the inequality of earnings. Occupations with the greatest income inequality among men have among the largest gender earnings gaps. The occupations with the highest income inequality are also those in which employees vie for clients, contracts, deals, and patients. They also have among the longest hours, with the most on-call and rush hours (consider the long hours of lawyers, surgeons, accountants, and those in the C-suite).

For all these reasons, occupations with high levels of income inequality are ones in which women, particularly mothers, will be less likely to earn the higher incomes. They will be paid considerably less than those who actively compete for the deals and less than those who put in the long and irregular hours to secure them.

With rising income inequality since the late 1970s more generally, jobs with the greatest demands on hours have paid more. Thus, those jobs that have been the most difficult for women to enter and have been the roughest for them are precisely those that have become the most lucrative in the last several decades. This impact may be one reason why the gender earnings gap, especially for the college-graduate group, has hardly budged in the last decade, even though women have improved their credentials. Women are swimming upstream, holding their own, but going against some strong economic currents.

———

Lilly Ledbetter, who called herself "the grandmother of equal pay," and women who share some of her experiences know that the gender earnings gap is real. It is among the most important issues of our day. What can be done about it? The various fixes mentioned earlier—ridding the labor market of biased managers and organizations, encouraging women to compete more, teaching them to bargain more effectively, and revealing to all what others earn—could narrow the gap somewhat. But those, and even the more challenging fix of eliminating all occupational segregation, would have only a modest impact.

Differences in earnings between the sexes exist within almost every occupation. They are more important to the overall gender earnings gap than are occupational differences between men and women. The gender earnings gap widens over time and increases at certain moments, such as after a birth. For the MBAs, the gap expanded for women in the aggregate. But it expanded far less, if at all, for those without children and for those who did not take a break of more than six months.

The culprit in the gender earnings gap story must be sought in two domains. One concerns the decisions made by ordinary couples, such as Isabel and Lucas, regarding how they share childcare responsibilities. The other is found in the cost of temporal flexibility at work that constrains all couples in their choices. The greater the cost, the more the members of a couple will specialize and forgo couple equity in childcare.

Let's bring our detective lens to the cases of the pharmacist and the lawyer, both of which further expose the underlying cause of the gender earnings gap and offer additional clues to how we could solve it.

9

The Case of the Lawyer and
the Pharmacist

IN THE EARLY 1960s, a popular TV legal drama followed the cases of fictional criminal defense attorney Perry Mason. Perry was a soft-spoken, deep-thinking, sensitive, and physically large man. Aided by his savvy legal secretary Della Street, Perry solved the crime at the end of every show, exonerating the falsely accused defendant. The riveting plots often came from the pen of the great storyteller Erle Stanley Gardner.

When Della was Perry's right-hand gal in the 1960s, the median female JD made just 57 cents on her male counterpart's dollar on an annual basis—if she landed a job as a lawyer at all. In the 1950s and early 1960s, many of the best female law school graduates—members of Group Three—could not get a foot in the door at most law firms. When Sandra Day O'Connor graduated near the top of her Stanford Law School class in 1952, she could not even find a firm willing to grant her an interview. Ruth Bader Ginsburg did not get a clerkship with Justice Felix Frankfurter because he didn't hire female clerks. Group Three women who tried to enter careers, even those with impeccable credentials, were few in number and often not taken seriously.

When the original *Perry Mason* last aired, in 1966, just 4 percent of law students were female. By 1987, a mere two decades later, more than 40 percent of JD recipients were women. By the time HBO's spin-off by the same name aired in summer 2020, men and women could be found in equal numbers on law school campuses across the nation. Practicing law as a lawyer in a law firm, as a corporate counsel, or otherwise is a popular profession. Relative to medicine, for example, there are almost three entering law students to every entering medical student. Doors have opened for female lawyers in various arenas: as members of private law firms, as in-house corporate attorneys, and as lawyers in the public sector. Today, Della Street could become a Perry Mason herself—she just wouldn't be paid like him, yet. (And she likely wouldn't have a secretary as smart and savvy as Perry was privileged to have as his sidekick.) Women's earnings in the field have advanced, too. But for a variety of reasons, they are still low, relative to men's. Today, the median female lawyer earns just about 78 cents on the median male lawyer dollar.

Though that's a major improvement, why can't attorney Della Street make the same money now as attorney Perry Mason? Is it because the senior partners won't promote her? As we learned in the last chapter, the gender pay gap is more complicated than noted discrimination. Of course, bias—explicit or implicit—may play a role. It most assuredly did in the past, when Sandra Day O'Connor wasn't even interviewed for a job or when Ruth Bader Ginsburg did not receive a Supreme Court clerkship.

But for today's Della and Perry, that isn't the whole story. A more insidious issue, seamlessly woven into the fabric of modern work, proves to be far more influential. The answer to the mystery in the imagined 2021 season of Della and Perry's partnership returns us to the heart of our vexing and persistent gender earnings gap.

———

Let's recast Della and Perry from their 1950s roles of secretary and attorney to more modern ones: an ambitious young couple from Group Five who met and fell in love on the law review of their top-ranked law school. Sometime after graduation, with JDs in hand, they both headed into practice.

Freshly minted law school graduates have a host of employment options. They can work in large corporate law firms or small practices that specialize in family law and estate planning. They can work as corporate counsel, in government and nonprofits, or they can teach in law schools.

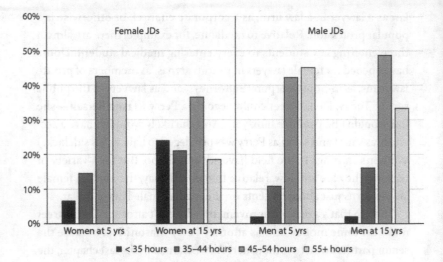

FIGURE 9.1. Percentage Distribution of Hours of Work for Female and Male JDs:
Five and Fifteen Years after Law School Graduation
See Figures and Table Appendix.

They can run for political office or work elsewhere outside the legal sector. Each of the options affords a range of amenities with different levels of compensation.

Della and Perry are young and ambitious, so they both decide to take demanding jobs in private firms (those law school loans aren't going to repay themselves). Five years out, they will be earning almost identical amounts. Earnings just after JD receipt are about the same by sex, and the slight gap in the raw data between male and female JD salaries five years after law school disappears when hours worked and job experience are taken into account.

As rookie lawyers at a private firm, however, their lives are demanding. Hours are long for all JDs at that career stage, and almost 80 percent of female JDs and 90 percent of male JDs work more than forty-five hours per week in their fifth year, as shown in figure 9.1. Those in large law firms or in the corporate sector work even more, with Perry working around fifty-one hours per week and Della working forty-eight. And the women stay in the game for now: just 6 percent of these young lawyers work part-time, and a miniscule 4 percent are out of the labor force by year five.

At the five-year mark, Della and Perry are a modern dream team, working essentially the same number of hours and making essentially the same amount of money. They're on track to be equals, in pay and responsibility. Given this promising beginning, in a decade or so they should both be on track to make partner in their firms. Right?

Wrong. In the next ten years of practice, one-quarter of the women will fall back to working part-time. A full 16 percent will leave the labor force. By contrast, only a tiny fraction of the men will work part-time (2 percent), and an equally small fraction (2 percent again) will have no employment. For both male and female JDs, around 20 percent will leave the law but remain employed, but the reasons given for doing so generally differ.

While Perry Mason will be about to make partner and maximize his earning potential, there is more than a one in three chance that the equally talented, hardworking, and employable Della Street will have left the law altogether, either to pursue another career or to be a stay-at-home mom. Even if Della does stay in her law career, she may not work as many hours as Perry. Fifteen years out from graduation, about 80 percent of male lawyers put in more than 45 hours a week, while just 55 percent of the women do the same. When they were just five years out, the fractions were much closer. Della's income will differ drastically as a result: at the fifteen-year mark, female JDs earn just a little over *half* (56 percent) of what male JDs earn.

What happened with Della and Perry? Where did this great divide in their careers come from? The spirited young couple started out with the same goals, aspirations, and qualifications. They were evenly matched five years into practice. What changed?

The easy response is, well, the field is such an old boys' club that to land the big client you have to smoke a cigar with them over a steak dinner and talk for hours about the latest baseball game. But it's not quite so simple. The gap between Della's and Perry's careers is not because Della doesn't like cigars, or that Perry and the male partners above him maintain a discriminatory practice of promotion and mentorship. It's not even because the law provides among the most extreme case of a gender pay gap. The root of the problem plagues a range of professions and careers, and it has less to do with labor market discrimination and everything to do with *time*. The culprit, as we witnessed in the story of Isabel and Lucas, is the very structure of work.

After fifteen years, by working fewer hours than Perry, Della has accumulated less legal experience. But even if she worked the same hours, she would be receiving only 81 percent of his earnings, as her hourly pay is now much lower than his. Much of the remaining difference is because, though she was an equally promising lawyer, Della took some time off from her legal career.

When we closely scrutinize compensation in the legal field, we learn something important: just how much putting in the time pays off in Della and Perry's chosen profession.

By year fifteen, the average lawyer who works sixty hours a week earns more than two and a half times what the lawyer working thirty hours a week earns. That jump in earnings with time occurs without regard to gender. Both male and female lawyers earn significantly more per hour when their overall hours increase. We've seen this before in the sketch of the lives of Isabel and Lucas, but these numbers are actual ones, computed from a large sample of lawyers.

When a lawyer's hours increase from thirty to sixty per week, the average hourly rate increases by almost a quarter. The more hours per week that lawyers work, the more each of their hours spent working is worth. If we hold hours worked constant for men and women, there is *no* gender component to the discrepancy.

We know the difference between what the genders earn is significant. But if the underlying cause of the gap is not their genders, what is it, and why does it fall along gender lines so prominently? To best understand the answer, we have to look deep into the structure of firms and the demands of their clients—as well as into who picks up the slack at home.

Five years out of law school, women work a little less than men—but not much less. By year fifteen, however, even women who work full-time put in considerably fewer hours than men, and fewer hours than

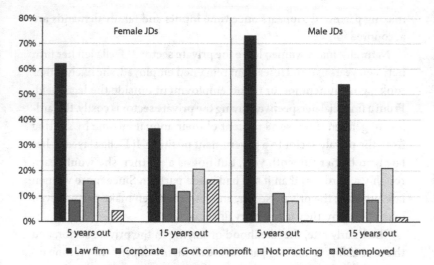

FIGURE 9.2. Percentage Distribution of Work Setting for Female and Male JDs:
Five and Fifteen Years after Law School Graduation
See Figures and Table Appendix.

the same women did at the start. Their reduced work time, moreover, didn't suddenly start at year fifteen. For any lawyer, working part-time or shorter hours means a lower probability of working with the richer clients. Just 18 percent of lawyers who worked part-time in year fifteen were in a firm that had a Fortune 500 client, but almost 30 percent of those who worked fifty-five hours and more a week were.

Lawyers also make more money in private firms. At year five, as shown in figure 9.2, most men and women worked for private firms. Ten years later, both groups have moved away from private practice. More women than men, however, shifted out of the private sector in that intervening decade. Only 37 percent of the women remained with private firms by the fifteen-year mark, compared with more than half the men.

The women who stuck with the private sector still had a good chance of making partner by their fifteenth year—just not as good a chance as the men. More than half the women made partner by year fifteen, while 70 percent of the men did. But the gender difference in the rate of making partner disappears once time inputs and family demands are accounted for.

Naturally, many women leave the private sector. If Della left her firm between years five and fifteen but remained employed, she likely either took a government job or found employment outside the legal field. From a financial perspective, leaving the private sector is costly. Regardless of gender, JDs lose 38 percent of their annual income by shifting from the private sector to a government position. If Della stayed at her law firm by her fifteenth year, but not as a partner, she would earn roughly a third less than if she had made partner. Since more women lawyers leave the private sector, and fewer women make partner even when they stay, they take a hefty financial hit.

The hourly rate, the likelihood of staying in the private sector, and the probability of making partner are all highly dependent on time inputs and family demands—but not as much on the gender of the lawyer. Bias exists in many law firms, but it is not the primary cause of gender differences in promotion and earnings.

Why, then, does time input diverge so greatly and have such a serious impact on the earnings and careers of women versus men? Almost all the women who exit the law profession between five and fifteen years after the JD have young children. But lots of female lawyers have children, you might argue, so there must be other factors determining who leaves.

Let's imagine that Della and Perry, perhaps seven to ten years into their careers, have one or two children. If Perry's income puts him in the top tier, it is much more likely that Della will leave her job and her profession than if Perry had the lower income of the two. Women with children who have wealthy husbands are three times more likely to be out of the labor force than women whose husbands have lower (but certainly not low) incomes. (By comparison, for women without children there are no differences in employment based on their husbands' differing incomes.)

So the change in Della's employment that results from Perry's extraordinarily high income comes about *if they have children*. Female lawyers do not leave their jobs just because they have wealthy husbands.

Their husbands are enabled to earn that much more, plus have a family to boot, because their wives leave their jobs. Perry can be at the top of his game, but only if his time and effort aren't taken up by household and childcare responsibilities. That isn't to say that Perry isn't a great father when he is around. He just doesn't have to be around as much as the on-call parent and the at-home manager.

Even if Della and Perry hired round-the-clock childcare, children require and deserve parental time. And most parents want to give them that time, which presents a quandary. Time spent with the children is time not spent with clients. Time spent managing daycare and the household help is not time spent writing briefs, in court, and getting promoted to partner. These tradeoffs have become even clearer in the COVID era, we will soon see, as work has shifted to a home that is also a childcare center, school, and lunchroom.

Della and Perry are faced with an extreme decision. They could both compromise and work full-time without putting in those forty-five-plus-hour work weeks and late nights. As we've seen, however, that would mean both would sacrifice a ton of money and a heap of experience, falling behind the pack in the private sector and facing a longer, harder route to partnership.

Instead of hamstringing both their careers and still lacking lots of time to spend with their children, Della and Perry do the very logical thing: they maximize their earnings potential as a couple. Della drops back from her career, perhaps working part-time or leaving legal work altogether, to do the work at home. That frees Perry from those time-consuming family and household responsibilities and allows him to put in the necessary long hours at work to accelerate to partner, maximize his hourly rate, and see the payoff for the family in that higher income.

At the end of every *Perry Mason* story, Perry and Della solved the crime. In this case, the crime they had to solve was how to have a family and maximize their household income. The real crime, however, is that the end of modern Perry and Della's story is essentially unchanged from that of their 1950s selves: Perry is the high-powered attorney, the one in the courtroom and the boardroom, while Della works part-time professionally and full-time at home, when the children are young. As the kids become more independent, Della increases her work hours, but she already sacrificed making partner in the lucrative law firm.

If Perry and Della were colleagues of the same high-earning variety, they could earn roughly the same amount, work the same hours, and have similar chances of making partner. But if they are—like so many people—a couple with similar educations and career goals who want to have children, then their careers won't stay in sync for long. Only one of them can reach that high-earning level. When their careers diverge, it is almost entirely due to women's desire for more flexible or fewer hours, and their retreat from the private and corporate sectors to literally find the time they need to do the work of raising children. Despite the progress toward gender equality in the profession, the legal field today still has one of the largest gender earnings gaps for any occupation in the American economy.

Della and Perry's conundrum is shared by many couples, like our friends Isabel and Lucas, across many professions. Highly educated people who settle down together—the doctor and the tenured professor, the CEO and the senator, the global consultant and the architect—will face a different version of the same problem.

The huge database we previously looked at, O*NET—produced by the US Bureau of Labor Statistics—gathers the detailed information we discussed about census occupations, offering some critical insights into the experience of the American labor force. We've seen that the data show that some job characteristics are closely related to the gender earnings gap, like the importance of the time demands of the job, the degree to which the job requires close contact with others (such as clients and customers), and the importance to the job of maintaining personal relationships. The greater the time demands of the profession and the greater the need for uninterrupted time with clients and others, the less likely some women will be to succeed in these jobs relative to men.

We now know that the occupations with greater time demands pay disproportionately more, *even per hour*, when employees work more hours and make themselves more available to clients. Employers such as law firms are willing to pay to entice people to work irregular, on-call, unpredictable, and just flat-out more hours because, among other

THE LAWYER AND THE PHARMACIST 185

reasons, individuals become indispensable to the firm's clients and its various deals. A client may demand a particular accountant or consultant. A lawyer involved in a big-ticket merger and acquisition may be viewed as essential to the transaction. Legal, consulting, and accounting firms may believe that the client will be forever lost if a particular person is not part of the deal every step of the way. Greater time demands lead to higher hourly wages, which is why some workers get paid a lot more to be "on call at the office."

But just because workers are on call and expected to work long and irregular hours doesn't always mean that they will get paid more for it. Like everything in economics, it depends on supply and demand. Firms want workers who will put in the long hours because having workers who are readily available to the client is good for business. But employees working long and irregular days get paid more because they demand the extra compensation to do so. The compensation is sort of like hardship pay.

Individuals whose careers involve making partner, or being promoted to tenure, also have severe time demands. But these are different. These employees must work intensely during a fixed period for a goal that is often a "winner-take-all" prize. In this case, the contemporaneous hourly wage does not increase. But expected earnings and future job security do.

When your pay per hour rises with the number of hours worked, you generally have an incentive to labor more hours. If the increase in pay is high enough, even those with responsibilities at home and desires to be with their families will have a significant financial incentive to spend more hours in the office. Given that both parents—regardless of their profession or occupation—cannot (and usually do not want to) contract out all parental duties to a nanny, one parent will, by necessity, work fewer hours in the office and spend more time at home. That parent will not get the paycheck premium on hours, even if she (or he) continues working.

Both parents could have taken the less predictable jobs and maximized family income. Or they could both have taken the more predictable and flexible jobs—maximizing time with their children but reducing their family income. Or they could have one take the high-paying job and the other take the flexible one, which is what they chose to do.

They maximized family income subject to the constraint that at least one parent had to be on call at home. They did that by having one parent be on call at work.

Men disproportionately take jobs with less predictable and more inflexible hours, which means that women, on average, earn less than men even if they put in as many hours. And when the more inflexible jobs have greater advancement, women get fewer promotions down the pike. Gender inequality results. Women disproportionately take jobs with more predictable and flexible hours, so they can spend more time taking care of child and household needs and emergencies. Couple inequity results. But, of course, gender norms are at the root of why women take the more flexible and predictable jobs in the first place.

As we've learned, having an authentic career outside the home is a relatively new phenomenon for women—one that developed over the course of our five groups. When viewed in the context of such rapid change, we can see that although the social acceptability of a woman having a career and a family has shifted considerably, the workplace still greatly rewards old-fashioned specialization. Individuals, and thus couples, have a major financial incentive to concentrate heavily on their career—and not compromise with responsibilities in the home. But if a family is also a goal, then something has to give.

The differences in earnings between men and women, according to the logic and data we're exploring, have little direct relationship to bias in the workplace or to a lack of family-friendly policies or to any of the other quick fixes mentioned. Those solutions are intended to give women what is due to them in their current positions. But the features of the jobs they have now are the reason why they are earning less. These are the aspects of jobs that make a particular worker—lawyer, accountant, consultant, financial advisor—indispensable to the account, client, deal.

The good news? It isn't *you*; it is the system. The bad news: it isn't you; it is the *system*. Even a woman who is getting a salary that could be verified as "fair and unbiased" may still earn less than a comparable man in the same profession if she is unable to put in the longer hours or be on call because of the constraints of family and children.

Despite our best intentions and many victories on the long road to equality, the earnings gap between men and women persists. These days, both Perry and Della flip through self-help books and articles, looking for the ten-step instructions on how to have a good career and a family *at all*, searching for advice on how to balance the two. The answer won't be found there, but the admission that a problem exists shows some progress.

As long as the difference in earnings between the two jobs is substantial, the average couple will opt for higher family income and, often to their mutual frustration and sorrow, will thereby be forced to throw gender equality and couple equity under the bus.

How can couples be encouraged not to abandon couple equity? Clearly, they need an option where it doesn't cost them so much to remain equals. Is it possible to achieve this by changing the system, or for the system to change on its own? The answer is yes—in fact, a handful of professions already have done so. Pharmacy, for one, tells a much different story.

———

Not only is the occupation of pharmacist egalitarian; it is also highly lucrative. Relative to women in all other occupations, female pharmacists rank fifth (out of almost five hundred occupations) in terms of their median earnings, as reported in the US census for full-time, full-year workers. (Lawyers are seventh among women.) Female pharmacists don't just have high incomes relative to other comparably educated women; they also earn almost the same as male pharmacists when adjusted for hours of work.

What accounts for the gender equality among pharmacists yet the large inequity remaining in the legal field? After all, both professions have experienced similar increases in the fraction of women entering the field, and both require specialized postbachelor's training, in which women have thrived.

The answer lies in the very structure of the work. These occupations once shared similar characteristics. Long and irregular hours had been an important feature of the lives of both pharmacists and lawyers. Each occupation involved a high degree of self-employment and carried the risk that ownership always entails. Whereas these features still define the situation of lawyers today, none of them applies to modern pharmacists.

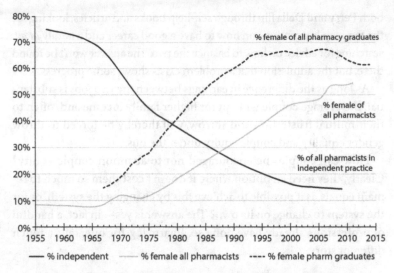

FIGURE 9.3. Percentage Female among Pharmacists and Pharmacy Graduates and
Percentage Working in Independent Practice among Pharmacists
See Figures and Table Appendix.

Vials is a recent, short-lived, funny sitcom set in an independent pharmacy called Gateway Drug. The store is owned by a cantankerous pharmacist named Rich and run by various technicians and Rich's rebellious daughter Lisa, a newbie pharmacist. A half century ago, pharmacies like Gateway Drug were the main way consumers got their prescriptions filled and their drugstore needs met. The pharmacists and pharmacy owners of the past were almost all men. In 1965, female pharmacists, largely those in Group Three, constituted less than 10 percent of all pharmacists (see figure 9.3) and were usually employed by a male pharmacist who owned the store. In that year, about 75 percent of all pharmacists were either owners of independent practices or were their employees (the other 25 percent worked in chains, hospitals, and the like). The female pharmacists earned 67 cents on the male pharmacist dollar, largely because they didn't own the stores.

Pharmacists who worked longer hours in those days (when even pharmacists were watching *Perry Mason* on TV) earned considerably more per hour than those who worked fewer hours. The self-employed were far more highly remunerated than were employees. Women with children must have earned far less than those without children, even if they worked the same hours, because they were unable to work particular hours on demand. The occupation of pharmacist in the mid-twentieth century seems a lot like some occupations in the financial sector today, and like today's lawyers and accountants.

The products that pharmacies sold and the services they offered were somewhat different from today's. Drugs were often compounded specifically for the client, and the relationship between pharmacist and client was more intimate. Pharmacists could even be roused at late hours to fill an urgent prescription for a familiar client.

Then things began to change. No longer were pharmacists distinct from one another. They didn't give as much personal service, and they didn't have to memorize their clients' individual medical needs. I doubt that anyone reading this page has gone to the pharmacy in recent years, handed over a refill request, and demanded that the pharmacist to whom they originally gave the prescription be the one to fill it. Yet when we see our tax accountants and divorce lawyers, we expect to deal with a particular professional, not their officemate.

What changed in pharmacies? Drugstores became big business, increasing both in size and in scope of operations across the twentieth century. From the 1950s to today the fraction of independent pharmacies plummeted, and with that transformation, the fraction of pharmacists working in independent practices dropped drastically too. Changes in our health care and health insurance systems reinforced these trends and produced an increase in the share of pharmacists working in hospitals and in mail-order pharmacies.

Each of these shifts reduced the number of self-employed pharmacists and increased the fraction working as employees of corporations. Whereas the corporate sector isn't generally viewed as an agent of progressive change, in this case it played exactly that role. The shift of pharmacies to the corporate sector meant that ownership was no longer relevant to a pharmacist's job. Since men had been the owners and women were primarily their assistants, the shift meant that men and women could be more equal as pharmacists. The person receiving the net profits from the enterprise was no longer the male pharmacist. It was the stockholders.

Several other transformations reinforced these changes. Drugs became far more standardized, and, with few exceptions, compounding was no longer needed. Information technology gave any pharmacist access to the list of all the prescription drugs a client was taking, and that knowledge allowed him or her to give appropriate advice on drug interactions to any client.

Personal contact with the pharmacist was no longer important for an individual customer's health and well-being. Late-night pharmacies meant that all pharmacists did not have to be on call. A close relationship with your pharmacist was no longer necessary to give you late night entrée to the drugstore.

Throughout these transformations, the job of a pharmacist did not become easier, and the position did not become less professional. Most recently, pharmacists have been called into the frontlines of managing and administering part of the COVID-19 vaccination campaign. In fact, drugs and medications have become far more complex than they were fifty years ago, and pharmacists have to know considerably more than they did in the past. The educational demands in the training of pharmacists increased. Whereas an undergraduate degree in pharmacy plus one year (and the passing of boards and some experience) was once sufficient to become a practicing pharmacist, since the early 2000s a six-year PharmD degree (two undergrad years and four grad years), plus boards and practical experience, have been required.

Fast-forward to the pharmacies of today. Gateway is an anomaly. Only about 12 percent of pharmacists work for independent local pharmacies. Huge national chains like CVS, Walgreens, and Walmart, and a multitude of hospitals, now employ the majority of pharmacists. Along with mail-order pharmacies, stores like these fill the bulk of our prescriptions.

More than 50 percent of all pharmacy graduates today are women, and that has been the case ever since the mid-1980s. Female pharmacists are no longer the sidekicks of the male pharmacist-owners. They are their equals. Both are primarily employees, not owners. Pharmacists today are largely the personnel of a corporate entity.

Together, these changes meant that one pharmacist could easily be substituted for another, and that meant that pharmacists, by and large, did not have to work long and irregular hours. There are, of course, some pharmacists who work evenings, weekends, and vacations—the ones who staff the twenty-four-hour pharmacies, the hospital pharmacies, and those that are mail order—and they often still earn hardship pay. But the midnight owls may be rarer in pharmacy than in other fields where a large fraction of professionals are on call. The main point is that because there is almost perfect substitution, no one pharmacist is worth a tremendous amount more if he or she gives extra time to the job. Yet all are still valued professionals.

As pharmacists became better substitutes for each other, the hourly wage penalty to working part-time just about disappeared. The median female pharmacist now earns around 94 cents on her male counterpart's dollar. Pharmacy is one of a handful of professional occupations in which there is no discernible part-time penalty. Managers in corporate pharmacies make more money than the nonmanagers, but most of the difference is because they work more hours. The pharmacist who works more hours gets higher pay but doesn't get much more per hour. Pharmacy pay is just about linear in hours worked—which means that if the number of hours doubles, earnings double (and the same happens for any multiple).

As a result, there is no discernible premium in hourly pay for pharmacists today who work long hours. If Lisa works sixty hours a week, she earns twice as much as a pharmacist who works thirty hours a week. If Lisa, or Della the pharmacist, wants to make more money, she works more hours. But her hourly rate doesn't change. As we saw, the same is not true among lawyers.

Because working more hours doesn't make your hourly pay go up, lots of female pharmacists—particularly moms—work part-time. Around one-third of female pharmacists work fewer than thirty-five hours per week when they are thirty years old and continue to do so for at least another decade. And because the occupation is flexible, few pharmacist moms take off a lot of time after they have a child. There are very few breaks in employment for female pharmacists relative to lawyers and financiers.

Yet another surprise about pharmacy is that each of the three big changes—the rise of the corporate sector, the standardization of drugs, and the use of sophisticated information technology—occurred because of reasons having little or nothing to do with the large influx of women into the profession. About 65 percent of all PharmD graduates are now women, as compared with 10 percent in 1970, an increase of 55 percentage points.

Pharmacists today are paid very well, and their incomes have increased relative to those of other professionals. From 1970 to 2010, the income of the median pharmacist—working full-time, year-round—increased relative to that of the median lawyer, doctor, and veterinarian (for male and female professionals). In sum, pharmacists became virtually perfect substitutes for one another. Pharmacy, in consequence, has become a highly egalitarian profession. Earnings are substantial, and pay did not decline as women entered the profession in record numbers, a contrast to the usual notion that when women enter an occupation, earnings plummet.

————

A broader conclusion emerges: substitution among workers is the key to reducing disproportionately high hourly pay for long and on-call hours. If two employees are very good—possibly perfect—substitutes for each other, then when one has to take time off, the other can seamlessly take the first one's place. Clients, patients, students, and customers can be handed off from one skilled employee to another with no loss of information, no change in the level of trust, and no difference in effectiveness.

This transformation required no revolution, social movement, or upheaval. It occurred in pharmacy organically, for several reasons—none of which was directly related to any agenda. That doesn't mean change in other sectors and occupations must, or will, occur spontaneously. Pharmacy teaches us the types of changes that can enhance gender equality and improve couple equity, not necessarily how they must come about.

The notion of having just one perfect (or near perfect) substitute has colossal implications for women and for couples. In studying pharmacy, we can see how the gender pay gap was nearly eradicated in that profession, and how it might be reduced in others. The lessons we can learn from it are critical.

If all occupations were like pharmacy, today's Della and Perry would not be in such a quandary. Della would not be the only one to scale back at work to take care of the kids. Perry would not be enticed to work long hours and on weekends to solve cases without Della. As a couple, they would not have to choose between one of their legal careers and having a family. They would be able to achieve both couple equity and gender equality.

The problem, of course, is that most occupations are not like pharmacy. When long hours are the only path to big hourly earnings, individuals implicitly pay more for the amenity of greater control over their work schedule, while couples are faced with a more difficult choice. The individual who takes the job with greater control over hours will earn far less, even hourly, than the individual who takes the job with less control. In the legal field, the differences are huge. Taking time off or working shorter hours or even simply working particular hours in the legal field means falling off a steep cliff in terms of hourly earnings. Taking time off in the pharmacy field involves no cliff. It is more of a leisurely stroll.

When workers in an occupation substitute for each other, everyone benefits. Consider what would happen if an employee had just one perfect substitute. The demanding client, the urgent meeting, the midnight M&A finale, or any moment that the worker is needed and cannot be there could be taken care of by the perfect substitute. Because the perfect substitute can take over in a pinch, she or he can smooth the time demands. There would be no reason why those who work long, demanding hours must get additional pay per hour because there would be no reason why the long, overly demanding hours would exist for a particular worker. The hours would be shared by two or more equally capable substitutes.

Several changes in the pharmacy sector enabled pharmacists to control their time with little loss in hourly pay. Each step forward involved technological changes, such as in information systems, that have similarly affected other fields and sectors.

Corporate entities took over the pharmacy sector, as well as many medical practices, some time ago. More recently, companies and private equity have made inroads into optometry, dentistry, and veterinary medicine by buying up small practices. The change from the friendly independent owner to the unfamiliar distant corporation has been a hard pill for many to swallow, even as it has saved many businesses.

Standardization of the product and better transmission of information gave pharmacists the ability to work with a wide range of clients and act as perfect substitutes for each other. Similar changes have also started to affect the banking and financial sectors, to some degree. For example, rather than providing premier clients with a personal banker, many large banks have switched to teams of personal bankers. How many times have you been told (correctly, I hope) that you will be equally served by the next available member of a team rather than by the person with whom you spoke before?

Having a substitute does not mean that an occupation, profession, or position is reduced to a commodity and to the lowest possible wage. The substitute isn't like a knockoff of an Hermès Birkin bag that lessens the value of the real thing. The physician, veterinarian, pharmacist, lawyer, financier, and accountant who have reasonably good substitutes will gain flexibility. Their earnings won't necessarily drop. A couple of doppelgängers don't diminish the value of the skill that these professionals provide. Pharmacy, in which there is an enormous degree of substitutability, is, as I noted before, a highly paid occupation.

The additional good news is that this change *is* occurring in other occupations—in a less organic fashion, but with results that complement those in pharmacy. In some fields, workers have demanded greater control over their hours and have forced firms, hospitals, and other institutions to provide it. In areas like consulting, accounting, and finance, companies have recognized that younger workers—both men and women—are leaving their jobs because hours are long and unpredictable. The threat of losing talent they've invested in developing may help spur these employers to change. In various technical and health occupations, work is inherently independent and requires few repeated personal interactions with a client or a patient, which means that employees with similar skills could substitute for each other. The increased demands on parents, particularly women, during the pandemic, have greatly amplified the value of having a good substitute at work.

At the end of every episode, Perry (often with Della there to assist) solves the crime by finding the guilty party. We have the guilty party, but we haven't yet freed the defendant. As we'll see, there are a range of occupations in the health, tech, and finance fields where the cost to employers of temporal flexibility for employees has decreased, and in which workers are being made better substitutes for each other.

10

On Call

MY DOG RARELY GETS SICK. But when he does, it is almost always at
eleven p.m. Off we race to a regional animal hospital, where he gets his
stomach pumped or a paw bandaged. Some decades ago, my canine's
late night dyspepsia and run-ins with the neighbor's cat would have involved an emergency call to our local veterinarian. No longer. Regional
veterinary hospitals have sprouted like mushrooms clear across the US
and function in a manner similar to emergency departments of hospitals that cater to human ailments.

Like the veterinarians of decades ago, many self-employed family
practitioners were once on call 24/7. *Marcus Welby, M.D.*, a popular TV
medical drama of the early 1970s, concerned one such physician. Welby,
played by Robert Young—the same actor who played the father in
Father Knows Best—worked in private practice and made house calls
with his medical bag and perennial smile.

House calls and after-hours veterinary visits have both vanished. Veterinarians are still largely employed by small neighborhood clinics, and
some physicians remain in private practice. But these practitioners are
rarely on call for private visits in the wee hours. Why?

The health needs of pets, children, and adults are now taken care of
through a two-tiered system. One tier operates mainly from nine a.m.
to six p.m., with half a weekend day thrown in occasionally. The other
is for emergencies and operates 24/7. Even though workers in the second group provide professional help round the clock, employees in
both tiers generally work predictable schedules. Some may have to take

the graveyard shift every now and then. But none of these professionals has to be on call every day. And their on-call life is also predictable.

The changes in who does emergency work have revolutionized health care. Most importantly (for the issues we've been exploring) is that these changes have altered the lives of those who occupy these professions. The modifications in time demands—with veterinarians and physicians not having to be on call at all times—have been accompanied by large increases in the fraction of these professionals who are women.

In 1970, at the start of Group Four's advances in the professions, just 7.5 percent of newly minted veterinarians were women. Today 77 percent are. In 1970, just 8 percent of all MDs were awarded to women. Now about half are. Some increase of women in these professions would have occurred in the absence of structural changes in time demands. But the increase of female degrees in both human and veterinary medicine would not have been as great without these changes. However, none of this means that the playing field in medicine has been leveled for female docs. Far from it.

———

The playing field for women and men in a host of other occupations— such as accounting, law, finance, consulting, and academia—is even less equal. Career progression in those fields has not changed much during the past half century or more, even as women have become almost half of these professionals. Promotion rules in each of these areas require substantial time inputs early on. At the end of a predefined period, employees (often known as associates) are evaluated. The hardworking (or lucky) ones are granted tenure or a partnership. The others are sent packing. These occupations are generally known as "up-or-out" positions. Those who are "up" can remain. Those who are "out" often go down a notch in the pecking order of firms, institutions, or universities.

Each of these occupations and sectors has distinctive hurdles and differently aligned clocks. But all have one feature in common. The big rewards, for those who get them, are now reaped by individuals in their mid- to late thirties. It wasn't always that way. But the time needed for

the advanced degree and the time required for the first promotion, partnership, or tenure have grown longer and later.

There was a time when college graduates pursuing an advanced degree went straight on to graduate and professional schools. But now,
almost all take a year or more after graduation to work in jobs related to
their eventual careers. In academia, most doctoral applicants first work
as research assistants directly following their bachelor's (positions
known as "predocs"). The MBA group generally works several years
before entering business school.

Getting a PhD now takes more time than ever before, and that is true
even in fields with tons of job opportunities. When I received my PhD,
the most usual time to degree in economics was four years. It is now six
years. Postdocs in the physical and biological sciences expand the training period, and these positions have become popular in other fields.

Years of schooling and training add up. But that's only the beginning
in the up-or-out world. The tenure clock in academia is about six to
eight years. Partnerships in law are decided in about ten years, and those
in consulting and accounting take six to nine years, depending on
whether one has an MBA. In investment banking, advancement from
junior banker to vice president may occur after five to six years.

So at a minimum, there are now thirteen years postbachelor's in academia, and probably more like sixteen years until one's career is cemented. There are at least ten in consulting and accounting before con-
sideration for promotion. Throw in a few more years for employment
before entering the MBA or JD programs. The first promotion in a
career, therefore, typically occurs in one's mid- to late thirties. Men and
women in Group Five are being considered for their first promotion
when they are about four to six years older than those in Group Four.

It is clear what the career-family squeeze is all about. At the end of the
quest for partnership or tenure, the college graduate who was once
twenty-two has aged considerably—to her mid-thirties, possibly older.
The median age at first marriage for college graduates is younger than that.

If the up-or-out decisions were made earlier, say before the early to
mid-thirties, a woman could work hard, make partner or be granted tenure, and then begin her family. But as the age for promotion has

increased, it has meant that either families are begun later, or the first big promotion decision is made when the children are in preschool. Career paths demand long hours that are often too intense for those with young children. Either option has its problems, especially for women.

Career clocks tick alongside biological and family clocks. Many women, and men, must begin their families before their careers are solidified. If they don't, they may never be able to have a family.

Why Pipelines Leak

In a host of professional occupations, the percentage of the newbies who were women greatly increased starting in the 1970s. Group Four launched the enormous advances in women's graduation from advanced degree programs of all types. But the fraction of women with tenure, partnerships, or some other advancement has not kept up. At first, it was thought that the low fraction in the higher ranks was because advancement took time. But we now know that is not the case. There has been enough time.

In my field of economics, women have been 30 to 35 percent of PhDs for the last twenty years. But they are 25 percent of tenured associate professors, and 15 percent of full professors. I was among the 8 percent of female assistant professors in 1974, which increased to 27 percent by 2018. The full-professor group was less than 3 percent female in 1974 and advanced to almost 15 percent in 2018. Though that's a huge gain, it was too slow. Had male and female candidates been promoted at the same rate, the fraction of women at the full-professor rank would have been greater. Part of the disparity is that women are promoted at lower rates given their publication records. Another is that they leave academia before promotion.

Lower promotion rates for women in fields such as academia, law, consulting, management, and finance have been attributed to "leaky pipelines," as the phenomenon is often called. The notion of the leaky pipeline is that women and men leave their positions before they are promoted, but a greater fraction of women than men exit at various junctures.

The reasons for women's greater attrition have been sought using various methods. After comparing men and women who are equally qualified in terms of publications, factors including bias, favoritism, and inadequate mentoring remain. But the primary cause for the leaky pipeline in most up-or-out professions leads us back to the question of time demands required for advancement. Intense careers are difficult for all. They are especially tough for young parents, and the parent who often slows down on the track to the top, while putting in the intensive family time, is the woman.

Take CPA accounting. Women have been 50 percent of new CPAs ever since the 1980s. Yet in 2017 they were just 21 percent of partners in CPA firms with one hundred or more CPAs. The gender disparity in partnerships is even worse. In the larger accounting firm category, they were only 16 percent of equity partners. In the smaller firms—those with fewer than a hundred CPAs—women were 42 percent of partners, which is much closer to the overall number of 50 percent. Very often, CPA women who do not make the grade in the larger firms take jobs in smaller CPA firms or in nonpublic (that is, non-CPA) accounting practices.

We saw similar pipeline leaks for the legal field. Just 18 percent of female law school graduates of the University of Michigan had made partner fifteen years after earning their JD, whereas 35 percent of their male counterparts had.

Much has been written about actual discrimination in these professions and the role of higher-ups picking successors to be like themselves. There is also much discussion about the related matter of the difficulty of mentoring women, minorities, and underrepresented groups. Each of these factors is important in the up-or-out decision, but there is more.

The biggest barrier to women in these professions concerns the familiar culprit of time demands—and not just in terms of hours. Time demands also concern the moment in life when the demands are the greatest. As we just saw, these pressures peak in one's mid- to late thirties.

Hours matter a lot for promotion, as can be easily proved in professions that track hours, such as law. Lawyers bill by the hour (even by the quarter hour), and firms keep tabs. We know that female lawyers make partner at lower rates than male lawyers. But until recently we haven't known why. An analysis of a large survey of lawyers assembled by the

American Bar Association (called "After the JD") that follows them through the ranks has demonstrated that there is a clear relationship between making partner and time inputs. Hours worked by the associate lawyers and the revenue they raise account for much of the difference in promotion rates between men and women.

With more women starting in these professions and more men who want equitable relationships with their life partners, there is a larger cost from the old way of doing things. Institutions don't want to lose talent, and the majority of the talent that is leaking out is female.

Universities, which have among the most draconian up-or-out policies, have become more generous in providing family leave and stopping tenure clocks, for male and female junior faculty alike. New positions have been invented that get around the strict up-or-out paths. Instructorships and adjunct positions are offered to those who can't endure the punishing hours to make tenure or don't think they can make the cut. In law and accounting, there are nonequity partnerships. And one can always go down the food chain and take a tenured position at a lesser institution or a partnership in a smaller, less lucrative law or accounting firm.

Not long ago, I met a senior partner of one of the nation's largest and most respected consulting firms. His job was to make certain that the newbies and other associates and consultants (those at the bottom of the firm's hierarchy) were not worked so hard that they quit at the end of their current projects. The young worker bees had to be reassured that their PowerPoints were great and their Excel spreadsheets were read, at least once before they were deleted. He was tasked with telling the hard-driving managers and partners if they were harming the firm by pushing younger staff too hard.

He went from office to office across the US, asking the associates and consultants whether they were overworked, treated unfairly, or underappreciated. Regardless of his role's efficacy, the fact that a large company has a person and a staff dedicated to policing the higher-ups means that they appreciate there is a problem. And the problem has a name: the principal-agent problem. Middle-level managers have an incentive to work their teams hard. The manager gets the credit for the great reports and contented clients. But the rest of the company suffers when talent exits and teams fall apart. The agents (middle-level managers and partners) are insufficiently incentivized to follow the directives of the principal (senior partners and the CEO).

Companies don't want to lose valuable, highly trained workers, particularly in professional-services industries, where client relationships abound and training (paid for by the firm) is often costly. Young workers without children have few personal time constraints and often want to impress the firm's partners and upper-level management. They put in long hours, often competing with one another. It's fine to work your tail off when you are twenty-three or twenty-five or even twenty-seven. But that isn't the life that many—especially women—want when they have young children. Upper-level management, especially the CEOs, would like to cut down on the long and often unpredictable hours that have become the norm for most of the younger workers. The senior partner I met was trying to solve this principal-agent problem.

The big guns of Wall Street—Goldman Sachs, J.P. Morgan, Citigroup, Bank of America, Morgan Stanley, Barclays, and Credit Suisse—have also decided to create better incentives and reduce the principal-agent problems that plague the retention of young blood in their firms. The behemoths of finance have begun to create rules about protected weekends and evenings, paid sabbaticals, mandated vacations, and faster paths to promotion.

Goldman Sachs began with a salvo in 2013: "We are committed to implementing these initiatives to better enable our junior bankers to have successful and sustainable long term careers at the firm." The rules were explicit, and there were to be few exceptions that had to be reported to the executive committee. "All analysts and associates are required to be out of the office from 9 P.M. on Friday until 9 A.M. on Sunday (begins this weekend). . . . All analysts and associates are expected . . . to take 3 weeks of vacation a year." And work was not supposed to move from the office to the home or the local coffee shop. A year later Credit Suisse banned Saturday work, and Bank of America Merrill Lynch recommended that junior bankers take at least four weekend days off per month.

Tech giants also know that long hours are destructive of a contented work environment. In 2016, Amazon, in search of an "environment tailored to a reduced schedule that still fosters success and career growth," announced that it was allowing a 25 percent reduction in the hours of tech employees, including managers, at a 25 percent reduction in salary. Workers were being docked, essentially, on a per hours basis.

The COVID world has led many firms, including those in the tech sector, to extend the work-from-home period. The acceptance of remote work may have long-lasting beneficial effects on all workers, especially parents. But, as we will see, the impact of partially open offices and on-again-off-again schools and daycare may accentuate previous gender disparities as one parent must be available at home even more so than in the pre-COVID era. There may be gains, but there may also be losses.

Some consulting and accounting firms have imposed rules that restrict the number of long-distance trips their younger workers must take. Others have set bounds on the hours their employees are supposed to work, and have curbed e-mails that can be sent after hours. These are notable measures, imposed by senior partners and CEOs who believe that some of their managers are working their younger employees so hard that they are driven to quit. Each of the managers and partners wants their project to get done, and they don't always consider the cost of hard driving to the entire firm. Successful or not, the large number of efforts to rein in overwork by young workers demonstrates that firms—and their employees—recognize that there are costs to hard driving.

In the early to mid-1990s, two of the nation's largest accounting firms realized that they had a big personnel problem. They were doing a great job recruiting women. Half of their entering group of CPAs were women. But too few of these women were making it to partner. They were, as some in the industry put it, hemorrhaging women. Most of the higher-ups did not think that anything could stem the flow. But the smart, inquisitive CEO of Deloitte, Michael Cook, demurred and commissioned an external review panel in 1992 to see why women were leaving.

The report found that women were leaving long before they came up for promotion. According to the report, Deloitte's culture was pushing them out. They did not receive the lucrative accounts, were not being entrusted with the difficult decisions, and were not seen as tough enough—at least not in the same way their male colleagues were. Under Cook's leadership, changes were made to alter the corporate culture. The fraction of new female partners at Deloitte increased.

Similar problems were noticed in 1997 at Ernst and Young (now EY) by CEO Phil Laskawy. Tactics were tried at EY such as flexible work schedules, mentoring, and women's networks. There, too, the fraction of females among its partners increased.

Deloitte and EY both increased the fraction of their partners who were female, but so have other firms in the industry with less enlightened policies. How much of the increase was due to the deliberate policies of Deloitte to change its corporate culture, or to EY's flexible work scheduling cannot be assessed. But there is other evidence indicating that more basic, structural factors are holding women back from rising to the top.

A group of clever researchers used audit reports to create data on the fraction female among CPA-firm partners. Audits are the prime business for CPA firms. The fraction female among the large CPA firms is not much different for Deloitte and EY than for many of their competitors.

None of the policies have done enough. It's been thirty-five years since half of all CPAs were female. It's been twenty-five years since the top firms, like Deloitte and EY, decided that they had to do something to keep women in their firms. Yet at the top firms, the fraction of partners who are women is nowhere near the 50 percent number achieved long ago for all CPAs. The problem isn't that these firms don't know about the disparity between the fraction female among all CPAs and the fraction female among their partners, or don't care, or aren't trying. The real problem is that the timing of promotion decisions and the time commitment of these positions create difficulties in the lives of couples who have or want a family. It has to do with the very way these occupations are structured.

Solutions have been inadequate in each of these professions. In law, accounting, and consulting, nonequity partnerships are considerably lower paying. In academia, although there are both male and female adjunct faculty, adjunct jobs are disproportionately held by women. They are often positions for trailing spouses—males and females. But, historically, women are more often geographically tied to their husbands' position. Even stopping tenure clocks has gotten a bad rap lately. Women, it has been shown, take the added semester to care for their families. Men take it to get more research papers published. Up-or-out systems do not mesh well with having and raising a family. They don't work for either sex but, given the realities, women pay the greater price.

Unsurprisingly, employees who work on-call, irregular, unpredictable hours generally earn more than those who work closer to regular hours. Of greater significance are the problems this premium creates for women's careers and for couple equity. The greater the hourly wage premium to jobs with long or on-call hours, the greater is the incentive for each member of the couple to specialize, especially if they have children.

By "specialize," I don't mean that one person washes the dishes while the other dries them. I mean something more pervasive. As we have seen throughout our journey, one person (generally the wife) gives more time to being on call at home, and the other (generally the husband) gives more time to being on call at work.

If the members of a couple with children don't specialize—meaning if they don't make the pervasive decision for one partner to be dedicated to being on call at home while the other partner is on call at work—they will be leaving money on the table. They can't both work the job with uncontrollable hours, because kids, like my dog, get sick and needy at odd times of day (and children are far more demanding than my canine).

When the income on the table isn't very large, based on what the couple desires, it could be left there. That is, both members could turn down the job with less predictable hours. That way, they would effectively purchase couple equity for the amount they forgo from a paycheck. But when the amount is large, the cost of couple equity may be too high to turn down. Couple equity might be ditched. But that wouldn't be the only casualty. *When couple equity is abandoned, gender equality in the workplace tends to follow.* Women will earn less than men, even on an hourly basis. The problem is both how work in the labor market is remunerated and how work and caring in the household are divided by gender.

The key is that gender (in)equality and couple (in)equity are two sides of the same coin, as we learned from the case of the lawyer and the pharmacist. The difficult decision we've been exploring—when one partner in a couple, most often the woman, decides to be on call at home—creates inequity for couples. It also means that women, in the aggregate, earn less, even on a per hour basis, than do men. That creates gender inequality. But there is a silver lining to this rain cloud. More people than ever are striving for couple equity and time with their families.

———

Firms want to make profits. To do that, they want workers to be on call and be willing to work irregular hours. But companies are in a pickle. Before COVID, they wanted high-quality employees to work demanding schedules at the office, but they didn't want to pay a princely sum for that work. Yet more and more workers with children wanted fewer weekend and evening disruptions, and they were demanding extra compensation to carry the additional load.

The COVID period has added to these problems in unforeseen ways. But our experience may also contribute to solutions, as flexible work has been shown to be feasible in many unforeseen settings and to not apparently reduce productivity. (I will return soon to the impact of the increase in parental hours during the pandemic with the shuttering of schools and much daycare.)

The increased demand for family time was already a major issue in the pre-COVID period, as parents began spending more hours per week with their children, especially the more educated and higher-income parents. Detailed data on how people use their time have been gathered for the past fifty years from a very large sample of US households. These time-use data were first collected in 1965 by the University of Michigan's Americans' Use of Time Survey. Since 2003, a similar methodology has been used by the US Census Bureau (sponsored by the US Bureau of

Labor Statistics) and is called the American Time Use Survey (ATUS). Various researchers have worked to make the time series from these two surveys comparable.

The findings reveal that college-educated fathers (twenty-five to thirty-four years old) spent twice as many hours per week caring for their kids in 2015 as they did in 1990 (from five hours to ten). Similar proportional changes have occurred for those without a college education, although the levels are lower (four hours to eight).

Dads haven't been increasing their time with kids because moms have cut back. Just the opposite. Mothers have also increased the time they spend with their children. College-educated mothers (twenty-five to thirty-four years old) spent thirteen hours per week with children in 1990 but twenty-one hours in 2015. For the noncollege group, hours increased from eleven to sixteen. Putting all of this together means that for a college-educated couple (twenty-five to thirty-four years old), time spent with their children increased from eighteen to thirty-one hours per week from 1990 to 2015.

Despite spending more time with their children, men are bemoaning the fact that they aren't spending enough time with them. According to a revealing Pew Research Center survey, 46 percent of all dads stated that they would like to spend *more* time with their children. Fewer college-graduate dads admitted that they spend too little time with their progeny, but 40 percent of them did. Less educated dads felt more negligent, apparently, with 49 percent reporting that they would like to spend more time with their children.

Mothers reported half the regret of fathers, consistent with their greater time spent with their children. But still, 23 percent stated that they would like to devote more time. The fraction is higher for working moms (27 percent), but there are few differences by educational attainment given employment.

Not only are today's parents spending more time with their children than similar parents did twenty-five years ago (and wanting even more); they see themselves as better mothers and fathers than their parents were. Around 50 percent stated that they spend more time with their children than their parents did. On average, they actually do. Just

20 percent stated that they spend less time. These findings hold for all education and gender groups. Although there isn't extensive evidence that fathers have been asking their employers for fewer weekend and evening hours, their time use and stated desire to spend more time with their children suggest that they may be doing so.

Mothers state that they value job flexibility a lot. When women were asked what they considered extremely important about their jobs, 53 percent of college-graduate women said "flexibility," whereas 29 percent of the college-graduate men did.

A promising and significant new reality is how many couples would like a more equitable division of labor in their marriage. Husbands have become less willing to want their wives to give up their careers to undertake household care. Among husbands with a college degree, 67 percent reported that the best marriage is when both husband and wife have jobs and both take care of the house and children. Female college graduates would like even more equity in their relationships, with 80 percent reporting that the best marriage is when both have jobs and both share household and childcare responsibilities.

So what is happening to make these desires a reality?

Silver Linings

One of the ways that employees tell employers to change is that they exit and sign on with other firms that provide better earnings, hours, and perks. For some women with high-income mates, that could mean exiting altogether. When the younger, recently trained group gets up and leaves, firms take notice. They invest in finding and securing employees at the time of hire, and they continue to invest heavily throughout their early years.

As employees have increased their preference for family time and for more equitable relationships, time demands that go beyond usual working hours require even greater compensatory payment from firms. Profit-maximizing firms naturally don't want to increase salaries. As a result, many firms are inventing ways to conserve the time of their most valued and expensive workers. There are a range of possibilities. Some render workers better substitutes for one another other so that they can hand off clients with greater ease or substitute for their colleagues in meetings. These firms can still have peak demands and hectic moments. But workers can better optimize their schedules and don't have to miss critical soccer games or parent-teacher conferences.

Companies don't necessarily contain humane, caring, and sympathetic managers. But that may not matter. Sometimes the planets are aligned so that what works for the firm also works for its employees. Demands for higher wages by men who are asked to work erratic and long hours may incentivize firms to come up with ways to conserve employees' time and not ask them to forgo family occasions.

If firms could find ways to operate the business effectively without asking workers to run faster and longer, they would not have to compensate them as much as they do for these extra hours. The increased pay for those who work the unpredictable and grueling hours would not take place. Doing so would both reduce the gender earnings gap and enhance couple equity. What works for the gander also works for the goose (and the goslings), as in the slightly rearranged proverb.

There are problems with this scenario, of course. Some workers don't have family responsibilities or are older workers whose children are grown. But a large chunk of the labor force consists of those with family responsibilities of some type.

These changes aren't happening all over the labor landscape, as the case of lawyers shows. And some of the largest changes, as in the case of pharmacists, occurred organically, rather than because of employee pressure. And of course, there is often more talk than action, more heat than light. But in some real cases, firms and institutions are inventing ways, often using novel technologies, to bring down the cost of temporal flexibility.

Two examples are in the health sector. One is an analysis of physician hours and earnings by subspecialty. The other does the same for veterinarians. Both require the use of detailed data that go beyond the information in the census. Even though the census lists lots of occupations, they are often highly aggregated. "Physicians and surgeons," for example, aggregates fifty or more subspecialties. In the case of veterinarians, the census sample is too small to be adequate. Using more detailed data, we can peer into these occupations more closely, to understand the role of time demands on gender (in)equality.

———

Female physicians do the impossible. The best of them go through arduous training for many years and work hard for their patients. Yet many manage to have more children than women in professions with the same or fewer years of training.

In the Harvard and Beyond Project data, a greater fraction of women with MDs had children fifteen years after their bachelor's than women who had received a JD, an MBA, or a PhD. Among female MDs who graduated in the early 1980s, about 84 percent had a child (or had adopted one) by their early forties. How do female doctors do it?

First off, MD mothers have more money than most others. They can purchase nannies, quality daycare, and other goods and services that substitute for their time. They may also have more equitable marriages. But just like other women who lack their superpowers and resources, female physicians cut back on their work time when they have children.

They work long hours, to be sure. But they work far fewer hours than male physicians in the aggregate and also than male physicians in the same specialties. Female physicians who are forty-five years and younger spend ten fewer hours per week at work than do their male counterparts. Average hours worked are still high, so it isn't as if female physicians are lying down on the job, so to speak.

These younger female physicians work 48.1 hours per week, and their male counterparts work 58.6 hours, so they differ by one very long day of work per week. As physicians age, women increase their hours relative to men. Male physicians reduce their hours, and female physicians increase them.

The numbers of female to male physicians vary widely across medical specialties. More than 55 percent of child psychiatrists are women, 62 percent of dermatologists are, and 75 percent of obstetricians and gynecologists are, among the younger group of doctors. In contrast, about 20 percent of those in cardiovascular disease are women, and just

10 percent of those in orthopedic surgery are. Female physicians sort more into specialties that have lower weekly hours demands. An exception is OB-GYN, which is majority female but is also hours-intensive. As a general rule, the higher the hours for male physicians in a specialty, the fewer female physicians that are attracted to it. That is, there is a strong negative relationship between average hours for male physicians and the fraction female in the specialty.

Comparing specialties with similar-length residencies helps elucidate the point. Male dermatologists in the younger age group work forty-eight hours per week, and 62 percent of younger dermatologists are women. Male physicians in the specialty of internal medicine work fifty-nine hours a week, and 44 percent are female, a smaller fraction than for dermatologists. Even though young female physicians sort into lower-hours specialties, that isn't the main reason why they work ten fewer hours per week. Most of the ten-hour difference in weekly hours between the female and male physicians is because female physicians work fewer hours in just about every specialty. Indeed, across almost twenty of the largest medical specialties, younger women doctors work fewer hours than do younger men doctors.

As female physicians age and their children become less demanding of their time, they ramp up their hours. Hours increase for female physicians older than forty-five in almost every specialty. Tellingly, the opposite occurs for men. Older male physicians work fewer hours than younger ones. Hours in cardiology decrease from sixty-seven to sixty. Similarly, large changes are found in the surgical specialties. Most of the other changes are smaller since initial hours are lower.

In almost every specialty, hours of work per week decrease for the older male physicians relative to the younger ones, whereas women generally work the same or more hours as they age. The difference in hours between older male and female physicians drops from 10 to 5 hours, and much of the change occurs because male physicians reduce their workweek by 3.9 hours and female physicians increase their workweek by 1.1 hours.

Having the flexibility to work a considerably shorter week is a key ingredient in how MD women can raise their children and have successful careers. Combining a high-powered job with the flexible schedule necessary to have a family is not without its downside, however. One of those shortcomings shows up in the pay gap, even correcting for hours worked. Female physicians still make considerably less than male physicians on an hourly basis. The gender earnings ratio reported earlier for medical doctors was a disappointing 67 percent. But, as mentioned, that analysis does not differentiate among the many medical specialties.

The data on physicians used here are more detailed than are those in the US census and include specialties. They reveal that much of the earnings penalty that female physicians experience is because of their choice of specialty, which is related to both usual weekly hours and length of training. Adjusting for hours, specialty, and years since receiving the MD increases the gender earnings ratio from 67 to 82 cents on the male physician dollar.

Some factors cannot be included. Other studies have shown that female physicians spend more time with each patient and can therefore see (and bill for) fewer patients. According to one large study, female physicians spend 10 percent more time with each patient, resulting in fewer patients seen and lower billings. But it is likely that even with these other factors, female physicians still earn less.

The shorter work weeks of women physicians, when they are young, probably factor into their lower remuneration later in life. They may not receive as many grants and may be passed over for departmental promotions later. And they may be unable to shift jobs to secure higher pay and better positions. Women use outside offers less than their male colleagues to bargain for higher salaries. Relative to men, they are more often tied to a particular geographic area due to their husband's job.

Well, then, where's that silver lining? One layer of it is that Group Five physicians across a host of specialties have more work flexibility than physicians once did. Relative to many other high-income occupations, physicians have a greater ability to work part-time. More importantly, changes have occurred in medicine that have decreased the cost of implementing flexible schedules. According to the latest available data, women were 47 percent of all young physicians, 71 percent of pediatricians, 64 percent of dermatologists, and 56 percent of family medicine doctors. Their demands are being felt—as are those of their male colleagues who want more time with their families.

Let's look at pediatricians. My brother-in-law is a pediatrician and has three children. When he worked at a hospital in Albuquerque and his children were young, he asked for a change in his schedule to spend more time with his family. That didn't happen to his satisfaction. He eventually left for Kaiser Permanente, which gave him the time off he wanted. He voted with his feet to get a less grueling and more predictable schedule. Such moves, collectively, can spark considerable change.

Pediatrics today has among the highest fraction of young physicians working short weeks, regardless of gender. The American Academy of Pediatrics reports that 33 percent of all female pediatricians work part-time, and a significant fraction of male pediatricians do as well. This ability of pediatricians, and several other specialties, to work short weeks has been accomplished through the formation of group practices that allow physicians to substitute for each other. Group practices, depending on how they are run, can enable physicians to have greater time flexibility and to share on-call and evening hours.

Anesthesiologists and obstetricians are members of practices that almost always function as teams to enable substitution. Even if your favorite obstetrician is Brett, you'd better get to know Jeanette and Safa since there is a reasonable chance that one of them will be delivering your baby instead. I'm amazed when a lawyer, accountant, consultant, or financier makes a case for the nonsubstitutability among professionals in his area, but can't answer why delivering a baby isn't the equivalent. Do the financial records of one company differ from any other's more than one woman's labor in childbirth is relative to any other's?

An anesthesiologist keeps you alive during a surgery. Yet you meet that lifesaving physician just minutes before you go under. It would be a planning nightmare to schedule a particular surgeon with a specific anesthesiologist for each surgery. During times of crisis, it would be impossible. The upshot is that surgery may have on-call moments, but anesthesiology does not have to involve long hours, similar to how fields like dermatology, psychiatry, and child psychiatry offer more predictable hours because they have fewer emergencies.

Another example of the cost-cutting measures of hospital management concerns the relatively new subspecialty of hospitalist. A hospitalist is a physician who coordinates the care of patients and conserves the time of primary care physicians by substituting for them. Patients want their primary care physician to be at their bedside in the hospital. But that's expensive. A hospitalist coordinates the patient's care with specialists and with the primary care physician. Patients are probably in better hands with the hospitalist, and the primary care doctors don't have to scurry about taking care of patients in various hospitals.

Just as in the case of pharmacists, some changes to the time demands of doctors have been cost-saving measures having little to do with employee demands. Hospitalists lower costs at the same time that they lower the on-call demands of regular physicians.

The bottom line is that physicians in many specialties can now work shorter weeks. Greater work flexibility enables female physicians to have families. They have children in greater numbers than do comparably trained women and even those with far fewer years of training. But they still pay a price. Female physicians earn less than male physicians in hospitals and private practices in terms of annual earnings, and they earn less even accounting for hours of work.

———

Veterinarians are incredible doctors. MDs may master the inner workings of *Homo sapiens*, but veterinarians master those of other species—even ones that fly and live under water. No professional field has undergone as great a change in its gender makeup as has veterinary medicine. Fifty years ago there were hardly any female veterinarians. Today, almost 80 percent of veterinary school graduates are women. Women didn't suddenly develop a fondness for animals. Part of what changed concerns a greater ability to control hours of work and a decrease in on-call hours.

Veterinary medicine shares many of the career benefits of its human counterpart in terms of prestige, hours, satisfaction, and the joys of helping patients and their caregivers. (But, as my veterinarian friends would have me add, it doesn't pay nearly as much.) Veterinary training, however, offers advantages over medical training for those who want a family. For one, veterinarians do not have to do a residency that would train them to specialize in a particular area.

Recall that veterinarians once had office practices with occasional evening, weekend, and vacation hours. They responded to emergencies. Now, the emergencies and after-hours cases are cared for just as they would be for humans. Urgent care units and emergency departments attend to the canine and feline members of your family just as they do for you and your children. How these changes came about is a bit of a shaggy dog story.

In brief, the changes started when groups of local veterinarians began to take turns covering for one another on weekends and during evenings. They created informal referral practices and took turns being on call. These informal groups later became more formal veterinary referral hospitals with permanent staffs. The model spread, and animal hospitals and urgent veterinary care clinics that are open 24/7 now exist across the US. In consequence, most local veterinary clinics have only daytime and weekday hours.

Even though veterinarians employed by emergency hospitals have to work odd hours on occasion, neighborhood and small-clinic veterinarians generally do not. These local clinics are often group practices. If your dog's favorite vet is busy or on vacation, you will be directed to a very good substitute. Animals and children get injured and fall ill at all hours.

A female veterinarian in a private clinic works in regular practice around forty hours per week, with an additional four emergency hours. Those are fairly low hours for a medical professional. Her male colleague labors eight hours more weekly, on a regular basis, with six hours of emergency work thrown in. About 20 to 25 percent of female veterinarians work part-time among those in private practice. Only 5 percent of male veterinarians do the same.

Moderate, regular, controllable hours, few on-call hours, and fewer years of up-front training than for physicians are just some of the reasons why women have increased their ranks in veterinary medicine. Still, their ownership rate and equity shares are much lower than those of their male colleagues. Between 30 and 50 percent of female veterinarians in private practice are owners, whereas 60 to 80 percent of their male colleagues are.

Since ownership entails longer hours and greater responsibility than being an employee, many women with families are reluctant to add to their time demands. But female veterinarians are now the majority of those in their late forties, and male owners, mainly those in their fifties and sixties, are finding it difficult to sell their practices to their younger female colleagues. The result of this mismatch has been the acquisition of clinics by the corporate sector and a shrinkage in the number of independent veterinary clinics.

In consequence, a change in veterinary medicine has occurred similar to what happened in pharmacy. For both cases, there are reasons to bemoan the trend toward fewer independently owned practices. But, as in the case of pharmacists, corporate ownership reduces the time burdens on professionals. Corporate ownership also reduces income difference by gender since fewer male veterinarians will receive the enhanced returns to ownership. The shift from private practice to corporate ownership, however, is still in its infancy.

Female veterinarians in the recent period earn only 72 cents on the male veterinarian dollar. But women work fewer hours per week and fewer weeks per year. Considering only the full-time, full-year group— and adding in aspects of their veterinary training—increases their remuneration to 82 cents on the male dollar. Accounting for ownership and equity differences increases the ratio further to 85 cents.

Changes in veterinary practice have transformed the field into what is arguably the most female-dominated profession today, as measured by the fraction female among new entrants. The field's requirements haven't changed much. If anything, they have increased. What has changed is that the organization of work allows for greater individual control over hours.

Veterinary medicine today is the almost perfect profession for gender equality and couple equity—with controllable hours and fairly good substitutability among its professionals. But the playing field is still not level.

Transforming Work

As we've learned across generations and occupations, time is the enemy of women's quest for career and family. On-call, rush, emergency, evening, and weekend time is demanded simultaneously from the home and office. The narrow age window when up-or-out promotions are made adds to the conflict between family and work. The end results of both often increase gender inequality and widen couple inequity.

Progress has been made in the first type of hours bind. Less self-employment in health care occupations and more teams of physicians and veterinarians have meant fewer on-call demands. Female physicians have gravitated to specialties with lower regular and more controllable hours. But this welcomed flexibility has its costs, and fewer hours for younger physicians hurts both current and later earnings and career progression.

The transformation is far from complete. Veterinary clinics are still independently run. There will always be some medical specialties, such as surgery, that require long hours and on-call time. Worker demand produced some of the transformations—such as for my brother-in-law, the pediatrician, who wanted to spend more time with his own children. But other changes came about because profit-maximizing firms wanted to reduce the costs of their high-priced professionals.

Less progress has been made in transforming up-or-out careers. Women have greatly increased their numbers as partners in law, consulting, and accounting firms and as tenured members of academic faculties. But even in fields in which women have been half of all entrants for decades, they are nowhere near close to being half of the winners in the up-or-out race to the top.

According to some in firms with up-or-out promotions, things are looking up. Douglas McCracken, who stepped down in 2003 as chief executive of Deloitte Consulting, noted twenty years ago that "young men in the firm didn't want what the older men wanted." The young men "weren't trying to buy . . . lifestyles so that their wives didn't have to work." Rather, they were trying to buy time to be with their families and didn't want to work the eighty hours a week of the average partner. But McCracken didn't seem to understand the tradeoffs many couples, even high-income couples, are willing to make. He claimed, "They weren't willing to give up their families and outside lives for another $100,000." Unfortunately, they are. The price of couple equity is too high (and $100,000 is really high).

Deeper change is needed. Among the most important is to get men on board. BCG (Boston Consulting Group) senior partner Matthew Krentz said of his firm's paternity leave benefit in the US that "more and more men are taking advantage of it. . . . With more dual-career couples . . . male participation [in the leave program] has to be a top priority." But first, firms have to get buy-in from everyone so that the men who take the leave aren't penalized down the road.

There is no simple solution, no one-size-fits-all policy. But knowing the issues can move us in the right direction. At the very least, we won't waste time on the quick fixes.

A Matter of Time

I often ponder the words of my student who proclaimed, "I want a man who wants what I want." Standing in the way of her vision of blissful harmony is that career and family are in conflict. Each is vying for the same time slots.

When two people are involved, there are more options. One member of the couple can specialize more in one activity, and the other can specialize more in the other. Because the labor market greatly rewards some degree of specialization, the member who specializes more in the market will reap certain career returns. But there are tradeoffs on the home front. Each parent might want to spend particular time with the children. But the parent who specializes more in the market will probably not be able to watch the swim meets on Tuesday mornings or the soccer games on Thursday afternoons. The conflict comes from both sides of the equation. Solutions do as well.

One solution is to reduce the cost of flexibility. Cheapen the trade-off. Make it so that couples don't have to face as difficult a compromise. If the greedy job does not pay as much for on-call, weekend, long-hours work, then Lucas would be less enticed to take it. Better yet, make the flexible job more productive, and have it pay more. Then Lucas would gladly switch from the greedy to the flexible job. And Isabel would earn more in the flexible position and be less likely to leave her job entirely.

The family will be slightly poorer in terms of their income, but they will be monumentally richer in terms of couple equity. Both parents would be able to spend the right amount of time with the children without impoverishing the family. The two lines in figure 1.1 would come closer together, as would the metaphorical people being represented.

A complementary solution is to lessen the cost of childcare for the parents. With more accessible care, the tradeoffs are less costly. Most other rich nations greatly subsidize childcare, spending three to four times the US level relative to their national income. Nations as diverse as France, Sweden, and the United Kingdom heavily fund childcare that is high quality. This is one reason why the labor force participation rate for prime-age women in those nations now exceeds that in the US, even though the US rate had exceeded theirs for most of the post-WWII years. And care issues do not stop with regular school hours. They also concern after-school and summer programs for the K–12 group. A separate set of policies addresses the care of parents, grandparents, and others.

Yet another solution is to alter societal norms, so that tradeoffs do not depend on gender. As I have noted before in the context of same-sex couples, that might serve to greater equalize economic outcomes by gender but would not fix the problem of couple equity. It would not enable both members of the couple to be at their respective bliss points.

As I was putting the finishing touches on this book, a jolt of gargantuan proportions struck the global economy, exposing inequities and deficiencies in our everyday lives, and the unequal burdens on women in particular. This unforeseen boulder has fallen in a way that—rather than obscuring the road just traveled—has made clearer the connection between the care sector and the economic sector. No nation today, certainly not the US, can restart its economy until its children can return to schools and daycare. Women are half of all workers, whereas in the last Great Depression women were but a small fraction. The economy can't run on half its cylinders.

Almost all employers today are grappling with how to make remote work more productive and how to factor in flexibility while maintaining efficiency. They are trying to make certain that Isabel doesn't leave the workforce, and that Lucas can be as productive at home as he was in the office. They are trying to get both of them back into safe and secure offices while remaining cognizant of the needs of their families.

The quest for career and family continues during this moment of global reckoning. The pandemic has not redirected the journey. It has magnified it, lending urgency to questions surrounding the tradeoffs between work and home, forcing the choice of where one's time is best spent. As we've seen, pioneering women have been asking themselves these same questions for well over a century. As they sought the answers, they have knocked over barriers, widened opportunities, narrowed gaps, and passed lessons learned to successive generations. They will continue to do so. But in order to achieve an ideal balance in our uncertain future, it is not merely the women or the families who need to change. Our nation's systems of work and care need to be reconsidered in order to repave the ground on which we stride. It's all a matter of time.

Epilogue

JOURNEY'S END—MAGNIFIED

ALL ERAS CONTAIN UNCERTAINTY. The age of COVID exhibits this in extreme measure. Unemployment, which exploded just a year ago, at the start of the pandemic, has decreased considerably. But many jobs and small businesses remain at risk. The nation's public schools are still not yet fully open, and daycare centers flicker on and off. Safe and effective vaccines have finally become widely available but are not yet in everyone's arm. Normal life appears to be on the horizon, but the horizon is a shifting destination.

COVID has been a scourge. It has taken lives; it has taken jobs. It will impact future generations. It has exposed inequities by race, class, and gender regarding who was infected, who died, who had to work on the frontline, who could learn, and who was responsible for care of children and the sick. It has divided a nation into haves and have nots. It has been an alarming magnifying glass, enlarging the burdens on parents and revealing tradeoffs between working and caregiving. It has magnified most of the issues that have been carved out during the journey across the five groups chronicled in this book.

The force of the pandemic economy has had an outsized impact on women. Women are often essential workers on their jobs and essential workers in their homes. They are new mothers with unsteady infants, older mothers with increasingly bored teenagers being educated online, poor single mothers who now rely on food banks, highly educated ones who were ascending a corporate ladder, and women of color—at a higher risk of contracting the virus—who felt marginalized long before the nation fell off a cliff.

We are living through a moment without precedent. We liken the labor of frontline workers to that of our soldiers in wartime. But never before have our frontline workers been asked to carry danger back to their families. Never before have we needed to shut down the economy to get it running again. Never before has a recession impacted women more than men. And never before has the care sector been so manifestly intertwined with the economic sector. Women are almost 50 percent of the labor force. We need to make certain that they do not sacrifice their jobs because of care issues and that they do not sacrifice their caregiving for their jobs.

This book has followed college-graduate women's quest for career and family, using them as guides because over the course of the past 120 years they have had the greatest opportunity to achieve both. They were once a small slice of the population, no more than 3 percent of young women a century ago. Today, college graduates represent almost 45 percent of all US women in their late twenties.

The anxieties and discontent of the college-graduate group are palpable. Newspapers and news feeds are filled with disquieting prophecies about the future of the younger members of Group Five: "Pandemic Will 'Take Our Women 10 Years Back' in the Workplace," "Pandemic Could Scar a Generation of Working Mothers," and "How COVID-19 Sent Women's Workforce Progress Backward." In the age of COVID, those with children and others to care for are struggling to put in the hours, publish the academic papers, write the briefs, and attend to demanding clients on Zoom.

According to these predictions, a rug is being pulled out from under those who were finally able to achieve historic rates of career and family. As Deb Perelman, a food blogger, put it, "Let me say the quiet part loud: In the Covid-19 economy, you're allowed only a kid *or* a job." Is Group Five being forced to relive the compromises once made by the women of Group One?

There is no question that women have felt the impact of the pandemic and the economic recession more than men (which is why it has been called a "she-cession"). But college-graduate women have had a greater ability to maintain employment, or the semblance of it, than women with less education. Education has given them the ability to work at home. It has protected their health and their jobs.

Comparing fall/winter 2020 to the same for 2019, the labor force participation rate among college-graduate women aged twenty-five to thirty-four with preschool children (younger than five years old) fell by just 1.2 percentage points (from a base of 75 percent). But the rate for mothers aged thirty-five to forty-four with elementary and middle school–aged children (five to thirteen years old) fell by 4.9 percentage points (from a base of 86 percent)—a lot more. The noncollege group, either with or without children, had large decreases in labor force participation since they had been employed in the most vulnerable industries.

Though this picture may not fulfill the doomsday scenario of the headlines, the data do show cracks that may grow with time. Reentering the labor force may be difficult, and the loss of job experience will impact later earnings. Even for those who remained employed, many ask whether mothers will be disadvantaged at making partner, tenure, and first promotion. Among academics, mothers have published fewer papers during the past year than have men and women without school-aged children. Plus, data don't reveal the frustration of many for whom WFH means "Working From Hell."

Discontent

We examined the aspirations of college-graduate women from a century ago, who were faced with the prospect of a family or a career and who confronted an abundance of constraints, even in prosperous times. Obstacles shrank across the decades. We met the college-graduate women from the 1970s who were increasingly eager for a career and a family but who knew that to realize both they would have to attain them in that order. And we explored the women of the 1990s, who—with further gains in their education and increased career opportunities—became more candid about their aspirations. They spoke openly about desiring success in the workplace and the home and achieving both, in no particular order. In the past several decades, they have made even greater strides in both spheres.

But almost a decade before the virus took hold in America, and several years in advance of the watershed #MeToo movement, discontent among women began to be expressed widely. Phrases such as "sex discrimination" and "gender discrimination," found by searching the news media, signal the rise of frustration with pay inequity and defiance concerning sexual harassment.

In the early 2010s, several high-profile incidents, such as Ellen Pao's gender discrimination suit against her employer, Kleiner Perkins, and salary disparities between male and female professional soccer teams made the headlines. Flagrant examples of gender pay disparities in Hollywood, on Wall Street, and in Silicon Valley came to light. Women's resentment grew with the many issues that arose during the 2016 Clinton-Trump presidential race, especially the lewd remarks heard on the *Access Hollywood* tape and their apparent lack of influence on the outcome of the election. The reporting of these incidents produced the second peak moment of gender discontent in the twentieth century (as expressed through news articles). The first peak was in the early to mid-1970s.

Sixty years ago, in the 1960s, there was almost no mention of "sex discrimination" in the *New York Times*, and the phrase "gender discrimination" was unknown until several decades later. Around 1971, articles about "sex discrimination" began to soar, and by 1975 articles containing the phrase hit a high point. Then, with some fits and starts, the use of the phrase declined, reaching a nadir at about one-fifth its 1975 level, some thirty-five years later, around 2010.

But just as it rose abruptly in the early 1970s, the measure of discontent began to soar again in the early 2010s and has since skyrocketed to its highest level ever. The #MeToo and Time's Up movements added to the increase, but only at the end of 2017. Even before #MeToo became a symbol of women's defiance and resistance to a demeaning status quo, the apparent measure of discontent had already begun its ascent.

It is easy to understand why the measure of discontent increased in the early 1970s. The gender gap in pay was enormous. Women earned 59 cents on the male dollar, and the ratio was stuck at that abysmal level for a very long time. Women were still excluded from various clubs, restaurants, and bars, and had only just been granted admission at the nation's elite colleges and universities. Title IX of the Education Amendments Act of 1972 guaranteed women equality in education and in sports—following an era of protest movements from civil rights to antiwar. Women's-liberation and consciousness-raising groups cropped up everywhere in those heady days. Women were finally given a voice, and they used it to express discontent loudly.

But why were similar levels of dissatisfaction and frustration expressed in news articles in the 2010s, when the gains in women's employment, earnings, and education had been so significant?

Expectations had been raised and aspirations changed. Women, especially college-graduate ones, assumed that they could have a career *and* a family. Those with less education believed that they should be treated fairly in the labor market. The college-graduate group aspired to the same level of achievement as their male spouses. They began to imagine not only gender equality in the workplace, but also couple equity at home.

The gender gap in earnings, as we saw, had narrowed considerably in the 1980s and 1990s for all workers, but then stalled for the college-graduate group beginning in the 1990s. Rising income inequality meant that those at the top were gaining at the expense of others, and a disproportionate number of college-graduate men were in that rarified group. Greedy work became greedier, and women with care responsibilities struggled to keep up.

Caregiving

All of that existed BCE, "Before the Corona Era." In March 2020, with great urgency and suddenness, parents were told to keep their school-children at home. Daycares were shuttered. My Harvard undergraduates left for spring break, and only a fraction have since returned to the Yard. Employees were asked to work from home unless they were deemed "essential" by the US Department of Homeland Security. The nation had entered the "During Corona" (DC) period.

The economic catastrophe that accompanied the pandemic impacted women more than men in a way that downturns generally don't. Women's jobs are mainly in the service sector and have been sheltered from offshoring, the China trade shock, and automation. But service-sector jobs in hospitality, travel, personal services, restaurants, and retail were hit hard. In-person services don't cut it in a world of social distancing, and indoor work is less healthy than outdoor work. Construction bounced back. Most manufacturing did as well. The hardest-hit groups of women have been single moms and those with less than a college degree. College-graduate women also saw unemployment rates soar, while their labor force participation rates fell, as I have just noted.

As in the world BCE, college-graduate parents have had it easier than others, since they are more likely to be able to work from home. Before COVID, according to estimates based on the characteristics of occupations, about 62 percent of college-graduate working women (twenty-five to sixty-four years old) could have worked from home. According to Current Population Survey (CPS) data from May 2020, around 60 percent did work remotely, and about the same fraction of their male counterparts did. Among women with just some college, 42 percent could work at home, and among those with no college at all, just 34 percent were able to do so. The actual fraction of non-college-graduate women who claimed to work remotely in May 2020 was just 23 percent.

Given their occupations, the college-graduate group was poised for lockdown. Those without a college degree were destined to be the majority of the essential frontline workers, be furloughed, or be fired. Unemployment rates of college graduates have always been the lowest among those in the labor force. During the economically bleakest month of the pandemic, April 2020, when unemployment nationwide hit a double-digit peak, the unemployment rate for college-graduate women aged thirty-five to forty-four was 7 percent, and an additional 5 percent were "employed but not at work." Unemployment for the non-college-graduate group was more than double that: 17 percent, with an additional 10 percent who were employed but not at work.

In the DC period, the ability to work from home has mattered a lot. However, working from home can still mean that the employee is presumed to be available at odd hours, and available whenever the client or the manager wants a job done. Working from home can involve constant interruptions.

For most parents with preschool- and school-aged children, the time demands of family in the COVID era have been overwhelming. Everyone is working harder at home. For those with children, home is now a daycare center and a school. For those with a sick spouse or sick children, home is a clinic and a hospital. The number of uninterrupted hours spent on one's paying job have plummeted.

America is now in the mixed mode that I term AC/DC, since in many ways it is "After Corona" but still "During Corona." Some firms, offices, and institutions have opened, and some schools and daycare facilities have as well. But many schools have only partially opened, and some have remained fully remote. For couples with children, hybrid schools or remote schools mean that children will be at home, with any luck studying, under the watchful eye of whichever parent has stayed home with them. And if history or the journey we've just taken serves as any guide, that parent is likely to be a woman.

Exactly how much childcare time has increased and how much paid work time has decreased during the DC era is not yet known for large, nationally representative samples. The usual sources to study time use, such as the American Time Use Survey (ATUS), were paused in March 2020 and were not begun again until May. Those data will not be released for some time.

I've created estimates for the BCE (prepandemic years) based on the ATUS for "sample" families of employed college graduates with at least one child under eighteen years old. Before lockdown, the mothers in the sample families performed an average of 61 percent of the childcare. (They also did almost 70 percent of the food preparation, cleaning, and washing.) For similar mothers who are not employed, the fraction is 74 percent.

During lockdown, with children no longer attending school, preschoolers having limited childcare, and many caretakers furloughed, the total parental time commitment greatly increased. Parents monitored their children's school day, helped them with homework, and took over for the presence of teachers, who were suddenly distant images on a screen.

The immediate impact of lockdown on the mothers in the sample families was to double the total time they spent with their children. But the fraction of all childcare done by mothers in two-parent households actually decreased. Fathers were also at home, and they increased their hours of childcare by quite a lot relative to what they did before lockdown. Survey evidence for April 2020 shows that mothers increased their childcare hours by 1.54 times and fathers increased their childcare hours by 1.9 times. In addition, each parent with at least one elementary- or middle-school child allocated about an additional four hours of remote-learning time per week. Those with their youngest in high school added about two hours more per parent.

Infants, not surprisingly, took the most parental time before lockdown. Couples with an infant spent forty-two hours per week in all childcare prior to lockdown. Mothers performed 66 percent of that total. During lockdown the weekly total ballooned to seventy hours. But the share done by mothers of the new, higher total declined to 61 percent, even as their hours increased to forty-three, from twenty-eight.

For those with their youngest child in elementary or middle school, weekly hours spent by the mother on childcare and remote schooling went from around nine to seventeen. But, as in the previous case mentioned, hours of both parents greatly increased, and the fraction of total childcare and remote-schooling hours done by the mother decreased during lockdown, from almost 60 percent to a bit more than half.

It might appear that lockdown has been great for couple equity, since women's share of total childcare and remote-learning time has decreased as men's has increased. It might also seem that when all of this is over, men will want to give more time to their children and will contribute a greater share of family time. About that, we do not yet know.

We do know that even though mothers in two-parent families decreased their share of the total, the aggregate weight of childcare and household work was crushing. It was almost equally crushing for fathers. But because women performed a greater fraction of ordinary housework, food preparation, and laundry, the time left for their paid employment was greatly squeezed. According to one survey estimate for England, working mothers in April 2020 experienced interruptions during half of their paid working hours.

What has happened in the AC/DC period, when some schools, much daycare, and certain firms have reopened? Because some forms of childcare and schooling have become available, total childcare demands are likely to be around halfway between those experienced at the height of the DC period and those at the lower BCE level.

We do not have hard evidence, but there is reason to believe that women's total childcare load stayed about the same, but that the fraction of the total they did increased. The reason is that schools and daycares throughout the US opened more cautiously than did workplaces. The upshot is that some workers could go back, all or part of the time. But someone had to stay home with the children. What women gained from more childcare and open schools they lost from having their spouse go back to work some of the time.

The gain has been uneven and erratic. Daycare facilities for preschoolers largely reopened, and many families rehired their furloughed childcare workers. But even as late in the school year as March 2021, as I am writing these words, many of the largest districts in the US are still not fully open, although each has a plan to fully open "soon." Some had opened and then suddenly closed, sending tens of thousands of children back home. Desperate families formed real or virtual learning pods with a parent or paid tutor at the helm.

As firms, offices, and a variety of institutions opened, workers could leave their homes and go to work as they had previously done (except more cautiously). In families with children, one parent would still need to be at home part of the time if school was still partly remote. And at least one would still need to be on call at home.

Each parent may want to go back to the office for a number of reasons. The worker who goes to the office will probably learn more, be able to get the more lucrative clients, and be assigned the more interesting projects. That person will be able to interact with colleagues in person and to work more effectively, without interruption, away from children trying to learn their multiplication tables.

Both parents could still work at home, just as Isabel and Lucas could each work the highly flexible job. But, like Isabel and Lucas, they would be leaving money on the table if they did that. Earnings might not differ immediately if one parent worked from home and the other went back to the office. But the parent who made it into the office, even part of the time, would gain. While plenty of guesses have been aired, we don't yet know what the results of this devastating forced experiment will be.

Again, as we've learned from history, it is likely that the parent who is going back to the new version of the old normal—working from the office, even if only a fraction of the time—will be the man. But we are not yet certain. We know from special questions asked in the CPS that by September 2020 about 60 percent of all college graduates had headed back to their workplaces at least part of the time. We also know that more men than women went back. But the evidence is still slender. There is always the glimmer of hope that our gender norms will be altered by our compulsory trial with at-home work, and that the penalty for not going into the office will decrease.

There are abundant pressures in some quarters to get workers back in the office. David Solomon of Goldman Sachs Group Inc. encouraged traders to return to their headquarters. Sergio Ermotti, when he was CEO of UBS Group AG, said, "It's especially difficult for banks to create and sustain cohesiveness and a culture when employees stay at home." The CEO of a major real estate firm noted, possibly in a self-serving way, "Those who don't go into a place of work may miss out."

Even though the total number of childcare hours spent by the sample families decreased as the economy slowly, hesitantly, and very incompletely opened up, the load carried by women has probably remained the same. Thus, total childcare and remote-schooling hours spent by women in the sample families in the DC and AC/DC worlds have been about 1.7 times their BCE levels. Since the total number of hours increased, but the helping partner is assumed to be back in the office part of the time, the fraction of the total that employed college-graduate women are doing increased from about 60 percent BCE to around 73 percent AC/DC.

Inequities in the division of childcare did not emerge yesterday. The labor marketplace has not suddenly experienced up-or-out competition. Rather, the COVID world has magnified their impacts. Far greater job and career setbacks have occurred to, or may await, mothers than their husbands (or partners) and the fathers of their children.

Solutions

Much of the economic hit for college-graduate women has been due to the closing down of the caregiving sector. Without a well-functioning care sector, the economic sector will sputter. If schools remain shuttered, a large fraction of parents, mainly women, will be unable to work effectively, if at all. This has been the first major economic downturn during which the care sector will determine the fate of the economic sector. It wasn't always that way in major downturns. But it is now because women are almost half the total US labor force.

The Great Depression of the 1930s had far worse unemployment and far greater loss in economic output than the recent pandemic. Beginning in 1935, the Works Progress Administration (WPA) of the New Deal set up day nurseries for the children of low-income families age two to four. The program was multipronged. It ensured that the poorest and most vulnerable Americans would receive nutritious meals and health care and were taught basic skills. It employed teachers and school nurses who had been furloughed. Although the WPA nursery schools enabled parents to work, the program was not set up with that policy goal in mind.

There was little sense in the 1930s that the caregiving sector and the economic sector were intricately linked. In fact, the 1935 Omnibus Social Security Act deliberately included Aid to Dependent Children (ADC), which in 1962 was renamed Aid to Families with Dependent Children (AFDC), welfare as we once knew it. ADC paid women not to work, rather than subsidizing daycare so that women could work. Because Black women had worked more than their white counterparts, the program was mainly for white women. There was no presumption that white women should work for pay. Rather, the thinking was that poor white children should be taken care of by their mothers, and the mothers should be paid to do it. That's not something we hear today.

In the 1930s, the labor force participation rate of mothers (particularly white mothers) was so low that women's employment was not considered an important economic lever. As we have seen, women with able-bodied husbands were not expected to take jobs and were discouraged from doing so, by marriage bars and various social norms. It took WWII for Americans to link the economic sector with the care sector. But that was done only as an emergency, stopgap measure.

The Lanham Act, passed in 1943, set up daycare centers for the two- to four-year-old children of working mothers, many of whom were employed in war-related firms (including the famous Kaiser shipyards). Without these daycare centers, most women with preschool children would have been unable to work, and the war effort would have been hampered. The Lanham Act is, to date, the only piece of federal legislation that has funded childcare facilities nationwide for the children of working mothers without regard to their income.

Today, the care sector and the economic sector are clearly interdependent. It has become a commonplace to note that until schools are open full-time, many women will not be able to work effectively, and many will not be able to work at all.

America has never embraced the notion that the care of young children is a community responsibility, as have countries like Denmark, France, and Sweden, where childcare is heavily subsidized and women's labor force participation is higher than in the US. Before COVID, there were stirrings of change on related policies. Family and medical leave was expanded in six states, and the District of Columbia and more than a dozen other state legislatures had proposed legislation to do so. Companies, even some lower-wage ones such as Walmart, had adopted family-leave policies. Pre-K programs expanded in states and municipalities, as did after-school programs.

Getting men on board with childcare today is a critical part of the solution, yet it was not always that way. Even the most supportive husbands in the past could not easily have worked around the constraints and barriers maintained by firms, institutions, and governments. Eleanora Frances Bliss Knopf, who received a PhD in geology in 1912, married fellow geologist Adolph, a Yale professor. But she couldn't get a faculty position since Yale did not hire women. She continued her work with the US Geological Survey, often from her husband's office. "Both were authorities in separate fields," according to his memorial. Yet he has a mountain named after him; she does not.

Some women who had careers were employed by their husband's firm or formed their own. Jennie Loitman Barron opened a law practice in 1914, the year she passed the bar. After marrying her childhood sweetheart, providentially another lawyer, they joined forces, had three children, and opened Barron and Barron in 1918, which they maintained until she was appointed assistant attorney general of Massachusetts in 1934. Sadie Mossell Alexander, as noted earlier, worked in her husband's law practice.

Few women had the fortitude and financial ability to leave marriages that were constraining. Nora Blatch, the granddaughter of Elizabeth Cady Stanton, was one. She was also the first woman in the US to earn a civil engineering degree and the first to earn a degree in engineering at Cornell University. She divorced Lee de Forest, inventor of the radio tube, when he wanted her to quit her job, and in 1919 she married Morgan Barney, a naval architect. But the vast majority of married women who may have wanted to pursue a career, or even a job, didn't leave confining marriages, and they have left nary a trace in accessible records.

Doors opened, and more positions for married women became available in the 1950s. The ability to have a family and then a job or a career increased with Group Three. For some husbands, it was difficult to resist the temptation to have a second income to pay the mortgage and send the kids to college. As women became more educated, the cost to men of opposing their wives' careers pushed many over the edge. They relented. In some very special cases, it was more than a concession.

Marty Ginsburg relished the fact that his wife, Ruth, was brilliant. "I think that the most important thing I have done is to enable Ruth to do what she has done," he once said. Yet they were still a classic Group Three couple in many ways. They met in college, married just after

graduation in 1954, and had their first child a year later. Ruth even transferred from Harvard to Columbia Law School to follow Marty to New
York City, and "when Marty was intent on becoming a partner in a
New York law firm in five years," Ruth took over at home. But the comparison with their contemporaries ends there. For most in Group Three,
the woman's career took a backseat to her husband's.

In 1964, three-quarters of male and female graduates of the class of
1961 agreed that men's careers took precedence over women's. But
change was afoot. By 1980, about 60 percent of college graduates of
either gender (up from 25 percent in 1964) believed that husbands and
wives should be given an equal chance to have a career (or get a "good
job"). By 1998, the fraction of college graduates who proclaimed that
there should be equality of opportunity exceeded 85 percent. That was
the last time the question was asked in the survey.

Men shifted to being on board with their wife's career goals just as rapidly as their wives began to assert that they wanted them. A sea change
had occurred in aspirations and objectives. But the reality would have to
work through other barriers, no longer those that were as visible as the
ones encountered by the earliest of our groups, but just as potent.

For women to achieve career, family, and equity, fathers will have to
make the same demands at work that women make, and they will have
to take charge at home so women can take charge at work. Some high-
powered couples have done just that by toggling who has the primary
career. Karen Quintos, chief customer officer at Dell, and her husband
have "both had to make compromises." Similarly for Jules Pieri, founder
and CEO of The Grommet, who described her home life as a "ballet"
in which she and her husband "alternated who took the lead."

Marissa Mayer, who famously had twins when she was CEO of
Yahoo!, noted that a woman often scales back when her children are
young, but later "her career takes off." The facts show, though, that many
of those whose careers resume later in life never gain much altitude. As
we saw in figure 7.1, women with children increase their employment
and earnings in their forties and fifties relative to men's, but they do not
come close to catching up to their male colleagues. Jobs may resume,
but careers often do not soar.

Douglas Emhoff is the perfect role model. The first "second gentleman" is doing what women have always done: providing the personal support for those who lead our country, giving a shoulder, a Kleenex, an ear, sympathy, and help. He could lead the way as a manly man who happens to be married to a superwoman who is the vice president of the United States, showing men how to be proud, not jealous, and enabling, not obstructive. We need more of that.

We need men to lean out at work, support their male colleagues who are on parental leave, vote for public policies that subsidize childcare, and get their firms to change their greedy ways by letting them know that their families are worth even more than their jobs. Dreams won't come true, aspirations won't easily be realized unless men are brought along for the rest of the journey.

———

We will come out of this pandemic. But it will be a long time before workplaces, restaurants, movie theaters, airplanes, hotels, parties, sports arenas, weddings, and life itself look the way they did BCE. The journey of college-graduate women will also continue. We don't know the damage that will have been done to nascent careers. We also don't know whether our forced trial with at-home work for both parents will jolt gender norms and restructure the way work is done. We do know a lot about the past gains, about what has held women back, and about what still does.

We've taken a journey from those in Group One, who chose between the two goals of career and family, to those in Group Five, who now aspire to, and often succeed at, both. Sadie Mossell Alexander earned an advanced degree but could not land a job in her chosen field. Hazel Kyrk and Margaret Reid implicitly chose careers above family since they could not have both. Most accepted the consequences of the constraints of their era, and some, like Dorothy Wolff Douglas, blossomed despite them. Jeannette Rankin and Amelia Earhart soared triumphantly at some moments, but lost ground at others.

Some lived long enough to enjoy serial lives that changed with the times, such as Ada Comstock, who married in her late sixties. Many in

Group Three who were emblematic mothers of the baby boom, like Erma Bombeck, Jeane Kirkpatrick, Phyllis Schlafly, and Betty Friedan, evolved over the years, changed with the period, and even altered history.

Many were faced with governmental laws, regulations, and institutional policies that restricted their employment. Some fought for change and won, as we saw with Anita Landy and Mildred Basden, whose efforts after WWII worked to vanquish marriage bars by school districts.

Margaret Sanger and Katharine Dexter McCormick, the mothers of the Pill, helped awaken the Quiet Revolution that set Group Four apart from Group Three. Mary Tyler Moore, as Mary Richards, was the popular face of a new group of independent young women who could delay marriage and motherhood. Yet she, like many women, experienced disparate treatment in the workplace. Lilly Ledbetter endured far more— sexual harassment, physical and emotional harm, employment discrimination, and pay disparities. She survived to claim victory decades later.

But we've learned that treatment in the workplace isn't the only issue. Another is couple equity in the home. Too many women with careers "forgot to have the children," as Tiny Fey *almost* does in her TV and movie roles.

Members of Group Four put off marriage and family and set their sights on achieving career first. Hillary Rodham married Bill Clinton at age twenty-eight. Group Five increased the marriage age even further. Clinton's successor as a New York senator, Kirsten Rutnik, married Jonathan Gillibrand at age thirty-five. Amy Klobuchar married at age thirty-three, and Kamala Harris, who has broken so many "firsts" and has just been sworn in as US vice president, married at age fifty.

The journey from Jeannette Rankin has cleared the air and revealed why highly educated and trained women continue to struggle to progress as far as their male counterparts. Childcare, elder care, and family care are disproportionately performed by women. Work is greedy, and the person who does the most gets the most. Couples with children optimize in a world of gendered norms.

Has our experiment with remote work been the shot in the arm that will drive down the price of work flexibility? The shift to remote work was more seamless than had been imagined, and most workers claim they would like to continue working remotely. Half of those with school-aged children had difficulty working without interruptions, but that should change as schools fully reopen. Among college graduates working from home, 46 percent had more flexibility in choosing their hours. The cost of flexibility to workers does appear to have decreased, at least in the short run.

The majority of those who can work from home say they would like to do so for at least two days a week after the pandemic. But it is not yet clear how that will affect productivity and overall costs. Although remote workers believe they have been more productive, the longer-run impact remains to be seen. Innovation requires teams and collaborative generation of ideas. Some firms have already indicated that those who return to the office more days per week will reap greater benefits, although companies are scaling back office space with resulting cost savings.

As with much else today, uncertainty surrounds these issues. But there is also hope that our trial by fire, by exposing disparities and revealing new ways of working and caregiving, will spark change for good. As we slowly emerge from the pandemic, with schools still operating remotely in many places and offices partially opened, we are seeing—in real time—how these actualities have worked to the detriment of women's careers. Margaret Gilpin Reid, the "ancient" I did not heed long ago, knew the value of the care sector to the economic sector. It is time that we paid closer attention to the baton that she and many others have passed along. But we also need to revise our system of work and repave the road on which our journey has progressed, so that my former student, and others, can have a career as well as a spouse who wants what they want.

March 2021
Cambridge, Massachusetts

ACKNOWLEDGMENTS

DURING MY FIRST YEAR at Harvard University, some three decades ago, my students wanted to discuss their aspirations for a career and a family. What did the past reveal about their futures? I didn't have an answer. My book *Understanding the Gender Gap* had just been published. It covered the growth of the female labor force across US history, but not college-graduate women's quest for personal and professional success. I had to do more research.

Prodded by their questions, in 1992 I wrote "The Meaning of College in the Lives of American Women: The Past Hundred Years," which concerns three groups of college-graduate women, each defined by a different era corresponding to Groups One, Three, and Five in the current book. A few years later, Francine Blau, the labor economist and an undergraduate classmate of mine at Cornell University, asked me to expand that paper and add Group Four (ours), for a conference she was planning. The result was "Career and Family: College Women Look to the Past" (1997). Those two papers are the foundations of this book, like the light from some distant galaxy that reaches Earth a gazillion years later.

I left that work for several decades to research the history of education and the roles of education and technological change in the rise of economic inequality. But I never abandoned my interest in gender—specifically, the power of the Pill, name change as a social indicator, a pollution theory of discrimination, the history of coeducation, and the Quiet Revolution, which was the theme of my 2006 AEA Ely Lecture. I also helped devise the Harvard and Beyond study, as well as one on MBAs, and I collected evidence on why women trailed men across a variety of professions.

My 2014 AEA presidential lecture, "A Grand Gender Convergence: Its Last Chapter," spelled out the enormous progress women have made over the past century and the remaining steps that must occur on the road to gender equality. The Arrow Lecture at Columbia University in 2015 was a turning point for this work. In preparing for that lecture, I realized that my then current work on the reasons for gender differences in careers was inextricably linked to my earlier history of the career and family progression among the five groups of college-graduate women. After the lecture, Bridget Flannery-McCoy, then of Columbia University Press, asked if I was considering writing up the lecture as a book. I wasn't. But her encouraging words stuck with me when I decided to write something bigger than the lecture. By the time I began to write this book, she had joined Princeton University Press.

In March 2020, when I was almost finished with the book, the pandemic struck, and the volume took on new urgency. If women fell behind in normal times, when schools and daycares were open, what would happen when care and educational facilities were closed? But if work became remote for most parents and greater flexibility in work arrangements developed, would women's careers be aided? Would we emerge from the lockdown with a new awareness of the importance of work flexibility and caregiving? In trying to resolve the pressing questions about our present circumstances, I realized that even the recent past can help us understand the road ahead in a post-COVID world.

At every stage of this project, from the seed planted in the distant galaxy to the era of the pandemic, I have been helped by coauthors, colleagues, research assistants, my agent and her editorial associate, and my editorial helper.

There are many to thank. At the top of the list is Larry Katz— my coauthor, fellow economist, Mr. Memory, dog enthusiast, birder, husband—my everything. What would I do without him? What would either of us do without the warmth of Pika, the amazing and talented golden retriever who is a titled scenting champion, a therapy dog, and the love of our lives?

The journey from idea to book began with my agent, Jill Kneerim, and her gifted editorial associate, Lucy Cleland, now a literary agent in her own right. Jill and Lucy taught me to add the human element, the stories, people, and color. They prodded, questioned, probed, and encouraged. They also insisted that I take on an editorial helper and strongly advised that it be Domenica Alioto. How did they know that two opposites would attract and bond? Domenica bettered every page and sent me a poem with every e-mail.

A long list of research assistants is to be thanked. The writing of the book began when Dev Patel returned to Cambridge to be my research assistant and dove into my project. He discovered data gems and exhumed data that had never been used to their fullest extent before, such as the *Great Aspirations* study. Even after he became a PhD student in economics at Harvard, he continued to shepherd the volume and read every page before I sent it to Domenica.

In reverse chronological order, I thank the most recent of my research assistants, Jennifer Walsh, for taking on a clean-up role in between her duties on another project, and Summer Cai for being a great last-minute gofer. The other research assistants to whom I am deeply grateful, listed with their main assignments, are: Ross Mattheis (Black teachers), Ayushi Narayan (fertility data), Namrata Narain (Who's Who), Jonathan Roth (HRS), Amira Abulafi (AEA presidential paper), Natalia Emanuel (AEA presidential paper), Chenzi Xu (pharmacy data), Tatyana Avilova (pharmacy data), Jane Lee (Community Tracking Study), Rebecca Diamond (MBA data), Naomi Hausman (MBA and Harvard and Beyond data), Lisa Blau Kahn (Ely paper), Crystal Yang (Ely paper), Boris Simkovich ("Career and Family" paper), and Kathy Snead (National Archives, Women's Bureau Bulletins).

My many coauthors on related projects are to be thanked for teaching me as we worked together. In reverse chronological order, they include: Claudia Olivetti, Sari Pekkala Kerr, Josh Mitchell, Marianne Bertrand, Ilyana Kuziemko, Maria Shim, and Cecilia Rouse. Daniel Horowitz, historian at Smith College, is to be thanked for providing valuable insights on Betty Friedan. Stanley Engerman read and commented on anything I would give him. Kathleen Gerson provided some last-minute help on the role of men in changing gender roles.

I refined my ideas by presenting them at many lectures. Among the most important to this work, presented after my 2014 presidential address, were the Arrow Lecture at Columbia University, the Bies Lecture at Northwestern University, the Lindahl Lectures at Uppsala University, Sweden, the Gorman Lectures at University College London, and the Feldstein Lecture at the National Bureau of Economic Research.

My editor at Princeton University Press, Joe Jackson, provided suggestions that have bettered the exposition, Kelley Blewster, from Westchester Publishing, was an exceptionally careful and thoughtful copyeditor, and Angela Piliouras was an extraordinary production editor. Seung Jin Kim was an insightful translator. I thank them all.

Data were provided by the many institutions and associations mentioned in the Source Appendix. I thank the many people behind these data collections. They include: Marianne Bertrand, a coauthor and the initiator of the MBA project that used administrative data from the Booth School of the University of Chicago; John Schommer at the University of Minnesota for the data on pharmacists; Terry K. Adams and J. J. Prescott for the University of Michigan Law School Alumni Research Survey Dataset, and Stephanie Hurder for helping me make sense of the data; Bryce Ward for helping create and produce the Harvard and Beyond survey instrument, and Naomi Hausman for making the data usable.

The journey that women have taken across the past century and more has been mine as well, and at the end of my journey, I met Domenica Alioto, who made my work more relevant and taught me to appreciate poetry. We each went through difficult times over the past nine months—the anxiety of a global pandemic, the death of my mother, the mental illness of a good friend, the toxic soot-filled air that greeted Domenica in California after she fled the virus in Brooklyn, and the 2020 election. That spring, summer, and fall, I soldiered on, wrote, taught, gardened, and read Domenica's edits and e-mails: "Between my finger and my thumb / The squat pen rests. / I'll dig with it" (Seamus Heaney, "Digging"). "Meanwhile the wild geese, high in the clean blue air, / are heading home again" (Mary Oliver, "Wild Geese"). The journey continues.

FIGURES AND TABLE APPENDIX:
SOURCES AND NOTES

Chapter 1

Figure 1.1. Gender Inequality and Couple Inequity
No sources. Notes are part of figure in text.

Chapter 2

Figure 2.1. A Century of Five Groups of College-Graduate Women
Notes: Desired or achieved family and career/job paths are given below the birth years. Groups that are still ongoing have "desired" family and career/jobs paths, and those that have completed their lives have "achieved" paths. These characterizations are for the aggregate. Heterogeneity within groups is explored in the various chapters.

Figure 2.2. Fraction of College-Graduate Women Never Married, by Age and Birth Group
Sources: 1940, 1950, 1960, 1970, 1980, 1990, 2000 micro data of the US Census of Population; 2000 to 2015 micro data of the American Community Surveys (ACS).
Notes: The marriage data provided are for white women because Black women were a small fraction of college graduates in the early years, but far more in the more recent period. To make certain that these distinctions are not affected by compositional change, the groups include only native-born women. Because the data come from a closed (native-born) population, the fraction remaining single should decline for each birth group as it ages, but differential mortality by marriage could alter that

relationship. The data point for 50- to 54-year-olds born in 1908 has been reduced by 0.8 for consistency with the remaining data. The data point for 1883 is for 55- to 59-year-olds. The construction of the five-year age groups is slightly different using the US Census of Population than using the ACS. For the census, the data are an average for each five-year age group by birth year. For example, the data for 35- to 39-year-olds born in 1953 are from the 1990 census. The year of birth is for the midpoint of the age bracket. For the ACS data, all five years of data are known and are for the exact birth year. The splice point for the two datasets is the year 2000. For those ages 25 to 29, the splice point is the 1973 birth year. It should be noted that the marriage fractions are relatively flat between 1973 and 1978; therefore, the difference in the calculation does not affect the data much.

Figure 2.3. Fraction of College-Graduate Women with No Births, by Age and Birth Group
Sources: US Population Censuses 1940, 1950, 1960, 1970; June Fertility Supplement of the Current Population Survey (CPS), 1973 to 2018.
Notes: US Population Census data are used for all years prior to the birth year of 1949 for the 25- to 29-year-old group, and 1934 for the 40- to 44-year-old group. Data for older age groups are used for the two earliest years for the 40- to 44-year-old group. Data from the CPS June Fertility Supplement, expressed as five-year centered moving averages, are used where possible. For other years, the US Population Census data are used. Linear interpolations connect between census years and link the two sources. Data are for all races.

Figure 2.4. Labor Force Participation Rates by Age and Birth Group: Ever-Married College-Graduate Women
Sources: Three sources are used: US decennial population censuses; CPS; ACS. Integrated Public Use Microdata Series (IPUMS), US decennial census of population, micro data, for 1940 to 2000. The ACS includes all years from 2000 to 2016. The US decennial population census uses the following samples: 1940 1 percent, 1950 1 percent, 1960 5 percent, 1970 1 percent "metro form 1" and "metro form 2," 1980

5 percent "state," 1990 5 percent, and 2000 5 percent. The CPS Annual Social and Economic Supplement (ASEC) includes all years from 1962 through 2017. College graduate is defined in all samples as four or more years of college.

Notes: Labor force participation is defined by the US Census as being employed during the census week or searching for work. All elements in each five-year matrix (e.g., 35- to 39-year-olds born between 1930 and 1934) are complete. Data for 25- to 29-year-olds for 1900–1904 have been extrapolated based on the change from subjects age 25–29 to subjects age 35–39 using the data for those born between 1910 and 1914.

Figure 2.5. College Graduation Rates for Males and Females (at Age Thirty)
Sources and Notes: 1940 to 2000 censuses IPUMS and CPS Merged Outgoing Rotation Groups (MORG) 2006 to 2016 are used. The procedure is the same as in Goldin and Katz (2008), figure 7.1.

Table 2.1. Marriage, Children, and Employment across Five Groups of College-Graduate Women
Sources and Notes: Cols. (A) and (B) use the birth years 1890, 1910, 1930, 1950, and 1960 for the five groups (rows). See also figure 2.2. Col. (C) data are those underlying figure 2.3. For the first three groups, the age group 45–49 is used. Cols. (D) and (E), see also figure 2.4. Census years used for col. (D) are 1940, 1960, 1980, and 1990 for Groups Two to Five. Census years used for col. (E) are 1940, 1960, 1980, 2000, and 2010 for Groups One to Five. Birth years used for Groups One to Five are 1890–1894, 1910–1914, 1930–1934, 1950–1954, and 1960–1964. The estimate for Group One col. (D) is an educated guess. Group One was in its late forties both during the Great Depression and during WWII, and their labor force participation rates greatly varied during those years.

Chapter 3

No figures, tables.

Chapter 4

Figure 4.1. Marriage and Children among All and Notable College-Graduate Women

Sources: The "Notable Sample" of college-graduate women was collected from all volumes of *Notable American Women*, but mainly from the two most recent ones. See James, James, and Boyer (1971), Sicherman and Green (1980), and Ware and Braukman (2004). For "All College-Graduate Women," see sources in chapter 2 for figures 2.2 and 2.3.

Notes: Demographic information is measured in the woman's fifties or, in the case of *Notable American Women*, toward the end of the woman's life. In the construction of children conditional on ever being married, the assumption for the "All" sample is that no women who were never married had biological children. Children can include adopted children but generally exclude stepchildren.

Figure 4.2. Marriage and Retention Bars for Public Schoolteachers: 1928 to 1951

Sources: National Education Association (1928, 1932, 1942, 1952).

Notes: The percentage is for the population in the various cities that had either a hire or a retention bar. The original data by size of city are weighted to obtain these numbers. The unweighted data are not very different from the weighted estimates.

Chapter 5

Figure 5.1. Fraction of Men or Women (All Education Levels) Who Agree with the Statement "A Preschool Child Is Likely to Suffer if His or Her Mother Works"

Source: General Social Survey (GSS) micro data from 1977 to 2016.

Notes: Five-year moving averages are given. The GSS data begin in 1977 and then jump to 1985. Therefore, the early birth groups are older, on average, at the time of the interview than the younger birth groups. Survey weights have been used.

Chapter 6

Figure 6.1. Median Age at First Marriage for College-Graduate Women by Birth Year: 1925 to 1988
Sources and Notes: CPS June Fertility Supplements and CPS Annual Social and Economic Supplement (ASEC). Three-year centered moving averages are shown. Dotted line is a freehand summary of the two series.

Figure 6.2. Employment Expectations and Attitudes of Female Youth by Age and Year
Sources: 1968 National Longitudinal Survey of Young Women (NLS68) and 1979 National Longitudinal Survey of Youth (NLSY). See Goldin (2005) for details. Higher Education Research Institute CIRP (Astin) Freshman Survey. See https://heri.ucla.edu/cirp-freshman-survey/. Notes are part of figure in text.

Figure 6.3. Fraction Female among Professional School Graduates: Medical, Law, Dental, and MBA
Sources and Notes: First-year law student data from the American Bar Association (ABA) website, http://www.abanet.org/legaled/statistics/femstats.html, when the ABA data are available, and US Department of Education, National Center for Education Statistics (NCES) *Digest of Higher Education* (online), when they are not. First-year medical student data from the American Association of Medical Colleges (AAMC) website, http://www.aamc.org/data/facts/enrollmentgraduate/table31-women-count.htm, when they are available, and US Department of Education, NCES *Digest of Higher Education* (online), when the AAMC data are not. First-year dentistry students extrapolated from dental degrees awarded lagged four years, from US Department of Education, NCES *Digest of Higher Education* (online). MBA first-year students extrapolated from MBA degrees awarded lagged two years, from US Department of Education, NCES *Digest of Higher Education* (online).

Figure 6.4. Occupations of College-Graduate Women, Thirty to Thirty-Four Years Old: 1940 to 2017

Sources: Integrated Public Use Microdata Sample (IPUMS) of the US Federal Population Census, 1940 to 2000; ACS 2012, 2017.

Notes: The solid line includes librarians, nurses, social and religious workers, secretaries (and other clerical workers), and (grade school) teachers. The dashed line includes lawyers, managers, physicians (including dentists, veterinarians, and so forth), professors, and scientists.

Chapter 7

Figure 7.1. Career and Family Success for Four Age Groups: 1931 to 1965
Sources and Notes: 1931–1957 Health and Retirement Study; 1958–65 NLSY79. See Source Appendix (Ch7): "Career and Family Success." Uses fertility data for the birth groups from the June Fertility Supplements of the CPS rather than from the HRS, to correct for overstatements of birthrates in the HRS. Also uses the fertility data from the June Fertility Supplements for the 1958–65 NLSY79 group, for consistency.

Figure 7.2. Career and Family by Advanced Degree, Harvard and Beyond Fifteen Years after College
Sources and Notes: See Source Appendix (Ch7): "Harvard and Beyond Project." Employment is 15 years after college graduation. Full-time includes full-year. MA = master's degree and does not include those with higher degrees such as PhDs. Some individuals have more than one advanced degree above an MA. None = no degree above an undergraduate degree. "Children" includes children adopted less than three years old.

Chapter 8

Figure 8.1. Female to Male Median Annual Earnings Ratio, Full-Time, Year-Round Workers: 1960 to 2018
Sources: All workers, 1960 to 2019: https://www.census.gov/library/publications/2020/demo/p60-270.html.

College-graduate workers, 1961 to 2019: computed from Annual Social and Economic Supplement (ASEC), Current Population Survey, US Census Bureau.

Notes: The computed series is shifted back a year for consistency with the published series because annual income is for the previous year. Three-year centered moving averages are presented for both series.

Figure 8.2. Relative Annual Earnings of College-Graduate Men and Women: Group Five, Born 1958 to 1983
Sources: US Census Micro Data 1970, 1980, 1990, 2000, and American Community Survey 2004 to 2006 (for 2005), 2009 to 2011 (for 2010), and 2014 to 2016 (for 2015). See Goldin (2014), figure 1, part b, updated to 2015.
Notes: Sample consists of college-graduate (16 years or more of schooling) men and women (white, native-born, nonmilitary, 25 to 69 years old), using trimmed annual earnings data (exceeding 1,400 hours × 0.5 × relevant federal minimum wage) corrected for income truncation (top-coded values × 1.5). Dependent variable is log(annual earnings) with controls for education beyond 16 years, log(hours), log(weeks), and age, entered in five-year intervals interacted with the dummy variable female. Lines connect the coefficients on the five-year intervals for each birth cohort. Only birth cohorts from 1958 to 1983 and only age groups to 55 years old are shown. The vertical axis is translated from logs into ratios. The midpoint of the birth years is given, thus c. 1963 is for those born from 1961 to 1965.

Figure 8.3. Ratio of Female to Male MBA Annual Earnings by Years since MBA Receipt
Source: See Bertrand, Goldin, and Katz (2010).
Notes: Year 13 means the years between 10 and 16 post-MBA. "Annual earnings" are defined as total earnings before taxes and other deductions, including salary and bonus, and is coded as missing when the individual is not working. Ratios are given for annual earnings corrected for MBA courses and MBA grades in a regression context with MBA cohort fixed effects. The "all MBA" bars are for all males and all females. The "MBA women with no kids" bars include only women who had no children to the year they were interviewed after receiving their MBAs and who had taken no time out exceeding six months.

Figure 8.4. Gender Earnings Ratio for College Graduates by Occupational Sector
Sources: American Community Survey, 2009 to 2016.
Notes: Sample consists of college graduates, 25 to 64 years old, who worked full-time, full-year (FT-FY) in the census year and who were in an occupation for which mean annual earnings of FT-FY male workers exceeded $65,000. Covariates include age in a quartic, usual hours worked per week, usual weeks worked per year, and education (above the bachelor's degree). See Online Appendix table 1A (Ch8), "ACS Occupations and Industry Groupings," for a listing of the occupations in each of the ten groups. Weights are the number of workers in each of the separate occupations.

Chapter 9

Figure 9.1. Percentage Distribution of Hours of Work for Female and Male JDs: Five and Fifteen Years after Law School Graduation
Source: See Source Appendix (Ch 9): "University of Michigan Law School Alumni Survey Research Dataset."
Notes: Includes JDs who graduated from the University of Michigan Law School from 1982 to 1992 and who were in the survey in year five and in year fifteen. "At 5 years" and "at 15 years" mean years since receiving a JD. The group is a longitudinal sample, so all who are in the "at 5 years" columns are also in the "at 15 years" columns.

Figure 9.2. Percentage Distribution of Work Setting for Female and Male JDs: Five and Fifteen Years after Law School Graduation
Source: See Source Appendix (Ch9): "University of Michigan Law School Alumni Survey Research Dataset."
Notes: Includes JDs who graduated from the University of Michigan Law School from 1982 to 1992 and who were in the survey in year five and in year fifteen and were not listed with a "missing" occupation in either year. "Years out" means years since receiving a JD. The group is a longitudinal sample, so all who are in the "5 years out" columns are also in the "15 years out" columns.

Figure 9.3. Percentage Female among Pharmacists and Pharmacy Graduates and Percentage Working in Independent Practice among Pharmacists

Sources: Goldin and Katz (2016) use the micro data from surveys of the Midwest Pharmacy Research Consortium (see Source Appendix [Ch9]: "National Pharmacist Workforce Surveys: 2000, 2004, 2009") and more conventional sources.

Notes: Fraction of females among pharmacy graduates is a three-year moving average. The other two series are at intervals and are not continuous series.

Chapter 10

No figures or tables.

Epilogue

No figures or tables.

SOURCE APPENDIX

ALSO SEE THE ONLINE appendix for longer descriptions, which can be found on the book's PUP webpage or at this link: https://assets.press.princeton.edu /releases/m30613.pdf.

Ch3: Radcliffe Alumnae Questionnaire of 1928

The Radcliffe Alumnae Questionnaire was distributed by mail in 1928 in honor of Radcliffe's semicentennial. It was designed to provide an overall profile of Radcliffe alumnae. The sample consists of women who had attended Radcliffe from its beginning, in 1879, through the time of the survey. About nineteen hundred Radcliffe BAs, who graduated from the 1880s to the 1920s, responded. See Solomon (1985, 1989).

Ch5: Women's Bureau 1957 Survey and 1964 Resurvey

Women's Bureau Bulletin no. 268, *First Jobs of College Women: Report of Women Graduates, Class of 1957*, is a report on a survey of about six thousand female college graduates of the class of 1957 across 131 institutions, and no. 292, *College Women Seven Years after Graduation: Resurvey of Women Graduates, Class of 1957*, is the 1964 follow-up, to which about five thousand of the original women responded (US Department of Labor, Women's Bureau 1959, 1966). The tabular material in the bulletins comes mainly from each of the surveys separately; just one table in the 1966 publication cross-tabulates the results.

To obtain longitudinal data, a sample of the surveys was collected from the National Archives and matched across the two years. The sample was collected in 1987. Because the National Archives kept the surveys in separate boxes, most but not all women who responded to both surveys could be matched. Of the 993 surveys sampled from 1964, 749 were matched to surveys in 1957. These data inform statements in the text about changes across the seven years by women's characteristics in 1957. In addition, all surveys from this group with comments written by the respondents were copied. The surveys are from Record Group #86, Boxes 739–767. See also Goldin (1990), Data Appendix.

Ch5: *Great Aspirations* Data

The "Career Plans and Experiences of June 1961 College Graduates," as the *Great Aspirations* data are formally called at the Interuniversity Consortium for Political and Social Research (ICPSR), is a panel study that surveyed college graduates in the spring of 1961 (Wave A), 1962 (Wave B), 1963 (Wave C), 1964 (Wave D), and 1968 (Wave E). Each survey wave contains questions about career plans and goals, often compared with the graduate's original plans, as well as attitudes about career fields. Additionally, Wave D contains a supplement for female respondents that assesses attitudes toward family and career decisions. Wave E, conducted seven years after graduation, includes many questions about respondents' retrospective experiences of and satisfaction with their undergraduate institutions.

The initial sample was selected from college seniors intending to graduate in June 1961 from 135 colleges and universities in the US. The sample was selected using a two-stage probability sampling technique, in which colleges were selected from a group of eligible institutions and students were then selected from those colleges. All told, 41,116 individuals received surveys. The final sample from universities, liberal arts colleges, and teachers colleges contains 35,527 respondents, who form an unbalanced panel across the years.

The five waves of the original data used by lead researcher James Davis were archived with the consortium as ICPSR 07344: "Career Plans and Experiences of June 1961, College Graduates." The original data were in ASCII form with no dictionary. To remedy that, I have added ICPSR 121481, an update to the original. The analyses using the *Great Aspirations* data reported in chapter 5 were done using the original data for all five waves. See Davis (1964) and the longer description of these data in the online appendix to this book on the Princeton University Press website.

Sample Sizes for the Five Waves of the *Great Aspirations* Data for Respondents from Universities, Liberal Arts Colleges, and Teachers Colleges

	All Waves	Wave A	Wave B	Wave C	Wave D	Wave E
All respondents	35,527	32,092	29,438	28,188	23,146	4,615
Female respondents	13,086	11,952	11,136	10,479	8,254	1,778

Ch5: Radcliffe College Centennial Survey, 1977

The centennial survey, part of Radcliffe College's hundredth-anniversary celebration, was sent to those who attended the college as undergraduates and graduates from the classes of 1900 to 1977. More than six thousand women completed and returned the questionnaire, a response rate of 48 percent. The survey included questions on further education, paid and volunteer work, career history, marital history and children, husband's education and work, and attitudes about women and education. The data are housed at the Henry A. Murray Research Center. See also Solomon (1985).

Ch7: Career and Family Success

To measure the degree to which women achieved a career and a family requires a definition of each. "Family" is defined as having a child (when possible including the adoption of an infant or young child). I created a definition of "career" using information about the person's employment history and earnings. The definition is related to the notion that a career is achieved across an extended period and involves (labor) earnings that exceed some level.

I use two extensive longitudinal datasets that allow me to estimate career and family success for both female and male college graduates born from 1931 to 1964 across their lives. In earlier work (Goldin 1997, 2004), I estimated the career and family success of college-graduate women in their late thirties to early forties. The National Longitudinal

Survey of Youth, 1979 (NLSY79) respondents are now old enough to track to their fifties. In the current estimates, I use the Health and Retirement Study (HRS) linked to Social Security Administration records to track the success of the women of Groups Three and Four to their early fifties, and I provide data for a comparable group of college-graduate men.

In all the estimates, I employ a career criterion that involves earning above the twenty-fifth percentile of the full-time, full-year distribution for males in the same age bracket and education level. The male earnings data were obtained from the Current Population Survey (CPS) for the relevant year. The earnings of a man at the twenty-fifth percentile is about equal to the earnings of the median female in most years.

To be deemed successful at a career, the income level had to be exceeded for some number of consecutive years (or nearby years if the survey was biennial). Thus, a college-graduate woman forty to forty-four years old would be deemed to have a career if she earned at least as much as a college-graduate man forty to forty-four years old who was at the twenty-fifth percentile in the male distribution. Since the respondents in the NLSY79 were surveyed every other year, a respondent would be interviewed three times in a five-year interval. Given that, she would be deemed to have a career if she exceeded the level two out of the three possible interviews.

I employ approximately the same definition using the HRS linked to Social Security Administration (and W-2) earnings data (Goldin and Katz 2018). The annual income data that have been linked to the HRS are annual, whereas the NLSY79 data are biennial. Therefore, one difference is that I define "career" in the HRS as meeting the earnings condition for at least three years in each five-year period. There is no overlap in birth groups for the NLSY79 and the version of the HRS available at the time of this writing.

In using the HRS, I divide the sample for convenience into four birth groups from 1931 to 1957. The earliest two of the birth groups map onto an "early" Group Three (born 1931–1937) and a "later" Group Three (born 1938–1944). More recent birth cohorts map into an "early" Group Four (born 1945–1950) and a "later" Group Four (born 1951–1957). For the 1951–1957 Group Four in the HRS, 79.9 percent of college-graduate women claim to have had at least one biological child by age fifty, whereas for the 1957–1964 NLSY79 cohort, 71.8 percent claim to have had a child by age thirty-nine to forty-six years. To correct for the possible overstatement of births in the HRS, I have substituted the total cohort fertility rates from the June Fertility Supplements of the CPS for the HRS birth groups in the final calculations of career and family success.

Ch7: Harvard and Beyond Project

The Harvard and Beyond Project provides detailed information on the education, career, and family transitions of thirteen classes of Harvard/ Radcliffe College students. The survey was done with the cooperation of, and funding from, Harvard University president Lawrence H. Summers. See Goldin and Katz (2008a).

The project surveyed the entering classes of 1965 to 1968 (most of whom graduated from 1969 to 1972), 1975 to 1978 (graduating 1979 to 1982), and 1985 to 1988 (graduating 1989 to 1992). Individuals who entered with these classes, or who transferred to Harvard, or who did not graduate on time were also included. In addition, women from the class of 1973 were included. Administrative data from transcripts were added. Because these were not in electronic form prior to the mid-1980s, they were coded from originals in the Harvard University Registrar's Office. More than sixty-five hundred replies to the survey were received.

Ch9: University of Michigan Law School Alumni Survey Research Dataset

The University of Michigan Law School Alumni Survey Research Dataset includes alumni surveys from 1967 to 2006 for persons graduating from 1952 to 2001 together with administrative data on each alumnus. The surveys were sent to graduating classes five, fifteen, twenty-five, thirty-five, and forty-five years after they received their JD. The survey was meant to be a set of repeated cross-sections, but because so many alumni filled out the survey at each of these milestones, a longitudinal dataset was assembled. Researchers wanting to use these data are encouraged to contact the University of Michigan Law School Alumni Survey Project.

Ch9: National Pharmacist Workforce Surveys: 2000, 2004, 2009

The National Pharmacist Workforce Surveys were collected in three years—2000, 2004, and 2009—by the Midwest Pharmacy Workforce Research Consortium. Tabulations are contained in Midwest Pharmacy Workforce Research Consortium (2000, 2005, 2010).

The primary purpose of the surveys was to collect reliable information on demographic and work characteristics of the US pharmacist workforce. The project obtained information from a nationally representative sample of pharmacists. The survey questionnaire covers employment status and situation (working or not, setting, position, years employed and in current position), compensation and hours worked, future work plans, and individual demographic background information. Observations are available for about 5,150 individuals across the three waves. See Goldin and Katz (2016). Researchers wanting to use these and other pharmacy surveys are advised to contact Jon Schommer of the consortium.

Ch10: Community Tracking Study

The Community Tracking Study (CTS), a project of the Center for Studying Health System Change (HSC), is a large-scale investigation of the US health system sponsored by the Robert Wood Johnson Foundation (RWJF). The Physician Survey portion of the CTS interviewed physicians in the sixty CTS sites and a supplemental national sample of physicians. There are four waves of the CTS physician survey: 1996, 1998, 2000, and 2004. In 2008, it was replaced by the HSC Health Tracking Physician Survey. Only the first four waves include detailed income data. The merged data contain almost fifty thousand observations.

Physician characteristics available include sex, age, race, Hispanic origin, year of MD, detailed specialty, hours, weeks, earnings, ownership, practice type, career satisfaction, and geographic place. Highly detailed information exists on the physician's practice and aggregate patient characteristics. There is no personal demographic information concerning marital status and children. The data are cross-sectional but have a longitudinal component since some physicians were interviewed in multiple waves. Specialties without a patient base, such as those in radiology and anesthesiology, are not included, since the purpose of the study was to track physicians and their patient communities. The data can be obtained from ICPSR. A restricted-use version contains detailed physician specialties and income.

Ch10: American Veterinary Medical Association (AVMA) Dataset for 2007 and 2009

The AVMA dataset contains both cross-sectional and retrospective information on veterinary training, practice hours, income, position, specialty, years in service, and clinic ownership by sex as well as by other demographic and geographic characteristics for 8,340 veterinarians in 2007 and 2009. The data were obtained from the American Veterinary Medical Association (2007, 2009).

Because the total number of active veterinarians in the nation is relatively small (probably around sixty thousand), the more usual sources, such as the Current Population Survey (CPS) and even the decennial census, do not yield sufficient information. In addition, the usual datasets lack information on training, specialty, and ownership, among other variables contained in the AVMA survey. The AVMA data are collected biennially; researchers are encouraged to contact the AVMA for these and more recent versions of the survey.

NOTES

The micro data of many large US national surveys have been used in these chapters to provide demographic and economic statistics and trends, through analyses of millions of observations. The data sources include: the US Population Census from 1900 to 2000, including the micro data of the "complete count" decennial censuses (1900 to 1940); the American Community Surveys (ACS) from 2000 to the present; and the Current Population Survey (CPS). The CPS sources include the basic monthly data, the Merged Outgoing Rotation Groups (known as the MORG), the Annual Social and Economic Supplement of the CPS (known as the ASEC or the March Supplement), and the June Fertility Supplement. The CPS micro data samples generally begin with 1962, although the MORG starts in 1979, and the June Supplement micro data in 1973. The micro data files have been accessed mainly through the IPUMS (Integrated Public Use Microdata Series, https://ipums.org/) but also through the US Census and National Bureau of Economic Research websites. A large number of other data sources and archival documents have also been used; they are described in the Source Appendix.

Chapter One

3   **greedy work**   The term "greedy work" was popularized by Claire Cain Miller. See "Work in America Is Greedy. But It Doesn't Have To Be," *New York Times*, May 15, 2019.

3   **In the late 1930s, firm managers told survey agents**   These quotations are from the original manuscripts of a Women's Bureau survey taken in 1939. See Goldin (1990), Data Appendix, 1940 Office Worker Survey. "Loan work is not suitable" was from Los Angeles Auto Bank; "women wouldn't be acceptable" was offered by Don Lee, Los Angeles automobile dealer; and "Would not put a woman" was listed by Jewel Marache and Co., brokerage firm.

3   **even during the tight labor market of the late 1950s**   These quotations are from the original manuscripts of the 1957 Hussey Report that surveyed firms in Philadelphia. See Goldin (1990), Data Appendix, 1957 Hussey Report. "Mothers of young children" is from Equitable Life Assurance Society; "Married women with" was offered by Penn Mutual Life Insurance Company; and "Pregnancy is cause" was given by Provident Mutual Life Insurance Company.

4   **two-thirds of the gender-based difference in earnings**   See chapter 8 and Goldin (2014) for the calculation.

4   **—if women were the doctors and men were the nurses** See the discussion of physician hours and pay by gender in chapter 10.

5   **In the first few years of employment, the pay gap is modest** See chapter 8 for a further discussion of the data for college graduates and MBAs.

5   **almost 45 percent of twenty-five-year-old women . . . for men is just 36 percent** Author's calculations using the data sources cited in the notes to figure 2.5; also those for Online Appendix figure 4A (Ch2), "College Graduation Rates for Males and Females by Race (at Age Thirty)," extrapolated to the 1998 birth year. (Unless otherwise attributed, all statistics in this chapter related to college graduation rates come from these sources.)

6   **more women than men have graduated** See Goldin, Katz, and Kuziemko (2006).

6   **So college-graduate women born around the early 1970s have a considerably higher birth rate** The data on births come from the June Fertility Supplements to the CPS. These will be discussed in detail in a later chapter. It is still too early to know the precise impact the COVID pandemic and the recessionary economy have had on conceptions and thus future births, but there is some evidence that a baby bust will soon be apparent.

7   **"It's hard—but do it."** Yohalem (1979), p. 52.

7   **the median age at first marriage . . . was about twenty-three years old** See figure 6.1, for which the median marriage age is graphed by birth year. Until around the 1948 birth year, the median marriage age was about 23, thus the turning point is about 1971.

8   **After 1970, the age at first marriage started to increase** See figure 6.1.

8   **The fraction of women with children has startlingly increased** See figure 2.3, which is given as the fraction without a birth by age. On the impact of assisted-reproductive methods, see chapter 7.

Chapter Two

18   **born in Hellgate Township, Montana Territory** 1880 US Census Manuscripts. The area was called Grant Creek and Hell Gate Valley in the 1880 census manuscripts and Hellgate Township in 1910.

18   **"As a woman I cannot go to war"** Office of History and Preservation, Office of the Clerk, U.S. House of Representatives (2006), p. 40.

18   **who were elected as US Representatives** The figure is for those elected, as opposed to those appointed, which is how some women at the time entered Congress after the death of their husbands who had held that House seat.

19   **Fast forward to Tammy Duckworth** Duckworth graduated from the University of Hawaii in 1989 and received an MA from George Washington University and a PhD from Capella University in 2015.

19   **Kirsten Gillibrand, born in 1966** Gillibrand graduated from Dartmouth College in 1988 and received a JD from UCLA School of Law in 1991.

19   **the other nine female members of Congress** Information on pregnancies and women in the House of Representatives is from: https://en.wikipedia.org/wiki/Women_in_the_United_States_House_of_Representatives#Pregnancies.

20   **when reliable, trustworthy sources were first recorded**   The US census for 1940 is the first that contains information on educational attainment. Prior to that date, information from college alumni and alumnae records can be used, and have been, by various researchers (Cookingham 1984; Solomon 1985). Such data are useful, and some will be employed here. But they are not large samples, are not national in scope, and are limited by the institution(s) in question.

21   **". . . Otherwise it is not a career but a job."**   Yohalem (1979), p. 54. The respondent had been, like all of Yohalem's subjects in 1974, a graduate or student at a Columbia University graduate division in the 1940s and was currently in her fifties. This particular respondent, like many in her group, never had children.

22   **". . . I haven't found a man who can cook."**   Sicherman and Green (1980), in the entry for Virginia Apgar.

22   **20 to 25 percent of economic growth since 1960**   See Hsieh, Jones, Hurst, and Klenow (2019).

25   **one half never had (or adopted) a child**   See Figure 2.3. Many of the statistics on children and marriage in this section come from Figures 2.2 and 2.3.

26   **less than 30 percent had children**   See figure 4.1.

29   **12 percent of college-graduate women divorced**   These data are from Isen and Stevenson (2010), table 3.1, who use the Survey of Income and Program Participation (SIPP). They are for white women. Black women's divorce rates were considerably higher than were those for white women for the group that married in the 1950s. Thus, their divorce rates were already substantial before the increase. There are no data given for groups that married before the 1950s. I have also used the SIPP data and find that among those born in the 1930s, 17 percent were divorced at ten years of marriage, and 32 percent were divorced at ten years for those born in the 1940s.

31   **". . . It's expected now,"**   Yohalem (1979), p. 52. The respondents had been graduate students at Columbia University in the late 1940s and were born from about 1919 to 1926.

31   **"The worst is to be left in middle age, . . ."**   Yohalem (1979), p. 53.

31   **29 percent did not**   Isen and Stevenson (2010), table 3.1, for white, college-graduate women. Among Black women, 32 percent were divorced before their twentieth wedding anniversary for those married in the 1960s, and 44 percent were for those married in the 1970s.

33   **The men in this group also increased in their own desire for those achievements**   The annual Higher Education Research Institute (HERI) CIRP Freshmen Surveys (also known as the Astin surveys) show that freshmen men and women increased their desire for both family and career from 1969 to the mid-1980s, when a plateau was reached where career and family were each proxied by answers to questions about various objectives. I thank Dev Patel for producing the trends from the micro data.

34   **data on same-sex unions and marriages**   The US Census first recorded same-sex partners with the 2000 ACS. Before that year, the US Census would generally have recoded the sex of one of the members of an unmarried couple of the same sex.

35   **the median age at marriage**   See figure 6.1, "Median Age at First Marriage for College-Graduate Women by Birth Year: 1925 to 1988." Such data can be reliably and consistently produced only starting with Group Three.

35   **Women who never attended college have had different marriage rates** See Online Appendix figure 1A (Ch2), "Fraction Never Married by Age and Birth Year for White Women with No College," and Online Appendix figure 2A (Ch2), "Difference in Fraction Never Married between College-Graduate and Noncollege White Women." The comparison being made is with women who received a high school degree and below rather than with women who did not graduate from college. The reason for excluding the "some college" group is because it is a group that changes composition across the century. Toward the end of the period, it appears more like the high school–graduate group. But early in the period, it includes those who went to teachers colleges. Until recently, it will include many who obtained RNs.

36   **but also remains low at older ages** There are many potential reasons why the fraction of Black college-graduate women who ever marry is considerably lower than it is for white college-graduate women, particularly for Group Five, for which it is about 10 percentage points lower at ages fifty to fifty-four. One is that Black men have not increased their fraction graduating from college to the same degree that Black women have. See Online Appendix figure 4A (Ch2), "College Graduation Rates for Males and Females by Race (at Age Thirty)."

36   **the fraction of births to unmarried, unpartnered** Lundberg, Pollak, and Stearns (2016), figure 3, p. 85. From 1980–1984 to 2009–2013, the fraction of births to college-graduate women, less than forty years old, currently unmarried and unpartnered (non-cohabiting), fell from 4 to 2.5 percent. The fraction of births to the same education and age group of women who were cohabiting rose from less than 1 percent to 7 percent. The underlying data come from the National Survey of Family Growth (NSFG). The most recent version of the NSFG, using a routine to include births to same-sex couples, also yields that only about 2.8 percent of all births to college-graduate women in 2014–2017 are from those without a partner.

36   **Adding adoptions increases the fraction** The higher frequency data come from the June CPS Fertility Supplements beginning in the early 1970s. Data on adoptions are derived from the American Community Survey for college-graduate women at forty-five years old born from the mid-1950s to the mid-1960s who had no biological children and no stepchildren.

37   **More than half the women in Group One** In computing these numbers, I have utilized data for two older five-year groups to extend the birth information for Group One to 1880. Not much of the group is observed for the forty- to forty-four-year-old age bracket. The reason is that the first national information on births and educational attainment is in the 1940 Population Census.

37   **More than 90 percent who married had a child** The calculation is based on the fact that 92 percent of these women ever married, and it assumes that no, or few, births occurred to women who never married.

37   **the average at peak fertility was 3.14 births** The data on the number of births is in Online Appendix figure 3A (Ch2), "Median Number of Births to College-Graduate Women," and is provided for the median without the zero-birth women and with them.

38   **The mean number of births is 1.8**   Compare with Group Four for which the mean number of births was just 1.6 and was 2.2 for those who ever had a birth.

38   **The labor force participation rates of ever-married**   The data have been gleaned from the decennial censuses from 1940 to 2000 and the ACS for subsequent years. Because the census is a decennial survey, employment data from the 1940 census will be influenced by the Great Depression and that from the 1950 census may have been impacted by the experiences of women during WWII. The discussion of the labor force data uses primarily information after those dates. Therefore, the conclusions are not as seriously influenced by those two major events. Group One cannot be included in the data analysis because the 1940 census data will only cover a small fraction of these women prior to their later ages.

38   **employment has increased almost steadily**   I will use the terms "employment" and "labor force participation" interchangeably. The labor force consists of those who are currently employed plus those who are unemployed and actively seeking work. If the unemployment rate is low, these are almost identical numbers.

38   **Consider employment rates . . . from age twenty-five**   The data begin with age twenty-five, allowing most to have completed their schooling.

39   **almost one in two females**   The actual number is 45 percent, but it continues to rise. Note that the data in figure 2.5 stop with the 1983 birth group, but the data can be extrapolated to the later birth years.

40   **two decades or more**   See Online Appendix figure 4A (Ch2), "College Graduation Rates for Males and Females by Race (at Age Thirty)."

40   **aberrant decrease was due to reductions in the draft**   The female series contains similar, but far less extreme, anomalies—even though women were not drafted. Women's college decisions were influenced by men's. Part of the influence concerned dating and marriage, and another had to do with whether families that sent a son to college would be more likely to send a daughter.

40   **the crossover point when more women**   Goldin, Katz, and Kuziemko (2006) explore the reasons for the relative increase in women's educational levels in the US and elsewhere in the world.

40   **considers individuals born around the same year**   The data series of those born around the same year was constructed using census household surveys.

41   **far more males than females in college**   The two series are given in Online Appendix figure 5A (Ch2), "Ratio of Males to Females in College by College Attendance Year and Birth Year." The comparison of the two series assumes that graduation occurred at age twenty-two, although many individuals did not graduate that young, especially when men were being drafted or women were returning to school after raising their children.

42   **Most of the excess men were returning GIs**   Korean War GIs account for part of the difference, but another portion is because the US had a peacetime draft, and some male college students had done military service.

42   **40 percent of females attended a single-sex school**   Online Appendix table 1A (Ch2), "Fraction of Male and Female College Students in Coeducational Institutions: 1897 to 1980." See also Goldin and Katz (2011), and the underlying data of that project, for information on coeducation in US college history.

43   **Radcliffe/Harvard College**   I use the name "Radcliffe" women even though they become "Harvard" women at some point, depending on one's definition. For some, the coeducational turning point is 1943, when Harvard men and Radcliffe women took courses together. For others, the transition is 1963, when the diplomas of both were conferred by the "President and Fellows of Harvard College." Yet other turning points include the early 1970s, when the admission processes were merged and dorms became coeducational, and the 1977 "non-merger merger," when admission to Radcliffe meant a woman was enrolled in Harvard College.

43   **reduced the need for special preparation**   Lemann (2000).

43   **early 1900s to those graduating in the late 1970s**   See Source Appendix (Ch3), "Radcliffe Alumnae Questionnaire of 1928"; (Ch5), "Radcliffe College Centennial Survey, 1977"; and (Ch7), "Harvard and Beyond Project." Marriage rates are given to the late 1970s so that only women who were already beyond their late forties are included.

43   **from around 1900 onward**   See Online Appendix figure 6A (Ch2), "Comparing Marriages and Births for Radcliffe/Harvard Graduates with All College Graduates." The earliest birth group provides an exception. The nonmarriage rate for Group One was higher for Radcliffe graduates than for all female college graduates in the US. For those born before 1900, an astounding 50 percent of the Radcliffe group were not yet married by age 50, whereas 30 percent of all college-graduate women were in that category.

43   **Similar changes can be seen in the birth data**   The fraction with no children was exceptionally low for the Radcliffe group in Group Three. It is possible that respondents to the survey were disproportionately those who had children. Reunions generally attract individuals who have children or who are famous (or both). But the Radcliffe Centennial surveys were mailed and were not circulated or collected at a reunion.

44   **female graduates of single-sex colleges accounted for a small portion of the total**   Online Appendix table 1A (Ch2) provides data on the fraction of males and females in single-sex versus coeducational institutions from 1897 to the present.

44   **succession of generations**   The term "succession of generations" is due to the labor economist John Dana Durand (1948).

45   **5 percentage points more likely to marry**   Online Appendix figure 2A (Ch2) provides the difference in marriage rates between the college-graduate and the noncollege women.

Chapter Three

46   **"one of the ancients."**   August 14, 2019, e-mail from Hugh Rockoff (University of Chicago PhD, 1972). "My memory [of Margaret Reid] is almost the same as yours. People would say: 'There goes one of the ancients. She was important and, amazingly, she is still doing research!' The only thing I remember about her work is that she was involved in the controversy over the cost of living index in WW2."

46   **Instead, I regarded her**   August 11, 2019, e-mail from James Smith (University of Chicago PhD, 1972) notes, "I did interact with [Margaret Reid] some; she did attend the Becker workshop." Therefore, students with serious interests in her field did have contact with her. My interest in the field blossomed sometime after I left graduate school.

48   **the National Bureau of Economic Research (NBER)**   In the late 1970s, the NBER moved to Cambridge, Massachusetts, and had a new mission. I have been one of its research associates since 1978 and directed one of its earliest program for twenty-eight years, from 1989 to 2017.

48   **Congress asked the NBER if it could borrow Kuznets**   US Congress (1934). The final report notes (p. xi), "Dr. Kuznets, who was in full charge of the work, was responsible for the preparation of the final estimates, as well as the organization and the text of the report."

48   **In his report to Congress, he noted**   US Congress (1934), p. 4.

49   **A central argument is that**   For a modern view see Folbre (2001).

49   **After a stint in the federal government**   From 1943 to 1944, Reid served as an economic advisor to the Division of Statistical Standards in the Bureau of the Budget, and from 1945 to 1948 she was the head of the Family Economics Division in the US Department of Agriculture.

50   **(although Kyrk raised her cousin's teenage daughter)**   At various times, Kyrk lived with the children of her female cousin Don Kyrk Strine (daughter of her uncle Luther), who eventually had five daughters and two sons. When Kyrk was living in Ames, Iowa, the 1925 Iowa State Census manuscripts list her living with the oldest of the Strine children, Ruth, age fourteen. Kyrk's entry in *Notable American Women* refers to Ruth as her "foster daughter." In 1940, when Kyrk was living in both Washington, DC, and Chicago, she is listed as living with both Margarite, age twenty-seven, and Mary Strine, age twenty-three. Ancestry.com provided the census entries. The name Strine is given as Struie in *Notable*. But members of the family are clearly listed with the name Strine in the censuses and in death records. But it should be noted that Elizabeth Nelson, who wrote the entry, communicated with Ruth, so it isn't clear whether this is a typo or a factual error.

50   **I have no statements, expressed earlier**   International travel documents do not reveal any instances of female companions for either Reid or Kyrk. Census documents do not list any female companions or roommates for Reid. In Kyrk's case, census documents show that she lived with her nieces for some period, and that she boarded in 1920 with the mathematician Mary Emily Sinclair and her young children during a brief stint at Oberlin College.

50   **they each supported themselves in college**   Kyrk is listed in the 1900 census manuscripts with her father, Elmer, a teamster. Her mother had recently passed away. Kyrk taught school before she went to Ohio Wesleyan, where she was an au pair for professor of economics Leon Carroll Marshall, who became dean of the University of Chicago Business School (now the Booth School). She went with his family to Chicago, where she received her bachelor's in 1910. She then taught at Wellesley College and returned to Chicago to pursue a PhD, which she combined with teaching at Oberlin College. WWI broke out, and she went to London with her advisor to work as a statistician. She received her PhD from the University of Chicago in 1920.

51   **30 percent never married and 50 percent never had children**   See figure 2.2.

51   **less than 12 percent**   Recall from an earlier discussion that the rate has been especially high for Black college-graduate women born since the 1960s.

51   **These differences are not due to selection**   See the earlier discussion that compares marriage and childbearing rates for Radcliffe/Harvard graduates to those for the entire college-graduate population in the US. That comparison demonstrates that selection into college had little impact on the changes in marriage and childbearing rates over time since the Radcliffe/Harvard group had fairly similar selection over time and yet its demographic changes are almost identical to those of all college-graduate women.

52   **But Amherst wasn't going to be**   According to the US Census manuscripts, Dorothy and Paul were in Chicago in 1930 with their four children. Dorothy is listed as a "teacher, college" and Paul as a "professor." Dorothy left for Smith College soon after. In the 1940 US Census manuscripts, she is at Northampton, listed as a "teacher college," with the four children, all teenagers, and Katharine Lumpkin, who is an "economic researcher." She and Lumpkin wrote *Child Workers in America* and remained together as a couple for thirty years.

52   **having both a career and a family was difficult**   Similar to US historical data, in many parts of Asia today young women with advanced degrees have very low marriage rates. Social norms often dictate that they should be housewives and not pursue time-consuming careers. Hwang (2016) discusses the "Gold Miss" phenomenon in Korea and Japan.

52   **high levels of infant and child mortality**   See Alsan and Goldin (2019).

52   **fully 9 percent experienced at least one infant or child death**   The 9 percent figure comes from the entries in the several volumes of *Notable American Women* (Sicherman and Green 1980; Ware and Braukman 2004) for the college-graduate women in Group One.

53   **even professors**   On the reasons for the long-term decline in infant and child mortality, see Alsan and Goldin (2019). Preston and Haines (1991) explore socioeconomic status and infant mortality in 1900.

53   **Each volume contains information on women who died during a set of years**   Sicherman and Green (1980) contains the biographies of those who died from 1951 to 1975; Ware and Braukman (2004) contains those who died from 1976 to 1999. The first three volumes contain biographies of all the women who died up to 1951. Members of Group One who died before 1951 are in the first three volumes. They are not part of the dataset and would have died from their fifties to early seventies.

53   **contain enough entries to be studied**   The women included from more recent birth groups would have died at relatively young ages. There are, thankfully, few of them.

54   **just 20 percent had no biological or adopted**   Among the notables who ever married, a lower fraction, 45 percent, had no children, and among all college-graduate women who ever married, the figure is 29 percent. The fraction for the notable group is a bit higher (36 percent) for those who married before age thirty-five. See figure 4.1.

54   **sabbatical leave during their infancy**   The 1920 US Census listing for Mary Emily Sinclair has her residing in Oberlin, Ohio, with two young children (incorrectly identified as her niece and nephew) and with Hazel Kyrk, identified as a boarder. See also https://www.agnesscott.edu/LRiddle/women/sinclair.htm.

55   **around 30 percent . . . and 17 percent had a career and eventually married by their fifties**   The calculation is described in Online Appendix (Ch3), "Calculating the 'Success' Matrix for Group One."

56 **a husband to drag to the event**   I am not considering the possibility that their husband predeceases them and they do not remarry.

56 **attended more often than those without**   The Radcliffe 1928 survey and that done in 1977 indicate a higher fraction who never married for those born before 1920 than for the nation as a whole but a lower fraction for those born after 1920. This disparity suggests that Radcliffe reunions in the 1950s disproportionately brought out those with children, but that there was less selection on having children before.

56 **most of their postschool years**   We know that fact from tabulating the fraction who were in the labor force in 1940 when they were in their forties. For all women with four or more years of college, 0.923 were in the labor force for those forty to forty-four years old, and 0.893 were for those forty-five to forty-nine years old. These are very high fractions.

57 **25 percent rate was exceptionally high**   Based on the SIPP (Survey of Income Programs and Participation), the divorce rate for marriages entered into during the 1920s is around 20 percent for those that lasted around fifteen years and for which the woman was a college graduate. The marriages for the notables in Group One were a bit earlier. See Stevenson and Wolfers (2007) for a description of the procedure used.

57 **a tireless crusader against child labor**   Both Edith and Grace Abbott, like Hazel Kyrk, had to earn money to attend college. After graduating from the University of Nebraska, Edith Abbott won a scholarship to attend the University of Chicago, where she was a student of another female social scientist, Sophonisba Breckinridge (1866–1948). Grace Abbott graduated from Grand Island College and also eventually wound up at the University of Chicago. The two Abbott sisters and Breckinridge worked together to assist immigrant women in training for employment.

58 **graduated a large number**   On the history of the Home Economics and Household Administration Department at the University of Chicago, see https://www.lib.uchicago.edu/collex/exhibits/exoet/home-economics/.

58 **when FDR was governor**   Perkins was initially named a member of the State Industrial Commission by New York State governor Al Smith.

58 **unfit for marriage and motherhood**   Cookingham (1984) contains a discussion of the claims and their proponents.

59 **The majority were schoolteachers**   Shinn (1895). Shinn was the first woman to receive a PhD from the University of California. The quotation is: "It may very safely be answered . . . that it is *not* because they crave a more exciting and public life; for the majority . . . are school-teachers" (p. 947).

59 **"unhappy marriages are virtually unknown . . ."**   Shinn (1895), p. 948.

59 **"dislike intellectual women."**   Shinn (1895), p. 948.

59 **"You must know again my reluctance . . ."**   Grunwald and Adler (2005), p. 516.

59 **A clear majority supported themselves financially**   Davis (1928). She notes that 46 percent were between thirty and thirty-nine years old, and that almost 80 percent were thirty years and older. She does not mention who did the survey and when it was done, but since it was a "questionnaire on the sex life of the normal unmarried college graduate out of college for at least five years," it was probably done by Davis, who was a researcher at the Bureau of Social Hygiene and headed the bureau from 1918 to 1928. Davis, it should be noted, was a eugenicist whose work at the Bureau of Social Hygiene

was mainly in the area of criminology and the possible genetic basis of criminal behavior.

60   **few would have been able to achieve that**   The questionnaire apparently allowed the respondents to give open-ended answers. Interestingly, 1.6 percent said that they did not marry because they had "homo-sexual relations." Davis did not note that her data came from her work on sexuality and that almost 30 percent of the sample of unmarried college women had had lesbian relations at some time (see 1929, p. 272). Not surprisingly, a larger fraction of the women who did not have lesbian relations said that they did not marry because they "never met the right man."

60   **"noted sociological worker."**   See "Katharine B. Davis Converted to Wets: Social Worker, Long Friendly to Prohibition, Now Favors Control by States," *New York Times*, May 26, 1930.

60   **particularly the study of prostitutes**   Not much has been written on Katharine Bement Davis. The best description of her life is in Gilette (2018).

60   **drawn from *her* survey on sexuality**   See Davis (1929, p. 272) for the table included in Davis (1928). One important difference is that in her book on sexuality she separates the women who had lesbian relationships from those who did not. In her group of twelve hundred unmarried college women, about 30 percent had self-professed homosexual relations. Her book devotes nearly a hundred pages to the subject of homosexuality.

60   **The survey reveals much**   The 1928 Radcliffe survey was distributed by mail during the semicentennial celebration of Radcliffe. Almost nineteen hundred Radcliffe BAs, who graduated from the 1880s to the 1920s, responded to the survey. The full sample is around three thousand but includes special students, graduate students, and those who transferred or did not graduate. The fractions giving a "yes" answer to "career and marriage" and "motherhood and marriage" being possible are interpreted as "unconditionally agreeing" since the "hopeful" group is listed as a "conditional yes." These questions were asked only of those who "ever married." The calculation treats a "no" answer as a negative. See Solomon (1985, 1989) and Source Appendix (Ch3), "Radcliffe Alumnae Questionnaire of 1928."

62   **due to racial discrimination**   "As soon as an [academic] employer discovered I was black, that was it," she remarked in an interview given in 1981 to a geriatric nursing group. See https://www.sciencedirect.com/science/article/pii/S0197457281800936.

Chapter Four

63   **"frank descriptions of sex, contraception and breast-feeding,"**   See Elizabeth Day, "*The Group* by Mary McCarthy," *The Guardian*, November 28, 2009, https://www.theguardian.com/books/2009/nov/29/the-group-mary-mccarthy.

63   **"quaint MacDougal Avenue and Patchin Place"**   All quotes in this chapter from *The Group* come from McCarthy (1963).

65   **to the birth years from 1898 to 1914 and the second to those from 1915 to 1923**   Women were included in the *Notable* volumes only if they met certain criteria and died up to the dates of selection. Since the women for the final volume, number five, were chosen in the late 1990s, those in the second Group Two collection would have died younger than

those in the first. The mean age at death for the first group is eighty but is just sixty-eight for the second group. There are also a lot more women in the first group than the second, as they had more time to become "notable." The median age at death is almost the same as the mean, so outliers are not pulling the mean for each group disproportionately up or down.

67   **nearly identical to those for all college-graduate women**   The data for noncollege women are given in Online Appendix figure 1A (Ch2), "Fraction Never Married by Age and Birth Year for White Women with No College." See also Online Appendix figure 2A (Ch2), "Difference in Fraction Never Married between College-Graduate and Noncollege White Women."

68   **less sensational innovations were enormous**   For an excellent, but complicated, interpretation of the impact of a host of household appliances and public utility innovations, see Greenwood (2019). Greenwood, Seshadri, and Yorukoglu (2005), Online Appendix, provides the data on household electricity diffusion and household electrical appliance adoption.

69   **until the early 1900s**   The 1900 Census of Occupations (US Bureau of the Census 1904) lists 327,586 female teachers (excluding those at the college level and of music and art) and a total of 431,179 in all professional service. The office and sales category was somewhat smaller, with 85,269 clerks and copyists, 86,158 stenographers and typists, and 74,186 bookkeepers and accountants.

69   **number in clerical work increased by more than 8 times**   In 1900 there were 431,179 women in professional service work (the majority of whom were teachers). In 1930 there were 1,526,234. In 1900 there were 260,963 clerical workers (clerks, typists, stenographers, telephone operators, and bookkeepers), but in 1930 there were 1,986,830 (US Bureau of the Census 1904, 1933).

69   **also the case for most other white-collar female workers**   US Bureau of the Census (1904, 1933). There were 327,586 female non-college teachers in 1900, and 853,987 in 1930.

70   **far greater impact on women than on men**   Rotella (1981) provides one of the best, earliest, and most comprehensive examinations of the rise of the clerical and office sector for women's employment.

71   **From 1910 to 1940, high schools mushroomed**   On the "high school movement" see Goldin and Katz (2008), chapters 5 and 6. The "academies" that preceded many of the high schools were not elite preparatory schools, many of which had been founded earlier, some in the eighteenth century.

72   **incentivize men to work in the labor market**   The norm was far less apparent for Black women and their families since they had high employment rates in agriculture and domestic service early on. It is not clear whether the absence of the norm meant that society did not care about the burdens on Black women or that there wasn't a need to incentivize Black men.

72   **the stigma regarding married women's employment decreased**   See Goldin (1990, 2006) on the reasons for the increase in the female labor force over the long run.

72   **The rise of the ordinary white-collar sector was a game changer**   The rise of clerical work was not a game changer in the 1920s for Black women, who often couldn't access those jobs even if they had the requisite education. In an extensive set of surveys of

firms hiring clerical workers in 1939, managers and human resource personnel admitted to extensive bias on the part of other clerical workers about working with Black women. See Goldin (2014a) for a discussion of the surveys and their content.

73 **Careful analysis demonstrates that around half the total change** Without constructing an elaborate model and testing for time effects versus group effects (which economists call "cohort effects"), we can do something simple and look at changes by age versus changes by time. About 25 percent of those born in 1902 were in the labor force at age thirty-two, but 37 percent were for those born around 1917. Similar increases are found for all age groups. At the same time, changes within a woman's life cycle are also great. All told, for the birth groups from 1900 to 1930, probably around half of the increase was due to changes across the life cycle and half to time-series changes. There was around a 20 percentage point change from age twenty-seven to age forty-two, and there was a 10 percentage point change for either twenty-seven- or forty-two-year-olds. (Data refer to ever-married, white, college-graduate women from the various US census micro data.)

74 **Marriage bars were the hiring and firing policies** The marriage-bar policies were not unique to the US and existed for teachers and other professionals in Great Britain, Ireland, and Australia, among other countries.

75 **The Depression did just the reverse** Goldin (1991) uses surveys from the 1930s and school district compilations for the early twentieth century to analyze the institution of marriage bars and its expansion during the Great Depression.

76 **policy that fired single women** Goldin (1991). The data come from the original manuscripts of a Woman's Bureau Bulletin. The almost two hundred firms were located in Philadelphia and Kansas City. Data for a third city—Los Angeles—are lower (25 percent and 10 percent).

76 **What data are available show that marriage bars** The earlier data are for 1931, and it is difficult to know whether the policies existed before the downturn. Because these were actual policies, it is likely that firms did not have enough time to frame new human resource regulations. The 1931 study included 178 firms in Chicago, Hartford, New York City, and Philadelphia. The means weighted by female employment are about five percentage points lower than those for 1940 for the marriage-bar policy, but are similar for the retention policy.

77 **In 1940, among the women in Group Two, about 65 percent of Black** These differences probably persisted back to the 1920s, if not before, but information on education and employment begins with the 1940 population census.

77 **far less than in the white community** See Goldin (1977).

78 **In 1920, the fraction married among Black schoolteachers** See Online Appendix table 1A (Ch4), "Fraction Married among Teachers by Age, Race, and Region."

79 **"The marriage of any lady . . ."** Pedersen (1987) provides a detailed account of the case with interviews of the two women. Quotations in this section regarding the case come from this source.

80 **"Effective immediately and until further notice: . . ."** IBM letter #3930 from A. L. Williams, Vice President and Treasurer, to WHQ Executives and Department Managers, and others. January 10, 1951, https://thesocietypages.org/socimages/2010/06/23/ibm-decides-to-let-women-work-after-marriage-1951/.

80   **"friendly skies" became a little bit friendlier**   See *Sprogis v. United Air Lines, Inc.*, 308 F. Supp. 959 (N.D. Ill. 1970), and *Romasanta v. United Airlines, Inc.*, 537 F.2d 915 (7th Cir. 1976). United was just one of many airlines in the 1960s that barred married female flight attendants. The Sprogis case was brought in 1966; the Romasanta case, a class-action lawsuit for back pay, was brought in 1970. United's slogan (initiated in 1965) is "fly the friendly skies."

81   **"married women should plan . . ."**   These quotations are from the manuscripts of a 1931 Office Firm Survey that I collected. See Goldin (1990), Data Appendix. "Less efficient after marriage" was written by Indemnity Insurance Company of North America; "men are too selfish" is by F. A. Davis and Company Publishing.

81   **"possibility of collusion . . ."**   Philadelphia Saving Fund Society (December 6, 1956), 1957 Hussey Report. See Goldin (1990), Data Appendix.

81   **"oleomargarine controversy"**   See Seim (2008) on the details.

83   **shift to true coeducation**   By "true coeducation," I mean the ability of women to take the same courses as men together with them (and vice versa). Harvard/Radcliffe was not fully coeducational in 1943, and many coeducational institutions also suffered from similar defects. Radcliffe women could not use Lamont Library, for example. But their ability to sit in most of the same classes was an enormous change.

Chapter Five

84   **"While you are my wife . . ."**   From the episode "Brother Ralph" (8:44), https://www.youtube.com/watch?v=OmadqPZvjoM.

84   **"It's out of the question"**   There are many episodes of *I Love Lucy* in which Ricky tries, often unsuccessfully, to prevent Lucy from being employed. See, for example, season 1, episode 30, "Lucy Does a TV Commercial," or season 3 episode 2, "The Girls Go into Business."

85   **"truly feminine women do not want careers, . . ."**   Friedan (2013, orig. pub. 1963), p. 14.

86   **"Fewer and fewer women were entering professional work."**   Friedan (2013, orig. pub. 1963). The quotations in this paragraph are from pages 14, 112, 15, and 15.

86   **The past wasn't rosier than the present**   In his fascinating biography of Friedan, Daniel Horowitz (1998) explored the veracity of her claims that she had been a suburban housewife and not a feminist prior to the writing of her book. He also noted that the responses from the survey of her Smith College class were more positive than she led on in her extensive summary (p. 209). According to Horowitz, Friedan reinvented herself and gave her respondents a more jaundiced view of their lives.

86   **Whereas 5.8 percent**   Graduating college is defined by either finishing four years of college or earning a bachelor's degree. See figure 2.5, "College Graduation Rates for Males and Females (at Age Thirty)."

86   **The fraction of college-graduate women receiving advanced degrees**   These facts have been gleaned from the National Survey of College Graduates (NSCG), 1993 to 2015, for individuals obtaining their undergraduate degrees from the 1940s to the 1990s. I compute the fraction of an undergraduate class by sex who later received an advanced academic degree (MA, PhD) or a professional degree (such as JD, MD, MBA). There

was considerable growth in that fraction from the 1940s to the 1970s for women. The fraction for men increased somewhat but then declined with undergraduate degree classes around the 1970s, probably because graduate work was no longer a draft deferment.

86   **expanded by three times**   The fraction of all women graduating from college increased from 0.058 to 0.12, and the fraction of those who graduated from college who received an advanced degree increased from 0.3 to 0.43. Therefore, the fraction of all women born around 1940 relative to those born around 1920 who received an advanced degree increased by three times = $(0.43 \times 0.12)/(0.3 \times 0.058)$.

86   **a greater fraction of elite college-graduate women**   See Online Appendix table 1A (Ch5), "Fraction of Radcliffe Alumnae with Advanced Degrees by Graduation Year: 1900 to 1969." Adding in master's degrees brings the total for the 1920s and 1930s graduating classes to 38 percent. But among those who graduated from college in the late 1950s, the figure is an astounding 57 percent.

87   **In fact, the dropout rate was actually lower**   The comparison is between those born from 1934 to 1945 and those born from around 1910 to the early 1930s. The dropout rate is computed as one minus the ratio of those who graduated college (in four years–plus) to those who attended at least one year of college, using data from the US Census and CPS. The ratio rises from 40 percent to 50 percent for groups born from 1934 to 1945. Although these numbers would seem to support Friedan's 60 percent dropout figure, the ratio for men, computed in the same manner, was around 50 percent. The reason both rates are so high is that some of these college-going students went to two-year colleges and did not actually drop out.

87   **7 percent in the 1950s and just 3 percent**   The data come from Radcliffe College Student Directories, http://listview.lib.harvard.edu/lists/drs-43586165. Many women left college during WWII to do volunteer work and returned after a year or more, creating problems with the dropout metric for the 1940s.

88   **Though their husbands were less opposed to their jobs**   From US Department of Labor, Women's Bureau (1966). See Online Appendix table 3A (Ch5). Just 83 percent of their husbands were not opposed.

88   **". . . the best thing to do would be to stay home. . . ."**   Both quotations in this paragraph are from 1957 Women's Bureau survey, resurvey comments in 1964. See Source Appendix (Ch5), "Women's Bureau 1957 Survey and 1964 Resurvey."

88   **Only around 30 percent**   Data for the graduating class of 1957 give a figure of 26 percent seven years after graduation for women with children less than six years old, and 37 percent for those with children less than six but older than one year. For the graduating class of 1961 three years after graduation, 37 percent were employed among those with children. *Sources:* US Department of Labor, Women's Bureau (1966); micro data sample from the National Archives; *Great Aspirations* micro data. See Source Appendix (Ch5), "Women's Bureau 1957 Survey and 1964 Resurvey"; (Ch5): "*Great Aspirations* Data."

88   **". . . it is not sensible to work just to pay a babysitter."**   1957 Women's Bureau survey, resurvey comments in 1964.

89   **Matters only got worse for married women**   For the data and facts cited about marriage bars, see Goldin (1991). See also figure 4.2.

90   **She took a position at Smith College**   Both Dorothy and Paul received PhDs in economics from Columbia University, he in 1920 and she around 1923. They divorced in 1930, and their four children remained with Dorothy in Northampton. See https://www.bowdoin.edu/economics/curriculum-requirements/douglas-biography.shtml.

90   **introduced her to radical economic ideas**   Horowitz (1998), p. 52. The course was Economics 319, which offered a relatively radical treatment of labor movements in US history. Friedan learned about the class struggle, the oppressiveness of capitalism, and other fairly left-wing notions. Most important to Horowitz's argument is that she was exposed to sophisticated feminist thought. According to Horowitz, Friedan's assertion that she knew little of feminism until she wrote *The Feminine Mystique* was given to conceal her left-wing, Communist background.

90   **By the 1950s, marriage bars were largely thrown out**   See chapter 4 of this book and Goldin (1991).

90   **"Previously, the personnel department did not favor . . ."**   1957 Hussey Report manuscripts. See Goldin (1990), Data Appendix.

91   **(Female graduation rates eventually overtook those of males . . .)**   See figure 2.5, "College Graduation Rates for Males and Females (at Age Thirty)."

91   **education "is security."**   1957 Women's Bureau survey, resurvey comments in 1964.

91   **Not in terms of the eventual education of the man she would marry**   See Online Appendix figure 1A (Ch5), part B, which shows the percentage of women by education level who married a college-graduate man. For a woman born in 1932, for example, the fraction is 70 percent for a college-graduate woman but 50 percent for one who dropped out after three years of college. The difference of 20 percentage points holds for all birth years from 1912 to 1950.

91   **And not in terms of her general well-being**   There is a large literature on the causal returns to college in terms of health and earnings. On the latter, see Zimmerman (2014). On the causal relationship between a woman's education and her children's education, see Currie and Moretti (2003).

92   **there were 2.3 men per woman in college**   These data come from Online Appendix figure 5A (Ch2), "Ratio of Males to Females in College by College Attendance Year and Birth Year." The peak of 2.3 for the ratio of men to women in college was reached just after WWII. In the mid-1950s the ratio was 1.7.

92   **The fraction stayed high for graduating groups**   See Online Appendix figure 1A (Ch5), "Percentage Marrying a College-Graduate Man by Woman's Education for Married Women Born from 1912 to 1980." To compute the year of graduation, I assume that women graduate college at twenty-two years old.

93   **Economic downturns generally cause**   See Easterlin (1980) on the role of economic downturns and the age at first marriage.

93   **Americans married earlier**   Similarly, those in other nations had a spike in fertility after WWII, but only in the US did the Baby Boom last for decades.

94   **Almost 60 percent of college-graduate women gave birth**   See figure 2.3.

94   **about 30 percent of the college group never married**   For information on how much later the noncollege group married and the fraction who never married, see Online Appendix figure 2A (Ch2), "Difference in Fraction Never Married between College-Graduate and Noncollege White Women."

95   **A college major usually indicates the job or career path**   The US Department of Education collected data on college majors beginning with the graduating class of 1968. Information on college majors in the past comes from a variety of sources. Although the general levels and trends are similar, there are slight differences. I have used all available surveys of the National Survey of College Graduates (NSCG) to obtain the fraction of college graduation groups with various majors.

95   **According to the class of 1957 survey**   The difference between the class of 1957 survey data (Online Appendix table 3A [Ch5], "Selected Demographic and Economic Features of Female College Graduates: Class of June 1957, Surveyed in January 1958 and 1964") and those from the NSCG (Online Appendix table 2A [Ch5], "Fraction of Female Graduates in Selected College Majors by Year of College Graduation"), in the estimate of the fraction of college graduates majoring in education, is probably because NSCG respondents listed education even if the major was in another subject but teaching credentials had been obtained. The NSCG respondents were listing a major that had been completed thirty or more years before the survey was taken, whereas the class of 1957 respondents had recently graduated.

96   **"is an ideal career for a woman who wants to have a family . . ."**   Yohalem (1979), p. 53.

97   **college-graduate women of the 1950s, by the end**   The notion that the members of the graduating classes in the early 1900s had lower eventual success rates for career than did those in the 1950s comes from evidence on their labor force participation rates when they were in their forties. I later present estimates of career and family success by group.

97   **Most planned their escape long before Friedan**   Steinmann et al. (2005) is a revealing compilation of the life stories of female graduates of the Cornell University class of 1950, written to dispel the "great myth, a prevailing—and quite erroneous—stereotype."

98   **In January 1958, the Women's Bureau**   For the sources of the data in this section, see Online Appendix table 3A (Ch5), "Selected Demographic and Economic Features of Female College Graduates: Class of June 1957, Surveyed in January 1958 and 1964."

98   **The initial survey of the 1957 class**   US Department of Labor, Women's Bureau (1959, 1966). The precise numbers of observations are 5,846 in the original 1957 survey (more than 70 percent of the initial 8,200 canvassed), of whom 4,930 responded seven years later in the resurvey (almost 85 percent of the original survey group). The survey and the resurvey were all accomplished by mail. See Source Appendix (Ch5), "Women's Bureau 1957 Survey and 1964 Resurvey."

99   **Just 7 percent of the entire group**   Another 8 percent were attending school and not working.

99   **confident that they would eventually return—**   Just 2 percent of the total group answered that they had no plans "to work in foreseeable future." Another 6 percent said they would work in the future "only as necessary—for economic reasons." Therefore, just 8 percent were doubtful that they would be employed at some future time.

99   **"I am a housewife and mother . . ."**   From the original 1964 survey documents in the National Archives. See Source Appendix (Ch5), "Women's Bureau 1957 Survey and 1964 Resurvey."

100   **just 20 percent of the women and 30 percent of the men**   The trends are almost identical for college-graduate men and women as they are for all individuals in figure 5.1, except that the responses of the college-graduate women are 10 percentage points lower for every birth group. The trend for the college-graduate men is almost the same as for all men, and the levels are only slightly lower at times. The college-graduate sample is small.

101   **83 percent of their husbands were not opposed . . . just 21 percent of the husbands**   From US Department of Labor, Women's Bureau (1966). See Online Appendix table 3A (ch5).

101   **her husband "considers my role of mother and wife . . ."**   From the original 1964 survey documents in the National Archives. See Source Appendix (Ch5), "Women's Bureau 1957 Survey and 1964 Resurvey."

101   **"I want a career in social work. . . ."**   Quotations are from the original 1957 survey documents in the National Archives. See Source Appendix (Ch5), "Women's Bureau 1957 Survey and 1964 Resurvey." The survey asked respondents to write comments especially "on ways in which your college work might have been made more valuable." That is why most of the comments in 1957 concern their college courses and majors.

103   **Insights from the class of 1957**   For the sources of the data in this section, see Online Appendix table 4A (Ch5), "Selected Demographic and Economic Features of Female Graduates: Class of 1961, Surveyed in Spring 1961, 1962, 1963, 1964, and 1968."

103   **more extensive survey was taken four years later**   *Great Aspirations* is a population-based sample of almost thirty-six thousand graduating seniors (including thirteen thousand women) of the class of 1961 from 135 colleges and universities across the US. Follow-up surveys were requested each year to 1964 and again in 1968. A special women's supplement was added in 1964. Some attrition occurred across the subsequent surveys, but all samples are reasonably large.

103   **one appropriately titled *Great Aspirations***   See Davis (1964).

103   **rediscovered this treasure trove of information**   As of 2018, all the survey materials, from 1961 to 1968, were discovered and reassembled by me and my research assistants. The reasons why the *Great Aspirations* survey was left unused for fifty years can be found in Source Appendix (Ch5): "*Great Aspirations* Data."

103   **Almost all intended to be employed upon graduation**   In spring 1961, just 9 percent said they would be a "housewife" upon graduation; 46 percent said they would do "full-time career work," and 25 percent intended to continue their education with or without employment.

103   **Most would marry soon after**   See Online Appendix table 4A (Ch5), "Selected Demographic and Economic Features of Female Graduates: Class of 1961, Surveyed in Spring 1961, 1962, 1963, 1964, and 1968."

103   **The majority planned to return to the workplace**   In 1962, just 20 percent stated that they realistically expected to be a housewife only, and 28 percent said they realistically expected to be a housewife with occasional employment. The rest, 52 percent, thought that they would eventually have employment.

104   **42 percent of the women were married less than a year out of college**   At the three-
      year mark, 67 percent of the 1961 class were married, and 63 percent of the married group
      had children.

104   **data on the achievements of all members of the 1961 undergraduate class**   Data on
      advanced degree completion for the class of 1961 are computed from the various waves
      of the National Survey of College Graduates, 1993 to 2015. Those data give about
      50 percent of the men and 40 percent of the women who received their undergraduate
      degree around 1961 having eventually achieved an advanced academic or professional
      degree. The spring 1962 *Great Aspirations* survey gives 15 percent for women and
      27 percent for men, but that would be less than the number who attended at any time
      during the year.

104   **About 60 percent of the women**   These data are higher than are those in figure 5.1,
      which is from the General Social Survey (GSS) for all individuals and thus would be
      even higher than for college graduates in the GSS. One reason is that the GSS data were
      collected more than twenty years after the data for *Great Aspirations* would have been.
      Another is that the GSS responses are binary, but I have grouped both "strongly" and
      "mildly" agreeing in the *Great Aspirations* responses.

108   **". . . Even under the 'so-called' merit system . . ."**   Quotations in this and the next
      paragraph are from the original 1964 survey documents in the National Archives. See
      Source Appendix (Ch5), "Women's Bureau 1957 Survey and 1964 Resurvey."

Chapter Six

110   **originally sparked by a federal antivice act**   These laws were legacies of a federal
      antivice act passed in 1873, known colloquially as the Comstock Act (the real name of
      which was Act of the Suppression of Trade in, and Circulation of, Obscene Literature
      and Articles of Immoral Use). That law was relatively unimportant, but it served to fuel
      the passage of state "Comstock" laws. The last of which, prohibiting the sale of contra-
      ceptives to unmarried individuals, was repealed in 1974 (*Baird v. Lynch* in Wisconsin
      Federal District Court).

110   **By 1974, that number expanded to twenty-seven states**   Goldin and Katz (2002)
      contains the years of the state law changes. These women could get the Pill de jure, but
      some women were entirely dependent on college and university health services to pro-
      vide it and may not have been able to obtain it easily.

110   **She was not entirely noble,**   On July 21, 2020, the *New York Times* reported that
      "Planned Parenthood of Greater New York will remove the name of Margaret Sanger, a
      founder of the national organization, from its Manhattan health clinic because of her
      harmful connections to the eugenics movement."

111   **received a BSc in biology from MIT in 1904**   Katharine Dexter was the first woman
      to graduate from MIT with an undergraduate degree in biology.

111   **more radical offshoots and factions**   The National Organization for Women
      (NOW) was founded in 1966. Soon after, a number of dissenting groups formed, in-
      cluding the NY Radical Women, the Chicago Women's Liberation Union, the Women's
      Equity Action League, and the Redstockings. Disagreement formed largely because

NOW had not sufficiently embraced the more radical issues of sexuality, the ERA, and reproductive rights.

113   **90 percent of the married female college graduates**   Based on the CPS, around 90 percent of ever-married, college-graduate women born 1933 to 1942 already had children by the time they were in their late thirties.

114   **around 20 percent of brides were pregnant**   See Smith and Hindus (1975). For the eighteenth and nineteenth centuries the authors link marriage and first birth records. These data are computed at wide intervals and are noisy. Some years (1770s, 1890s, late 1950s) have higher levels of premarital pregnancy, and some have lower levels. Even though there are large ups and downs in the historians' estimates for 1700 to 1950, the 20 percent figure is a reasonable long-run average. For the latter part of the twentieth century, the authors use data from the CPS, which has the dates of marriage and birth. The cutoff used for the difference is about eight months. Any birth that occurs within eight months of the marriage is deemed a premarital pregnancy. More recently, as the stigma to premarital sex has declined, premarital pregnancies have soared, particularly among lower-educated women.

114   **By 1970, the age at first intercourse decreased to eighteen and a half . . . by 1990 it was sixteen and a half**   Goldin and Katz (2002, figure 6). See also Finer (2007) for similar estimates using the same source. Note that these figures provide the median age for a population and do not require that the entire population ever had sexual intercourse.

115   **reduced divorce by increasing the marriage age**   Rotz (2016) evaluates the impact of later marriage ages on the probability of divorce.

116   **she stood a fairly high chance—around 30 percent—of ever marrying . . . less than 10 percent—of ever bearing a child**   For college-graduate women born around 1940, according to the data in an earlier chapter, 19.7 percent did not yet have a child by around age thirty-seven, and 17.9 percent would not by their mid-forties. That gives Mary just a 9.4 percent chance of ever having a birth. For marriage, around 10.5 percent of those born around 1940 hadn't ever married by their late thirties, but 7.4 percent would not have ever married by their late fifties. That gives her a 30 percent chance of ever marrying. Both probabilities are, separately, conditional on reaching age thirty-seven having not yet married and having not yet had a child.

117   **The age at first marriage continued to increase . . . has increased to around twenty-eight years old**   A similar increase in the age at first marriage also occurred to women who attended but did not graduate from a four-year college.

118   **spent less than 65 percent of those twenty-five years married**   See the calculation in Goldin (2006, figure 9). These data are for all women, not just those who graduated from college.

118   **Couples in the 1970s reacted to the adoption of unilateral divorce laws**   Why divorce increased is a more contentious issue. Some had initially thought the increase was due entirely to the legal changes of the 1960s that relaxed divorce statutes in various states and allowed unilateral divorce. Others posited, along the lines of the Coase Theorem, that legal changes should not have mattered. The empirical literature shows that the immediate effect of the laws was to increase divorce, but that after a decade, divorce rates reverted to their initial levels. For a summary of the debate and an empirical

analysis of the short- and long-run effects of legal changes regarding divorce, see Wolfers (2006).

119 **had fewer children, had greater employment, and contributed less** Stevenson (2007) identifies the effect of the change in divorce laws by observing the behavior of couples in their first few years of marriage relative to the behavior of couples in the same states before they changed their laws, and relative to couples in states that did not change their laws.

119 **until the appearance of Gloria Steinem's *Ms.* magazine** Usage of the appellation "Ms." spread rapidly, but there was initial resistance, even at the *New York Times*. In 1984, the *Times* reported that "proceeds from [Gloria Steinem's fiftieth birthday] dinner will go to the Ms. Foundation . . . which publishes Ms. Magazine where Miss Steinem works as an editor" (*New York Times*, May 24, 1984, p. C10). Two years later, the *Times* changed its policy: "Beginning today, *The New York Times* will use 'Ms.' as an honorific" (*New York Times*, June 20, 1986, p. B1).

119 **retained their surnames at marriage** The topic is explored in Goldin and Shim (2004), who use data from the *New York Times* Style section, college reunion books, and Massachusetts birth records. The fraction of college-graduate women who kept their names declined somewhat during the 1990s for reasons that are not clear.

120 **increased their scores on standardized tests** Goldin, Katz, and Kuziemko (2006).

120 **the "age of majority" had been lowered to eighteen years old** The Twenty-sixth Amendment to the Constitution, ratified in 1971, extended the voting age to individuals eighteen years old and thus lowered the age of majority to eighteen. It was spurred by the Vietnam War slogan "Old enough to fight, old enough to vote." The rallying cry originated in World War II, and various states lowered their voting age to eighteen for state and local elections before 1971.

121 **did not greatly alter their lifetime fertility** Bailey (2006, 2010) investigates the fertility consequences of the Pill. Although the Pill enabled women to control their fertility, it did not reduce the number of births by much, if at all. Rather, it enabled couples to control the timing of births.

121 **others could afford to wait** Goldin and Katz (2002) describe the model that generates an increased age at first marriage with the diffusion of the Pill, and provide evidence concerning the timing of the Pill's spread among young women.

122 **compelled Betty to write an e-mail to DeLong** E-mail from Betty Clark, a petroleum geologist, written to Brad DeLong (September 2010), when she "accidently stumbled into [his] introductory economics class having found the Berkeley webcasts." Personal correspondence from Brad DeLong. Emphasis in original.

122 **This was not a coup d'état** Collins (2009), in her sweeping and engaging volume, comes to the same conclusion.

124 **greater labor force participation was not** See Goldin and Mitchell (2017) for changes in the labor force participation of women since the 1960s.

124 **participation for women with infants soared** March Current Population Survey, for white non-Hispanic women. The participation rate of women with an infant increased from 0.20 in 1973 to 0.62 by 2000 and has been at about that level ever since.

126 **increase from 33 percent to 80 percent** The actual employment rate for a thirty-five-year-old woman in 1978 was 56 percent. The female employment rate increased, but the expectations of the younger group had increased a lot more, and their new expectations were consistent with their later employment. Note that the change in employment expectations holds at all ages for the survey respondents. The response to the question from a fourteen-year-old was almost identical to that from an eighteen-year-old.

126 **"... go out and get a job."** From ethnographer Mirra Komarovsky's (1985) interviews with freshman women in 1979 and her follow-up interviews with them as seniors in 1983. "I wouldn't want ... ," p. 172; "My mother never worked ... ," p. 173; "My mother was home full time ... ," p. 139; "I often wished ... ," pp. 148–49.

126 **participation rate was about 75 percent** Actual labor force participation rates are from the CPS and are for married, white women averaged for ages thirty-four to thirty-six. The figure of 30 percent for their mothers is for 1962. Data from the two NLS surveys are for white females because the Black sample is very small.

126 **exceeded 80 percent** For college-graduate women, see Goldin and Mitchell (2017).

126 **The revised expectations ... (and there is some evidence that it did)** Goldin, Katz, and Kuziemko (2006) find that among female precollege teens (who were fourteen to eighteen years old in 1968), those who stated that they would be in the labor force when they were thirty-five had eventual college graduation rates that were 14.3 percentage points higher than those who said they would be "at home, with family" at age thirty-five. Those in the former group had a mean graduation rate of 32.8 percent, whereas the mean graduation rate for the latter group was 18.5 percent.

127 **By about 1990, girls ... and were considerably ahead in reading** The relative increases in math and science courses and math and reading aptitude test scores are from a comparison of the NLS-72 and the NELS-88 (NLS = National Longitudinal Study; NELS = National Education Longitudinal Study). The changes are consistent with those from the National Assessment of Educational Progress (NAEP), although somewhat larger, and from US Department of Education transcript surveys. See Goldin, Katz, and Kuziemko (2006).

128 **but not by much** The difference was much less because the levels were so much lower.

128 **Half of all women ... would have had to switch** The calculation involves constructing a simple index of inequality for male and female college majors at graduation. See Goldin (2005).

128 **Their stated career preferences as freshmen** This calculation uses the Higher Education Research Institute (HERI) survey data (also known as the Astin data) on career intentions among college freshmen to construct an index of dissimilarity. From 1985 until 2015, the index has remained at around 25 percent but declined from 50 percent in the late 1960s.

128 **In 1970, ... majored in a combination of education and the liberal arts** See Online Appendix table 2A (Ch5), "Fraction of Female Graduates in Selected College Majors by Year of College Graduation."

128   **both men and women shifted out**   In 1982, 17 percent of men majored in the two fields, and 34 percent of women did.

128   **By 1982, 21 percent were**   The increase for men was from 24 percent in 1967 to 28 percent in 1982. Female business majors were more often in accounting, human resources, and marketing; male business majors were more often in finance.

130   **The timing of the changes**   Another piece of evidence that legal and societal factors were at play concerns the returns to experience, mainly to Group Three women. From the 1970s to the 1980s, financial returns to experience greatly increased for women more than they did for men, given their education. On the increase in returns to experience, see Blau and Kahn (1997), Olivetti (2006), and O'Neill and Polachek (1993). Olivetti shows, for a somewhat longer period (comparing the 1970s with the 1990s), that women's returns increased by around 25 percent and men's by 6 to 9 percent.

130   **Solid evidence regarding the positive impact**   It has also been noted that even *within* cohorts, the earnings of women increased relative to those of men, suggesting that change may have diffused to those in their middle age and was caused, at least in part, by changes within the labor market or imposed by antidiscrimination legislation.

131   **As Group Four women . . . they remained employed far longer**   See Goldin and Katz (2018).

132   **". . . endorse the principle of equal pay . . ."**   See Rubin (1994), pp. 81, 83. She had conducted a similar study two decades earlier. Her later work makes comparisons to her earlier one.

132   **more on-the-job learning**   O'Neill and Polachek (1993) decompose the increase in relative earnings for women and find that increased returns to experience account for a larger fraction of the difference than the increase in years of work experience. They do not, however, explain the increase in returns to experience in terms of better preparation for the labor market or better treatment by the labor market.

132   **an even higher fraction without a birth—around 33 percent**   These data are highly reliable and come from the June Fertility Supplements of the Current Population Survey.

Chapter Seven

133   **". . . You're the dad."**   Infertility and the quest for parenthood were themes on *Friends* and *Sex and the City*, two highly popular sitcoms of the late 1990s and early 2000s. Monica and Chandler marry on *Friends*, have trouble conceiving, and rapidly find a surrogate who gives birth before the series ends. Charlotte on *Sex and the City* has trouble conceiving. *Private Life* (2018), a Netflix movie, concerns a married couple whose lives become consumed with their infertility problems and treatments. Jennifer Lopez, in *The Back-Up Plan* (2010), has a child through artificial insemination and then meets the perfect guy. Jennifer Aniston, in *The Switch* (2010), has a turkey-baster baby whose father is not the one whose sperm she thought was in the baster. The list could go on. It is clear that the collective anxieties of Group Five are reflected in its entertainment.

134   **28 percent . . . did not have a birth by the time they were forty-five years old**   See figure 2.3. In addition, about 1.7 percentage points more were able to adopt by the time

they were forty-five, computed for women born c. 1955 using the American Community Survey (ACS). (Almost the same number is computed for the group born from 1965 to 1969.) This means that 26.3 percent (28–1.7) of those born c. 1955 did not have a birth or an adoption.

134   **considerably more transparent (and increasingly generous)**   On firm-provided parental leave policies, see Goldin, Kerr, and Olivetti (2020).

134   **aspirations to attain both career and family**   Komarovsky (1985) notes that the answers she received in her study of one graduating class of 1983 were very different from those she recorded before. Fully 85 percent of the seniors stated that they wanted to achieve career and family fifteen years after graduation, whereas the previous numbers from the same college, admittedly from forty years before, were much smaller.

136   **Although there have been criticisms**   John Bongaarts, senior research associate at the Population Council, questioned certain aspects of the French study but especially its conclusion that women should be counseled to start having their children earlier. See *New York Times*, March 21, 1982. The original article reporting on a French fertility study of 2,193 women is in *New York Times*, February 18, 1982.

136   **without a husband or partner**   Manning, Brown, and Stykes (2015), using the National Survey of Family Growth data for births from 2009 to 2013, report that 3 percent of all college-graduate women who had a birth were not currently married or partnered.

136   **from the procedure was low in the early 1960s, according to a rough estimate**   The American Medical Student Association publication *New Physician* reported a figure of around eleven hundred for AI births in the US in 1962, according to *New York Times*, December 8, 1962.

136   **legal limbo into which the child would be born**   Reported in an article by Georgia Dullea, *New York Times*, March 9, 1979.

137   **Most of the articles in the 2000s**   The search engine for the National Center for Biotechnology Information, US National Library of Medicine, was used. All articles containing the words "human," "female," and "infertility" were counted, and the denominator was given by the number of articles with the neutral word "January"; therefore, relative numbers over time are more accurate than the absolute numbers. The first uptick in articles on infertility concerns the issue of age. The second, much larger uptick concerns infertility treatments.

137   **A search of the word "infertility" . . . reveals a fivefold increase**   The "fivefold" figure comes from a Google Ngram of (infertility + IVF) using the "American English 2009" corpus. The series increases from around 1970, but that after 1980 is much greater.

137   **articles about infertility in the *New York Times***   These data come from a search of all articles containing the words ("female" or "woman") and "infertility" divided by all articles that contain the word "January." January is used as a neutral word to scale the total number and length of articles.

137   **which had reached a frenzied peak in the late 1980s**   The frenzied peak occurred around 1986 to 1987, when an academic article by David Bloom, an economist and demographer, appeared, demonstrating that women who had children before age twenty-two had lower earnings later in their life than women who delayed childbirth until age

twenty-seven. Bloom and coauthor James Trussell had also written extensively on child-lessness and delayed childbearing, and also with coauthor Anne Pebley. Bloom with coauthor Neil Bennett had written a controversial article on the consequences of delayed marriage. These were all widely cited articles about the various consequences of delayed childbearing.

137   **about 12 percent of even healthy twenty-five-year-old women and men**   Menken, Trussell, and Larsen (1986) discuss the many biases in current data on infertility, and conclude that actual sterility is lower than in most estimates (likely 6 percent in the early twenties and 16 percent by the early thirties). The fraction of couples having trouble conceiving is higher.

138   **193 pages stapled together in four sections**   See Boston Women's Health Book Collective (1970).

138   **"delay[ing] childbearing into their thirties, . . ."**   Boston Women's Health Book Collective (1984), p. 420.

139   **Whereas 31 percent of Group Four . . . just 22 percent of Group Five did**   Data from the CPS June Fertility Supplements. Group Four are college-graduate women born 1948 to 1957; Group Five are college-graduate women born 1960 to 1985.

139   **5 percentage points for those with an advanced degree**   The data in this paragraph are from an analysis of the CPS June Fertility Supplement micro data (from 1973 to 2018). Professional degrees and doctorates are those above a master's.

139   **recent data for Group Five . . . almost identical to those for women with just a bachelor's**   Among women born from 1949 to 1953 who received a professional degree (MD, JD, and so forth) or a doctorate, 39 percent did not have a child (living at home) from ages forty to forty-four, according to the micro data in the National Survey of College Graduates (1993 to 2017). But the figure drops to 22 percent among women born after 1969.

140   **but also from new state mandates**   Bitler and Schmidt (2012) analyze the impact of state requirements mandating that private health insurance plans cover various infertility procedures. They find that in the fifteen states with mandated coverage, older and more educated women greatly increased their use of infertility treatments. See their table 1 for the years the state laws were enacted, which were mainly in the late 1980s.

141   **Between 37 percent and 50 percent . . . can be accounted for by advances in reproductive technologies**   An assumption in the comparison between Groups Four and Five is that no woman in the earlier group had a first birth due to a reproductive technology. Therefore, the 50 percent figure is an upper bound. The calculation uses actual birth data from the CDC, but those data begin in 2011. I estimate that the total number of first births to college-graduate women born c. 1976 was 550,000, of which about 20,000 were "assisted," or 3.6 percent. If 80 percent of all college-graduate women born c. 1976 had a first birth, but 74 percent of those born c. 1956 had a birth, then the 20,000 "explains" 50 percent of the difference. If the earlier birth cohort used assisted reproductive technology at a quarter of the rate of the later generation (say, 5,000 births), then ART would explain 37 percent.

142   **the definition and computation of "career"**   See Source Appendix (Ch7), "Career and Family Success."

144   **longitudinal survey data for those born 1980 to 1984**   Calculations use the NLSY97.

146   **". . . I don't think he was as sensitive then."**   Office of History and Preservation, Office of the Clerk, US House of Representatives (2008), p. 596. These remarks were taken from an interview Rep. Clayton did with Marian Burros, the *New York Times* food columnist, that appeared in the article "Rep. Mom," *Chicago Tribune*, June 20, 1993.

146   **elected to Congress when they were around fifty-three**   In fact, Group Three women were actually a bit younger when I account for differences in the amount of time each had to be elected. To do that, I create a Group Three of the same length as Group Four (assuming they were born from 1930 to 1943) but with a chance to be elected to Congress only until 2005, giving them the same number of years that Group Four has had to be elected. That way, Groups Three and Four are comparable. The result is that Group Three now has a mean age at election of 51.9 and Group Four remains at 52.7.

146   **mean age is higher for Group Four**   To make Groups Four and Five comparable, I keep Group Four as born from 1944 to 1957 but create a Group Five of the same length, born from 1958 to 1971. I measure their age at first election to Congress if Group Four had only until 2005 to be elected, which gives it and Group Five the same number of years. Mean age for Group Five is 48 and for Group Four is 47.1 years.

146   **largest group of women, thus far, elected to Congress**   In 2018, thirty-three women were newly elected to the House and three to the Senate. Plus, one was elected to the Senate in 2019 in a special election. The next-highest year was 1992, when twenty-four women were newly elected to the House and four were to the Senate. Almost tying that record, twenty-six were elected to the House and one to the Senate in 2020. Both 2018 and 1992 have been termed the "year of the woman." The 117th Congress has a record number of women serving, more than 140.

147   **We called the project Harvard and Beyond**   See Source Appendix (Ch7), "Harvard and Beyond Project." Also see Goldin and Katz (2008a) and the following for further information on the project: https://scholar.harvard.edu/goldin/pages/harvard-and -beyond-project.

149   **another project . . . that dives deeper into the world of work in the corporate and financial sectors**   See Bertrand, Goldin, and Katz (2010).

Chapter Eight

152   **"Everything at Goodyear was top secret,"**   Ledbetter and Isom (2012), p. 115. Many of the details in this section come from a reading of this autobiography.

152   **Eleventh Circuit Court of Appeals**   "By the fall of 2005, the Eleventh Circuit Court of Appeals . . . reversed the jury verdict, stating that my case was filed too late" (Ledbetter and Isom 2012, p. 202).

152   **Ruth Bader Ginsburg's dissent**   550 U.S. _____ (2007) Ginsburg, J., dissenting, Supreme Court of the United States No. 05-1074, *Lilly M. Ledbetter, Petitioner v. The Goodyear Tire & Rubber Company, Inc.*, May 29, 2007, p. 19.

153   **It widens as men and women age**   The gender earnings gap stabilizes and then narrows somewhat. The age when the gap starts to narrow is younger for earlier cohorts of college-graduate women, probably because they had their children earlier. It starts to

narrow at an older age for college-graduate women from later cohorts, most likely because they have had children at a much later age.

153 **The ratio conveniently . . . conveys a relative difference** The gender earnings difference is often expressed mathematically in logs, and the ratio in log terms is a difference. The reason is because the log of the ratios is the difference of the logs: $\log(x/y) = \log(x) - \log(y)$.

154 **According to a 2017 survey, 42 percent of women** See Pew Research (2017).

155 **Others . . . have espoused debiasing entire organizations** On the debiasing of organizations, see Bohnet (2016).

155 **Starbucks . . . to provide antibias training for all its personnel** The proximate cause was a racial incident in Philadelphia. For the story on Starbucks, see: https://www .vox.com/identities/2018/5/29/17405338/starbucks-racial-bias-training-why-closed.

155 **orchestras and the use of screens in auditions** Goldin and Rouse (2000).

155 **free salary-negotiation workshops for women (not men)** For information on the Boston mayor's negotiation initiative, see: https://www.boston.gov/departments /womens-advancement/aauw-work-smart-boston#about-the-workshops.

155 **disclose their prior earnings** The details of the act can be found at: https://www .mass.gov/service-details/learn-more-about-the-massachusetts-equal-pay-act. The act also mandates equal pay for comparable work, a complicated concept.

156 **The phenomenon is . . . "occupational segregation,"** Occupational differences by gender are measured by a construct known as the "index of dissimilarity." The index of dissimilarity is given by $I = \frac{1}{2} \Sigma_i |m_i - f_i|$ where m_i (f_i) is the fraction of male (female) workers in each of i occupations in the economy. If males and females are distributed equally across the occupations, then the index is zero. The index gives the fraction of female (or male) workers that would have to shift occupations to get an equal distribution by gender. If there is no occupational overlap, then the index is one and all women (or all men) would have to shift. Note that computing the fraction of each occupation that is female (or male) requires information on the total number of males and females in the workforce. If there are equal numbers of males and females, then the fraction of females in occupation i would be $[f_i / (m_i + f_i)]$.

156 **many firms had strict policies** Goldin (2014a) presents evidence from a large number of firm-level surveys done in 1939 about which occupations were restricted to women only and which to men only, and the reasons for these often complicated restrictions. Men were often allowed to enter lowly positions such as "mail boy," from which women were barred. Women were often allowed to enter higher positions, such as stenographer, from which men were barred.

157 **50 percent (either male or female) would have to shift** There are many calculations of the index of dissimilarity. For example, see Hegewisch and Hartmann (2014) for a time trend of the index from 1972 to 2011.

157 **one-third of all gender earnings inequality would be eliminated** See Goldin (2014). In a regression context, from 22 percent to 30 percent of the earnings gap would disappear. The smaller number is for all workers, and the larger one is for college graduates in a regression that contains variables such as age as a quartic, education categories,

hours and weeks worked, and a female dummy. Occupation dummies are added and the estimate given is the change in the coefficient on female. If one, instead, did the simpler experiment of giving women that male occupational distribution or giving men the female distribution, the gap would decrease for the college-graduate group by 30 percent to 40 percent.

157 **earnings gap . . . exists within just about every occupation** There are about five hundred occupations in the US census. Some are narrowly defined, whereas others are broad. "Physician" is a broad category and includes specialties that vary from surgeon to psychiatrist. A "lawyer" could work in a large firm, in a small firm, in government, or as corporate counsel, to mention a few settings. That is, an occupation is not necessarily the same as a job. It is more like a métier.

158 **By using the median, it is less affected** Mean earnings, on the other hand, would be more affected by the fact that, relative to women, men's earnings contain more extraordinarily high values. Because CPS earnings are truncated, the extremely high earnings are of less importance to the calculation.

159 **college-graduate men were the biggest winners of all** See Goldin and Katz (2008).

160 **disparity in their earnings was no longer mainly due** Blau and Kahn (2017), table 4, give estimates of the wage gap for 1980 and 2010 and the part of the gap that can be accounted for by differences in education and work experience. In 1980, the gender earnings gap was 0.62, and 29 percent could be accounted for by differences in education and work experience, what economists called "human capital" factors. Fully 52 percent could be accounted for by differences in "human capital" factors and the occupations and industries of the workers. In 2010 the gap had narrowed to 0.79, and just 15 percent could be accounted for by "human capital" factors. According to their estimates, a larger fraction in 2010 than in 1980 can be accounted for by occupation and industry. The main takeaway here is that a much larger fraction of the earnings gap in 1980 can be accounted for by "human capital" differences than in 2010. Note that these estimates are for all workers and not just the college-graduate group.

160 **difference also shrank considerably over time** Blau and Kahn (2017), table 2, give average years employed full-time and for at least twenty-six weeks for men and women ages twenty-five to sixty-four in the Panel Study of Income Dynamics (PSID). Men were employed for almost 7 years more than women in 1981, but just 1.4 years more in 2011.

160 **lack of competitiveness** See the extensive work of Muriel Niederle, for example Niederle and Vesterlund (2007).

161 **gender earnings gap (or ratio) is graphed for those in Group Five** I should note that the gender earnings ratios (in figure 8.2) are, essentially, the ratios of the means and will be somewhat lower than the ratios of the medians. The ratio of the medians was depicted previously because it is a standard measure and is less sensitive to very high earnings.

162 **the gap widens with age** As in Goldin (2014), the widening of the gender earnings gap stops, and then the reverse sets in somewhat after women reach their forties or fifties, the precise age depending on the birth group considered.

162 **many confounding factors are already held constant** The study was conducted by Marianne Bertrand, a professor at the Booth School, Lawrence F. Katz, and me. See Bertrand, Goldin, and Katz (2010).

162   **shorthand of thirteen years** The sample of MBAs includes those who graduated from 1990 to 2006. We aggregated the group that graduated ten to sixteen years before. In discussing that group, I will refer to them as graduating thirteen years ago rather than ten to sixteen years. We surveyed the graduates in 2006, and the University of Chicago Graduate School of Business provided administrative data on the individuals when they were students and at the time of their admission.

162   **for women who did not have a child** The requirement is also that the women never took any leave exceeding six months. The dark bars are all the women in the sample relative to all the men. The light ones are only those women who did not have a child up to that point. Therefore the sample for the light bars changes over time.

162   **Although there is variance in the light bars . . . there is little trend** It appears that MBA women who have children soon after receiving their MBAs, and continue to work, are positively selected. What that means is that they were, for unobservable and thus nonmeasurable reasons, more likely to earn more. After they have children, their earnings actually are higher than are those for women without children. As more women have children, earnings differences due to the demands of motherhood become more dominant.

164   **at thirteen years . . . is 64 cents . . . grows to 73 cents . . . increases even more** See Online Appendix figure 2A (Ch8), "Ratio of Female to Male MBA Annual Earnings around 13 Years (10 to 16 years) since MBA Receipt."

164   **The average woman . . . had taken 0.37 of a year off. . . . The average man had taken just 0.075** The job exits had to exceed six months each and do not include paid maternity and family leave.

164   **17 percent of the MBA women . . . higher than that experienced by other college-graduate women** The statement that MBA women take off more time after their highest degree during their first decade of work comes from the Harvard and Beyond study. See Goldin and Katz (2008a) for general information about the study. In the Harvard and Beyond data, for those graduating Harvard around 1980, 97 percent of the MDs, 94 percent of the PhDs, 91 percent of the JDs, and 87 percent of the MBAs were employed fifteen years after their bachelor's. The results differ slightly for those graduating around 1990 (96 percent MD, 94 percent PhD, 87 percent JD, and 85 percent MBA).

165   **College-graduate women generally don't opt out of the labor force** The term "opt out" was popularized by Lisa Belkin in her 2003 *New York Times Magazine* article "The Opt-Out Revolution" (October 26). It was followed by a large number of academic articles refuting the notion that opting out had increased and other articles in the post-great-recession period arguing that it could have increased.

166   **That figure, while not zero** All of the gender earnings gaps mentioned in this paragraph correct for skills at the time of MBA receipt. These skills include their courses and grades in business school.

166   **But there is compelling evidence** See Cortés and Pan (2020), who conclude that two-thirds of the overall gender gap in earnings is due to the difference in parental penalties in the labor market.

166   **earned above the median salary for MBA men** For the MBA men in our sample, $200,000 was the median annual salary seven years after MBA graduation. MBA men in the sample earned somewhat more than the husbands of the MBA women. The $200,000

income level of MBA husbands includes about 40 percent of the MBA women (respondent years) who were married with children.

166   **After five years, she was 32 percent**   Bertrand, Goldin, and Katz (2010), table 9. The estimation includes individual fixed effects.

166   **Women who have high-earning husbands but no children**   Bertrand, Goldin, and Katz (2010), table 6.

167   **my coauthors and I discovered that the earnings**   Goldin, Kerr, Olivetti, and Barth (2017).

168   **teams of researchers have produced such studies**   See Angelov, Johansson, and Lindahl (2016) on Sweden, and Kleven, Landais, and Søgaard (2019) on Denmark.

168   **estimates how the birth impacts couple's earnings**   The last birth year the authors could use is 2002 because they needed fifteen years to track the impact of the birth.

168   **The Danish study does a similar analysis**   Kleven, Landais, and Søgaard (2019) also analyze the impact of the grandparents to estimate intergenerational transmission of gender norms that would lead one couple to have greater specialization in childcare than others.

168   **husband earns 32 percent more than his wife**   Using the regression results of Angelov, Johansson, and Lindahl (2016), table 3, with a full set of controls, annual earnings widen within couples by 0.279 log points (or by 32 percent) at year fifteen after the first birth. If the husband and wife had equal earnings prior to the birth, the husband would earn 1.32 times his wife's earnings at year fifteen. That is, the ratio of female to male earnings is reduced from 1 to 0.76. If he had earned 1.18 times her earnings before the birth, he would now earn 1.56 times. In that case the ratio of female to male earnings would be reduced from 0.85 to 0.64.

168   **there are many reasons to believe they would be larger**   See Kleven et al. (2019), which compares child penalties across many countries.

169   **Almost half of all fathers surveyed**   Pew Research (2012), N = 2,511.

169   **The penalty for MBAs is 1.4 times**   Goldin and Katz (2008a) estimate penalties to taking time out and standardize them to eighteen months at fifteen years after graduating college. An MBA would earn only 60 percent, a JD or PhD would earn only 71 percent, and an MD would forgo the least and earn 84 percent of annual earnings.

169   **a huge dataset from the American Community Survey**   See Online Appendix (Ch8), "American Community Survey (ACS) Occupations and O*NET Sample." Eight ACSs, 2009 to 2016, are used. I chose to use full-time, year-round workers to create comparability between the samples of male and female workers.

169   **from some of the most prestigious to many that are less exalted**   Few production, protective service, and transport occupations are included, which is not surprising given that only college graduates are included.

170   **Women in tech earn 94 cents on the male tech dollar**   I use engineering for "tech," although tech would also include the math and computer group.

173   **low time demands and limited personal interactions**   Online Appendix table 2A (Ch8), "O*NET Values and Gender Earnings Ratios," provides the means (unweighted and weighted) for the O*NET characteristics and the log(gender earnings ratio), from the regression, by occupational group.

174   **An average of the six characteristics . . . goes a long way to "explaining" the gender earnings gap by occupation**   The O*NET characteristics are measured by an index created by the BLS using information gathered from various sources, including from

workers in the occupation. To take a simple average of the values for each of these characteristics, I first have to standardize them (with mean = 0 and standard deviation = 1) because each of the characteristics is measured differently, and some have large variances and some small.

174 **Occupations with the greatest income inequality . . . the largest gender earnings gaps** Online Appendix figure 1A (Ch8), "Earnings Inequality and the Gender Earnings Gap," gives the relationship between the 90-10 measure for male earnings inequality and the gender earnings gap for each of the 143 occupations. The 90-10 measure is the annual earnings of a male worker at the 90th percentile divided by that of a male worker at the 10th percentile. The statistic is generally computed, as it is in the figure, as the log of the earnings at the 90th percentile minus the log of the earnings at the 10th percentile. The earnings used are the residuals from the earnings regression described further in the Online Appendix. The gender earnings gap measure is the same as used elsewhere in this chapter.

Chapter Nine

176 **the median female JD made just 57 cents** Medians are for full-time, full-year workers and come from the US Census for 1970, and the American Community Survey (ACS) for 2014–2016. Note that full-time means thirty-five hours or more, and men work more hours than women.

176 **Ruth Bader Ginsburg did not get a clerkship** Lepore (2018) notes that Frankfurter's decision was despite the fact that he was informed that Ginsburg did not wear "pants."

178 **Earnings just after JD receipt** These results, and others in this chapter, use restricted-access data on law school alumni tracked at various intervals after their JD. See Source Appendix (Ch9), "University of Michigan Law School Alumni Survey Research Dataset." The raw numbers reveal that female JDs earn 90 percent of what male JDs make five years out. But once time worked and job experience are accounted for, no difference in earnings can be detected. In addition, although women work somewhat fewer hours at five years out, the differences in hours are small.

179 **stay in the game for now: just 6 percent** On hours, see figure 9.1. Part-time is defined in the usual manner, as less than thirty-five hours per week. On labor force participation, see figure 9.2.

179 **five years out, the fractions were much closer** Recall that at five years out, 80 percent of the women worked more than forty-five hours a week, and 90 percent of the men did.

179 **female JDs earn just a little over *half* (56 percent)** For the 56 percent figure, see Online Appendix: table 1A (Ch9), "Earnings Equations for JDs: University of Michigan Law School Alumni Survey, Longitudinal Sample."

180 **it has less to do with labor market discrimination and everything to do with** *time* See also Azmat and Ferrer (2017) for a similar explanation for the gender earnings gap among lawyers using the American Bar Association's sample from the "After the JD" survey in 2006, six years after passing the bar. Their findings support an explanation that men do better because they work more hours and bring in higher-revenue clients. But the authors can only study these lawyers up to six years out.

180   **she would be receiving only 81 percent of his earnings**   The regression results that
provide the 81 percent estimate, as well as the 56 percent one, are in the Online Appendix
table 1A (Ch9), "Earnings Equations for JDs: University of Michigan Law School
Alumni Survey, Longitudinal Sample," and come from Goldin (2014), table 1.

180   **hours increase from thirty to sixty per week, the average hourly rate increases by
almost a quarter**   The results on hourly pay are in the Online Appendix table 1A
(Ch9), "Earnings Equations for JDs: University of Michigan Law School Alumni Survey,
Longitudinal Sample."

181   **gender difference in the rate of making partner disappears**   The probability of making partner is estimated for all who worked in law firms in year five and includes hours
worked in year five, academic record variables, the existence of children in year fifteen,
an interaction of children with female, and a female dummy.

182   **all highly dependent on time inputs**   See Online Appendix table 1A (Ch9), "Earnings
Equations for JDs: University of Michigan Law School Alumni Survey, Longitudinal
Sample." The coefficient on female in the hourly fee regression is insignificant from zero
once hours worked contemporaneously are added.

182   **If Perry's income puts him in the top tier**   Interestingly, the median for the male
lawyers at year fifteen—around $200,000 (in 2007 dollars)—is approximately the mean
for the husbands of the female JDs. Because the male income distribution has a long right
tail, the husbands have a lower mean than all the lawyers. Note that the husbands are not
all lawyers. Note that the median in the MBA sample (in 2006 dollars) was also $200,000.

184   **one of the largest gender earnings gaps for any occupation**   The gender earnings
ratios are for the median full-time, full-year female and male. Using the coefficients from my
earlier analysis, which hold hours, weeks, age, and other factors constant and produce mean
ratios, lawyers are ranked twenty-ninth from the bottom out of the 143 occupations.

186   **Couple inequity results**   Note that couple inequity can, and does, exist for same-sex
couples. It is costly for any couple with family responsibilities for both members to take
the job with more flexible hours.

188   **67 cents on the male pharmacist dollar**   The "67 cents on the male dollar" figure is
for the median female pharmacist working full-time year-round relative to males in 1970.

191   **94 cents on her male counterpart's dollar**   The 94 cents figure is an average of two
estimates. A 96 cents figure is from an analysis of the medians using the 2014–2016 ACS
data. The regression analysis in a previous chapter gives a figure of 92 cents.

191   **no discernible part-time penalty**   The evidence to back up these points is in Goldin
and Katz (2016), table 4.

192   **From 1970 to 2010, the income of the median pharmacist**   Median earnings are wages
and salary plus business income for twenty-five- to sixty-four-year-olds working full-time,
full-year. The data are from the 1970, 1980, 1990, and 2000 US population censuses and the
2009–2010 ACS.

Chapter Ten

197   **just 7.5 percent of . . . Today 77 percent are. In 1970, just 8 percent**   For data on the
fraction female among recent professional school graduates, see figure 6.3. The fraction
female among veterinarians by age can be found in Online Appendix figure 2A (Ch10),

"Veterinarian Fraction Female, Part-Time, and Owner by Age Group." Those data understate the fraction female in recent classes since they are about a decade old.

199   **women have been 30 to 35 percent of PhDs**   CSWEP *Annual Reports* (various years). Only academic institutions with a doctoral program were surveyed. The fraction of PhDs in economics awarded to women has ranged from 30 percent to 35 percent for at least the past twenty years.

199   **advanced to almost 15 percent in 2018**   Data from Ginther and Kahn (2004) and the CSWEP *Annual Reports* (various years), for departments with doctoral programs.

199   **women are promoted at lower rates**   Ginther and Kahn (2004) use data collected by the National Science Foundation (NSF) known as the Survey of Doctoral Recipients (SDR) to make the point that women are advanced at lower rates than are men in various academic fields, and economics is one of them.

200   **Take CPA accounting**   The largest category comprises firms with one hundred or more CPAs, and the smallest is two to ten CPAs. CPA firms vary widely by employment. In 2016 there were around 42,000 CPA firms in the US. Of those, 41,600 had fewer than twenty employees. But the largest of the firms, known at the Big Four (Deloitte, PWC, EY, KPMG), each had more than three thousand CPAs and many more employees. The largest of them (Deloitte) had more than fifty thousand employees, and KPMG, the smallest of the Big Four, had more than thirty thousand. Employment figures also include employees of other divisions of the company, such as consulting. The Big Four do not advertise the gender breakdown of their partnership numbers.

200   **they were just 21 percent of partners**   The 21 percent figure and the other figures of the fraction female partners in large and small accounting firms come from the CPA firm gender survey (AICPA 2017). Burke, Hoitash, and Hoitash (2019) use audit data to show that women are 17.7 percent of audit partners in the four top accounting firms.

200   **take jobs in smaller CPA firms or in nonpublic**   The AICPA studies do not report the fraction of firms in each size class that are surveyed. Almost all the CPAs in their study are working at firms with one hundred or more CPAs.

201   **Hours worked by the associate lawyers . . . promotion rates between men and women**   Azmat and Ferrer (2017).

202   **". . . to take 3 weeks of vacation a year."**   The statement is attributed to David Solomon, https://dealbreaker.com/2013/11/goldman-sachs-spells-out-new-saturday-rule-for-junior-employees/.

202   **Bank of America Merrill Lynch**   Bank of America acquired Merrill Lynch in 2009 but dropped the name in 2019 and is now known as Bank of America.

203   **announced that it was allowing a 25 percent reduction**   On the initial announcement, see: https://www.washingtonpost.com/news/the-switch/wp/2016/08/26/amazon-is-piloting-teams-with-a-30-hour-work-week/?noredirect=on&utm_term=.217f3557a09d. For an update, see: https://www.forbes.com/sites/kaytiezimmerman/2016/09/11/what-amazons-new-30-hour-work-week-means-for-millennials/#5da95c896ae4.

203   **in 1992 to see why women were leaving**   See McCracken (2000) and Molina (2005). In 1989, Deloitte & Touche LLP was created through the merger of two accounting firms, Deloitte Haskins & Sells and Touche Ross & Co.

204   **the fraction of females among its partners increased**   See Hewlett (2008).

204   **not much different for Deloitte and EY**   Burke, Hoitash, and Hoitash (2019) use publicly available data on CPA audit partners due to a recent ruling that requires CPA firms to disclose the identity of the partner in charge of each audit. For 2017, Deloitte (number one in size) had 17.4 percent female partners, PWC (number two) 18.7 percent, EY (number three) 19.9 percent, and KPMG (number four) 13.7 percent.

204   **nowhere near the 50 percent number achieved long ago for all CPAs**   The top CPA firms hire a small fraction of all CPAs, so the fraction of all CPAs who are female can be 50 percent but the fraction of the largest CPA firms can be considerably lower.

205   **Men take it to get more research papers published**   See Antecol, Bedard, and Stearns (2018).

207   **spent thirteen hours per week . . . but twenty-one hours in 2015**   Ramey and Ramey (2010); 2015 data estimated by author from 2010 to 2018 ATUS. The numbers given here were read off their graphs and come from a regression analysis on adults twenty-five to sixty-four years old with age, year, education, and sex dummies. Time spent with children includes "maintenance" and education, recreation, travel, and others.

207   **increased from eighteen to thirty-one hours per week**   Guryan, Hurst, and Kearney (2008) also provide evidence on time spent with children for 2002–2003 and show a strong gradient with respect to education in the US and elsewhere. More-educated parents spend considerably more time with their children.

207   **23 percent stated . . . more time. The fraction is higher for working moms (27 percent)**   Pew Research (2012), N = 2,511. Micro data have been used: http://www.pewsocialtrends.org/datasets/. The results are for q26a: "Do you think you spend too much time with your children, too little time or the right amount?" Only parents with a child eighteen years and younger were asked the question. Sample weights are applied.

207   **Around 50 percent . . . Just 20 percent stated that they spend less time**   Pew Research (2012). The information given is from q26b.

208   **53 percent of college-graduate women said "flexibility," whereas 29 percent**   Pew Research (2012). The information given is from q40a to q40d. The only other attribute that was more important than job flexibility for college women was job security.

208   **Female college graduates would like even more equity**   Pew Research (2010), N = 2,691. Micro data have been used and sample weights have been applied. The information given is from q17. In the Pew Research report, these findings are compared to a CBS/*NYTimes* poll in 1977 for which the fraction stating that the best marriage was the more sharing one was 48 percent, compared with 62 percent for 2010 (p. 26).

210   **Among female MDs . . . about 84 percent had a child**   The Harvard and Beyond Survey was taken in 2006. The classes that graduated c. 1990 were still too young to obtain completed fertility. However, the female physicians in those classes had more children at that time than did those with other postgraduate degrees. Adoptions of children less than three years old are included. Interestingly, male doctors in the sample did not have more children than those in other fields. Although they had more children than the female physicians, they had fewer than male MBAs and JDs.

210   **ten fewer hours per week at work**   I use the Community Tracking Study (CTS), restricted-use version. The CTS does not have much demographic information on

physicians, such as marital status and number and ages of children. All analyses on the CTS in this chapter are conditional on listing work hours between twenty and one hundred per week, and being employed at least forty weeks per year. See Source Appendix (Ch10), "Community Tracking Study." Because no detailed information on earnings is given in 2008, the analysis is generally restricted to 1996 to 2004.

210 **they differ by one very long day of work per week** These means are for physicians working twenty to one hundred hours per week (the hours distribution has been trimmed), and for at least forty weeks per year. The difference in the physician workweek by gender would be even larger if information on children were available. The division between "younger" and "older" physicians is age forty-five. Note that the CTS excludes physicians who do not have their own patients and is not a random sample of all physicians.

210 **More than 55 percent . . . among the younger group of doctors** Current American Medical Association data on the specialties of recent graduates have a higher fraction of women in various specialties than does the CTS data, in part because the AMA data are more recent.

211 **the higher the hours for male physicians in a specialty, the fewer female physicians** I use male physician hours as the reference so that the statement is more causal.

211 **strong negative relationship between average hours . . . and the fraction female** The relationship between fraction female and mean hours worked for males less than forty-five years old is strong among the nineteen specialties with enough women to analyze. There are two outliers: OB-GYN and pediatrics. These specialties have a higher fraction female than would be predicted on the basis of the relationship between hours and fraction female. Without the two outlier specialties, the correlation coefficient between fraction female and weekly hours for males is around -0.8. For the entire sample it is -0.66.

211 **a smaller fraction than for dermatologists** The fraction female in each specialty is from the American Medical Association (2013), but the hours data are from the CTS data. The AMA 2013 data are used to be more consistent with the older CTS data.

211 **younger women doctors work fewer hours than do younger men doctors** See Online Appendix figure 1A (Ch10), "Physician Hours by Specialty, Sex, and Age," which gives the relationship between the hours of male and female physicians by specialty and age group.

212 **67 to 82 cents on the male physician dollar** The CTS does not have actual job experience, and these estimates use information on time since receiving the MD. The CTS also does not have information on children and other family variables. For the calculation of the gender earnings gap, see Online Appendix table 1A (Ch10), "Physicians and the Gender Earnings Gap," where the dependent variable is log(annual earnings). Note that the figure of 0.67 comes from col. (1), since $\exp(0.408) = 0.665$, and the 0.82 figure is from col. (4), since $\exp(0.203) = 0.816$.

212 **female physicians spend 10 percent more time** Medscape (2018), to which more than twenty thousand physicians responded across twenty-nine specialties. The distribution of minutes is given by bins. To compute mean times, I generally used the median of the bin. For the upper bin (> 25 minutes), I used 32 minutes and for the lower bin, 8 minutes.

212   **According to the latest available data, women were 47 percent**   Physician specialties are from American Association of Medical Colleges (2018) and refer to 2017 data.
"Young" refers to less than forty-five years old.

213   **33 percent of all female pediatricians work part-time, and a significant fraction of
male**   Part-time employment among pediatricians increased during 1993–2000 from
24 percent to 28 percent (American Academy of Pediatrics 2002). Data from the CTS
give 30 percent part-time for young female pediatricians in 2008 using a thirty-five-hour
cutoff. According to Cull et al. in the *Journal of Pediatrics* (2016), 35 percent of all female
pediatricians worked part-time, and 9 percent of all male pediatricians did.

213   **anesthesiology does not have to involve long hours**   Anesthesiology is not one of
the specialties in the CTS dataset because anesthesiologists generally do not have their
own patients. The CTS is a survey of physicians about themselves and their "community" of patients.

214   **almost 80 percent of veterinary school graduates are women**   The fraction female
by the age of veterinarians is provided in Online Appendix figure 2A (Ch10), "Veterinarian Fraction Female, Part-Time, and Owner by Age Group," part A, for the year 2008.
The fraction female among twenty-five- to thirty-one-year-olds was 0.72 but was 0.16 for
those age fifty-seven to sixty-one.

215   **with an additional four emergency hours**   These data come from confidential survey
data on veterinarian training, hours, earnings, and ownership provided to me by the
American Veterinary Medical Association (AVMA) for 2007 and 2009. Although some
information could have changed in the last decade, these are the latest data available. The
profession is too small to use US census data. See Source Appendix (Ch10), "American
Veterinary Medical Association (AVMA) Dataset for 2007 and 2009."

215   **with six hours of emergency work thrown in**   These are medians of the hours distribution by sex.

215   **5 percent of male veterinarians do the same**   The AVMA data show that whereas just
5 percent of female veterinarians age twenty-seven to thirty-one work part-time,
22 percent of those age thirty-two to forty-six do, increasing to 30 percent by age sixty.
A mere 5 percent of male veterinarians work part-time to age fifty, when the fraction
begins to rise. See Online Appendix figure 2A (Ch10), "Veterinarian Fraction Female,
Part-Time, and Owner by Age Group," part B.

215   **Between 30 and 50 percent . . . whereas 60 to 80 percent of their male colleagues
are**   See Online Appendix figure 2A (Ch10), "Veterinarian Fraction Female, Part-Time,
and Owner by Age Group," part C.

216   **72 cents on the male veterinarian dollar**   The 0.72 figure holds year of graduation
constant.

216   **increases their remuneration to 82 cents on the male dollar**   The other variables
included in all estimations are the survey year, size dummies for the community, and
number of years since the veterinary degree. Full-time is defined as forty or more hours,
and full-year is forty-five weeks or more. Holding hours and weeks constant produces
the same results. Additional variables concerning veterinary training and employment
are board certification, residency programs, and employment sector (e.g., government,
industry, academia, private practice).

216 **increases the ratio further to 85 cents** Married male veterinarians earn more than unmarried male veterinarians, but the opposite is true for female veterinarians, a finding that echoes those in many other studies across all occupations. The difference reveals the way home burdens play out differently by sex. Such differences are difficult to measure using just the number of hours worked. Including marital status and an interaction with female increases the ratio further to 0.90. The rest of the gap, similar to that found in many other studies, is hard to explain with the observables. It is possible that measuring the number of hours is a poor substitute for the ability to alter hours. For those not in private practice, gender earnings gaps are smaller.

216 **most female-dominated profession** I am excluding K-12 teaching, which might be higher.

217 **"They weren't willing to give up their families and outside lives for another $100,000."** McCracken (2000), p. 5.

218 **"more and more men are taking advantage of it. . . ."** Krentz (2017). As of this writing, the majors in consulting, including Deloitte Consulting and BCG, have a sixteen-week fully paid maternity and paternity leave policy.

219 **Most other rich nations greatly subsidize childcare** See Olivetti and Petrongolo (2017), table 1, for the ratio: (government spending on early childhood education and childcare)/GDP. The US figure is 0.4, but the figure for France is 1.2, Sweden is 1.6, and the UK is 1.1. Nations with higher ratios of government spending on childcare to GDP also generally have higher female labor force participation rates.

219 **This is one reason why the labor force participation rate** Federal Reserve chair Jerome Powell has said the same thing to bolster support for childcare policies that will increase women's employment rates. See Jeanna Smialek, "Powell Says Better Child Care Policies Might Lift Women in Work Force," *New York Times*, February 24, 2021.

Epilogue

222 **the future of the younger members of Group Five** I had earlier defined Group Five as having been born from 1958 to 1978 so that I could trace them to their forties. But, as I noted then, Group Five includes women who are even younger, and its end date is not yet clear.

222 **"Pandemic Will 'Take Our Women 10 Years Back' . . ."** Amanda Taub, "Pandemic Will 'Take Our Women 10 Years Back' in the Workplace," *New York Times*, September 26, 2020.

222 **"Pandemic Could Scar a Generation of Working Mothers,"** Patricia Cohen and Tiffany Hsu, "Pandemic Could Scar a Generation of Working Mothers," *New York Times*, June 3, 2020.

222 **"How COVID-19 Sent Women's Workforce Progress Backward."** Julie Kashen, Sarah Jane Glynn, and Amanda Novello, "How COVID-19 Sent Women's Workforce Progress Backward," Center for American Progress, October 30, 2020, https://www.americanprogress.org/issues/women/reports/2020/10/30/492582/covid-19-sent-womens-workforce-progress-backward/.

222 **". . . you're allowed only a kid *or* a job."** Deb Perelman, "In the Covid-19 Economy You Can Have a Kid or a Job. You Can't Have Both," *New York Times*, July 2, 2020. See also Allyson Waller, "Woman Says She Was Fired Because Her Children Disrupted Her Work Calls," *New York Times*, July 8, 2020.

223   **fell by just 1.2 percentage points . . . fell by 4.9 percentage points**   Monthly CPS data on labor force participation were used by comparing rates for September 2020 to January 2021 with those for September 2019 to January 2020. "Children" are those of custodial mothers. Black women with less than a college degree, thirty-five to forty-four years old, with at least one child five to thirteen years old, had a decreased participation rate that greatly exceeded that of non-Blacks with the same demographics.

223   **Among academics, mothers have published fewer papers**   Deryugina et al. (2021) surveyed academics from May to July 2020 and showed that research time decreased for all parents, but more for women. Flaherty (2020) analyzed Elsevier journal data and showed that publications of women lagged those of men, except in the life sciences, in the early months of the pandemic.

223   **Plus, data don't reveal the frustration**   For a similar point, see Garbes (2021). See also Jessica Bennett, "Three Women on the Brink," *New York Times*, February 4, 2021, on the "Primal Scream."

224   **articles about "sex discrimination" began to soar**   I searched for both "sex discrimination" and "gender discrimination." The word "sex" is used far more than "gender" until around 2010. I deflate the counts of the phrase with a neutral word (in this case "January") to control for the size of the newspaper. In that way, I create an index. See Online Appendix figure 1A (Epilogue), "Gender Discontent: *New York Times* Phrase Searches, 1960 to 2019." Google Ngram (using US English 2019) shows a similar trend from 1960, but the increase for the more recent years is less pronounced.

224   **Even before #MeToo became a symbol**   The #MeToo movement began in 2006 but gained national (and even global) recognition in 2016 with Gretchen Carlson's allegations of sexual harassment against Fox News chairman and CEO Roger Ailes and the many women who came forward with similar claims. Allegations regarding Bill Cosby appeared in 2015. But the *New York Times* did not give the #MeToo movement much coverage until 2016.

226   **62 percent . . . could have worked from home**   These estimates match the occupation of the individual in the IPUMS CPS (2017 census classifications) to one of twenty-two, two-digit aggregate occupation groups from the Bureau of Labor Statistics (BLS) 2018 Standard Occupational Classification (SOC) categorization. The separate BLS occupations were categorized by Dingel and Neiman (2020) in terms of the fraction of jobs that could be done at home using various items in O*NET. They aggregated to the two-digit level using the BLS 2018 Occupational Employment Statistics. I could have used the ability to work from home for each of the more than five hundred occupations listed and then aggregated. But the numbers would not have been very different.

226   **around 60 percent did work remotely**   The CPS from May to December 2020 asked whether the respondent "worked for pay remotely due to the pandemic." The percentage answering in the affirmative fell to 43 percent by December 2020.

226   **additional 5 percent were "employed but not at work"**   Unemployment and "employed but not at work" numbers are computed from the CPS, April 2020.

227   **with at least one child under eighteen years old**   Families are categorized according to the age of the youngest child. There could be more than one child in the family.

227   **an average of 61 percent of the childcare**   That may seem like a low fraction, but the sample families all have employed mothers.

227   **For similar mothers who are not employed**   The mothers are all not working and have a spouse who is working and at least one child less than eighteen years old. The fathers are all working and have a spouse who is not working and at least one child less than eighteen years old.

228   **impact of lockdown on the mothers . . . was to double**   The increase in childcare time has been estimated using large-scale surveys (e.g., Andrew et al. 2020) conducted during the lockdown period, to provide a reasonable sense of the increased burdens on those with preschool and school-aged children. See Online Appendix figure 2A (Epilogue), "Childcare Hours of College-Educated, Employed Mothers with College-Educated, Employed Husbands by the Age of Their Youngest Child."

228   **declined to 61 percent**   These calculations accept the number of hours of childcare given by men. There is considerable evidence from many studies that men overstate their hours of work in the home, especially childcare. But the ATUS makes certain that total hours sum to the total in the day, so any exaggeration for childcare would have to come out of another use of time.

228   **For those with their youngest child in elementary or middle school**   Parents with their youngest child in elementary or middle school had put in fifteen hours per week, and mothers did 58 percent of the total before lockdown. With lockdown, the total amount more than doubled, to thirty-three hours a week, but mothers now did 52 percent of the total for that group.

229   **According to one survey estimate for England**   See Andrew et al. (2020). Pew Research (2020) reports that in October 2020 half the mothers and the fathers working at home experienced interruptions.

229   **What has happened in the AC/DC period**   See Online Appendix figure 2A (Epilogue), "Childcare Hours of College-Educated, Employed Mothers with College-Educated, Employed Husbands by the Age of Their Youngest Child," for estimates done two ways. One method assumes that total parental hours in the AC/DC period are halfway between those in BCE and DC but fathers revert to their BCE hours. The other method has hours for parents with preschool-aged youngest children closer to BCE hours and those with school-aged youngest children closer to DC hours, reflecting the fact that daycares were open when public schools were not.

230   **about 60 percent of all college graduates had headed back**   One of the special questions asked of employed persons in the CPS beginning in May 2020 is "Have you teleworked or worked at home for pay at any time in the last four weeks because of the coronavirus?" In May 2020, 60 percent of all college graduates answered that they had been working from home. In September 2020, just about 40 percent were. The published data are not broken down by gender, but a higher fraction of women in general were working for pay from home than were men in both months.

230   **"It's especially difficult for banks . . ."**   Elisa Martinuzzi and Marcus Ashworth, "Banker Culture Slips in the Pandemic," Bloomberg Opinion, September 25, 2020, https://www.bloomberg.com/opinion/articles/2020-09-25/why-wall-street-wants -bankers-back-in-the-office.

230   **"Those who don't go into a place of work . . ."**   Handley (2020).

230   **in the DC and AC/DC worlds have been about 1.7 times . . . from about 60 percent BCE to around 73 percent AC/DC**   See the previous discussion of the AC/DC

calculation. The AC/DC aggregate numbers are invariant to the two types of assumptions used in the Online Appendix figure 2A (Epilogue) cited above.

231   **women are almost half the total US labor force**   Women are 48 percent of the US civilian labor force, computed from the CPS, January to March 2020. They are also 48 percent among those from eighteen to sixty-four years old.

232   **The Lanham Act, passed in 1943**   The funding for the childcare centers came from the 1941 Defense Public Works law (Title II of the 1940 National Defense Housing Act), which was designed to help communities with various basic needs. It was called the Lanham Act, and the name has stuck.

233   **"Both were authorities . . ."**   Coleman (1968).

233   **Jennie Loitman Barron opened a law practice**   Details from the Jewish Women's Archive Encyclopedia at www.jwa.org.

233   **first woman in the US to earn a civil engineering degree**   "Mrs. Nora S. Barney, Architect, 87, Dies," *New York Times*, January 20, 1971.

233   **". . . the most important thing I have done . . ."**   https://www.npr.org/templates /story/story.php?storyId=128249680.

234   **"when Marty was intent on becoming a partner . . ."**   https://www.mic.com /articles/110848/9-quotes-prove-ruth-bader-ginsburg-has-all-the-relationship-advice -you-ll-ever-need.

234   **In 1964, three-quarters of male and female graduates**   *Great Aspirations* survey of the college class of 1961. (See Source Appendix [Ch5], "*Great Aspirations* Data.")

234   **By 1980, about 60 percent of college graduates**   The General Social Survey (GSS) asked whether respondents agreed that "it is more important for a wife to help her husband's career than to have one herself." Among college graduates of all ages in 1977, 33 percent agreed (same for men and women), and from 1985 to 1990 around 20 percent did, somewhat lower for women than men. The number of observations is small (around 250) for the college graduates in each survey. The last GSS survey to ask the question was in 1998, when about 14 percent agreed.

234   **"both had to make compromises" "alternated who took the lead."**   https:// knowledge.wharton.upenn.edu/article/high-powered-women-and-supportive-spouses -whos-in-charge-and-of-what-2/.

234   **"her career takes off."**   https://knowledge.wharton.upenn.edu/article/high-powered -women-and-supportive-spouses-whos-in-charge-and-of-what-2/.

234   **do not come close to catching up to their male colleagues**   Women in Group Five in figure 7.1 who were 40 to 44 years old have a career and family rate of 22 percent which increases to 31 percent when they are 50 to 54 years old. But comparable men (college graduates) had a career and family rate of around 63 percent for both age groups.

237   **most workers claim they would like to continue . . . Half of those with school-aged children had difficulty working . . . 46 percent had more flexibility**   Pew Research (2020), pp. 4, 14, 23. Note that the data for this study were collected in October 2020.

237   **Some firms have already**   See, for example, "Return-to-Office Plans Are Set in Motion, but Virus Uncertainty Remains," *New York Times*, March 4, 2021.

REFERENCES

AICPA (Association of Independent Certified Public Accountants). 2017. "2017 CPA Firm Gender Survey." Discussed in AICPA, "Women's Initiative Executive Committee." https://www.aicpa.org/content/dam/aicpa/career/womenintheprofession/downloadabledocuments/wiec-2017-cpa-firm-gender-survey-brochure.pdf.

Alsan, Marcella, and Claudia Goldin. 2019. "Watersheds in Child Mortality: The Role of Effective Water and Sewerage Infrastructure," *Journal of Political Economy* 127(2): 586–638.

American Academy of Pediatrics. 2002. Division of Health Policy Research. "Pediatricians Working Part Time: Past, Present, and Future." https://www.aap.org/en-us/professional-resources/Research/Pages/Pediatricians-Working-Part-Time-Past-Present-and-Future.aspx.

American Association of Medical Colleges. 2018. *Physician Specialty Data Report*. Data are from the AMA Masterfile. https://www.aamc.org/data-reports/workforce/interactive-data/active-physicians-sex-and-specialty-2017.

American Medical Association. 2013. *Physician Characteristics and Distribution in the United States*. American Medical Association Press.

American Veterinary Medical Association (AVMA). 2007. *AVMA Report on Veterinary Compensation*. Schaumburg, IL: AVMA.

American Veterinary Medical Association (AVMA). 2009. *AVMA Report on Veterinary Compensation*. Schaumburg, IL: AVMA.

Andrew, Alison, Sarah Cattan, Monica Costa Dias, Christine Farquharson, Lucy Kraftman, Sonya Krutikova, Angus Phimister, and Almudena Sevilla. 2020. "How Are Mothers and Fathers Balancing Work and Family under Lockdown?" Institute for Fiscal Studies (IFS), London, England. May.

Angelov, Nikolay, Per Johansson, and Erica Lindahl. 2016. "Parenthood and the Gender Gap in Pay," *Journal of Labor Economics* 34(3): 545–79.

Antecol, Heather, Kelly Bedard, and Jenna Stearns. 2018. "Equal but Inequitable: Who Benefits from Gender-Neutral Tenure Clock Stopping Policies?," *American Economic Review* 108(9): 2420–441.

Azmat, Ghazala, and Rosa Ferrer. 2017. "Gender Gaps in Performance: Evidence from Young Lawyers," *Journal of Political Economy* 125(5): 1306–355.

Bailey, Martha. 2006. "More Power to the Pill: The Impact of Contraceptive Freedom on Women's Lifecycle Labor Supply," *Quarterly Journal of Economics* 121(1): 289–320.

Bailey, Martha. 2010. "Momma's Got the Pill: How Anthony Comstock and *Griswold v. Connecticut* Shaped US Childbearing," *American Economic Review* 100(1): 98–129.

Bertrand, Marianne, Claudia Goldin, and Lawrence F. Katz. 2010. "Dynamics of the Gender Gap for Young Professionals in the Financial and Corporate Sectors," *American Economic Journal: Applied Economics* 2(3): 228–55.

Bitler, Marianne P., and Lucie Schmidt. 2012. "Utilization of Infertility Treatments: The Effects of Insurance Mandates," *Demography* 49(1): 125–49.

Blau, Francine D., and Lawrence M. Kahn. 1997. "Swimming Upstream: Trends in the Gender Wage Differential in the 1980s," *Journal of Labor Economics* 15(1, Part 1): 1–42.

Blau, Francine D., and Lawrence M. Kahn. 2017. "The Gender Wage Gap: Extent, Trends, and Explanations," *Journal of Economic Literature* 55(3): 789–865.

Bohnet, Iris. 2016. *What Works: Gender Equality by Design*. Cambridge, MA: Harvard University Press.

Boston Women's Health Book Collective. 1970. *Women and Their Bodies: A Course*. https://www.ourbodiesourselves.org/cms/assets/uploads/2014/04/Women-and-Their-Bodies-1970.pdf.

Boston Women's Health Book Collective. 1984. *The New Our Bodies, Ourselves: A Book by and for Women*. New York: A Touchstone Book, Simon & Schuster.

Burke, Jenna, Rani Hoitash, and Udi Hoitash. 2019. "Audit Partner Identification and Characteristics: Evidence from U.S. Form AP Filings," *Auditing: A Journal of Practice & Theory* 38(3): 71–94.

Coleman, Robert G. 1968. "Memorial of Adolph Knopf," *American Mineralogist* 53(3–4): 567–76.

Collins, Gail. 2009. *When Everything Changed: The Amazing Journey of American Women from 1960 to the Present*. New York: Little, Brown and Company.

Cookingham, Mary E. 1984. "Bluestockings, Spinsters and Pedagogues: Women College Graduates: 1865–1910," *Population Studies* 38(3): 649–64.

Cortés, Patricia, and Jessica Pan. 2020. "Children and the Remaining Gender Gaps in the Labor Market." NBER Working Paper No. 27980. October.

CSWEP (Committee on the Status of Women in the Economics Profession). Various years. *Annual Reports*. https://www.aeaweb.org/about-aea/committees/cswep/survey/annual-reports.

Cull, William L., Mary Pat Frintner, Karen G. O'Connor, and Lynn M. Olson. 2016. "Pediatricians Working Part-Time Has Plateaued," *Journal of Pediatrics* 171: 294–99. https://www.jpeds.com/article/S0022-3476(15)01652-2/fulltext.

Currie, Janet, and Enrico Moretti. 2003. "Mother's Education and the Intergenerational Transmission of Human Capital: Evidence from College Openings," *Quarterly Journal of Economics* 118(4): 1495–532.

Davis, James A. 1964. *Great Aspirations: The Graduate School Plans of America's College Seniors*. Chicago, IL: Aldine Publishing Company.

Davis, Katharine Bement. 1928. "Why They Failed to Marry," *Harper's Magazine* 156 (March): 460–69.

Davis, Katharine Bement. 1929. *Factors in the Sex Life of Twenty-Two Hundred Women*. New York: Harper and Brothers. https://archive.org/details/factorsinsexlifeoodavi/page/n25.

Deryugina, Tatyana, Olga Shurchkov, and Jenna E. Steans. 2021. "COVID 19 Disruptions Disproportionately Affect Female Academics." NBER Working Paper No. 28360. January.

Dingel, Jonathan I., and Brent Neiman. 2020. "How Many Jobs Can be Done at Home?" NBER Working Paper No. 26948. April; revised June.

Durand, John Dana. 1948. *The Labor Force in the United States, 1890–1960.* New York: Social Science Research Council.

Easterlin, Richard A. 1980. *Birth and Fortune: The Impact of Numbers on Personal Welfare.* New York: Basic Books.

Finer, Lawrence B. 2007. "Trends in Premarital Sex in the United States, 1954–2003," *Public Health Reports* (Jan/Feb): 73–78.

Flaherty, Colleen. 2020. "Women are Falling Behind." *Inside Higher Ed.* October 20.

Folbre, Nancy. 2001. *The Invisible Heart: Economics and Family Values.* New York: New Press.

Friedan, Betty. 2013. Orig. pub. 1963. *The Feminine Mystique.* 50th Anniversary Edition. New York: W.W. Norton and Company.

Garbes, Angela. 2021. "The Numbers Don't Tell the Whole Story." *New Yorker.* February 1.

Gilette, Moriah. 2018. "Profile of Katharine Bement Davis." In A. Rutherford, ed., *Psychology's Feminist Voices Multimedia Internet Archive.* Retrieved from http://www.feministvoices.com/katharine-bement-davis/.

Ginther, Donna K., and Shulamit Kahn. 2004. "Women in Economics: Moving Up or Falling Off the Academic Career Ladder?" *Journal of Economic Perspectives* 18(3): 193–214.

Goldin, Claudia. 1977. "Female Labor Force Participation: The Origin of Black and White Differences, 1870 to 1880," *Journal of Economic History* 37(1): 87–108.

Goldin, Claudia. 1990. *Understanding the Gender Gap: An Economic History of American Women.* New York: Oxford University Press.

Goldin, Claudia. 1991. "Marriage Bars: Discrimination against Married Women Workers from the 1920s to the 1950s." In Henry Rosovsky, David Landes, and Patrice Higonnet, eds., *Favorites of Fortune: Technology, Growth, and Economic Development since the Industrial Revolution.* Cambridge, MA: Harvard University Press: 511–36.

Goldin, Claudia. 1997. "Career and Family: College Women Look to the Past." In R. Ehrenberg and F. Blau, eds., *Gender and Family Issues in the Workplace.* New York: Russell Sage Foundation Press.

Goldin, Claudia. 2004. "The Long Road to the Fast Track: Career and Family," *Annals of the American Academy of Political and Social Science* 596(November): 20–35.

Goldin, Claudia. 2005. "From the Valley to the Summit: A Brief History of the Quiet Revolution that Transformed Women's Work," *Regional Review* 14(Q1): 5–12.

Goldin, Claudia. 2006. "The 'Quiet Revolution' That Transformed Women's Employment, Education, and Family," *American Economic Review* (Ely Lecture), 96(2): 1–21.

Goldin, Claudia. 2014. "A Grand Gender Convergence: Its Last Chapter," *American Economic Review* 104(4): 1091–119.

Goldin, Claudia. 2014a. "A Pollution Theory of Discrimination: Male and Female Differences in Occupations and Earnings." In Leah Boustan, Carola Frydman, and Robert A. Margo, eds., *Human Capital and History: The American Record.* Chicago: University of Chicago Press: 313–48.

Goldin, Claudia, and Lawrence F. Katz. 2002. "The Power of the Pill: Oral Contraceptives and Women's Career and Marriage Decisions," *Journal of Political Economy* 110(4): 730–70.

Goldin, Claudia, and Lawrence F. Katz. 2008. *The Race between Education and Technology.* Cambridge, MA: Belknap Press.

Goldin, Claudia, and Lawrence F. Katz. 2008a. "Transitions: Career and Family Life Cycles of the Educational Elite," *American Economic Review: Papers & Proceedings* 98(2): 363–69.

Goldin, Claudia, and Lawrence F. Katz. 2011. "Putting the 'Co' in Education: Timing, Reasons, and Consequences of College Coeducation from 1835 to the Present," *Journal of Human Capital* 5(4): 377–417.

Goldin, Claudia, and Lawrence F. Katz. 2016. "A Most Egalitarian Profession: Pharmacy and the Evolution of a Family Friendly Occupation," *Journal of Labor Economics* 34(3): 705–46.

Goldin, Claudia, and Lawrence F. Katz. 2018. "Women Working Longer: Facts and Some Explanations." In C. Goldin and L. Katz, eds., *Women Working Longer: Increased Employment at Older Ages*. Chicago: University of Chicago Press.

Goldin, Claudia, Lawrence F. Katz, and Ilyana Kuziemko. 2006. "The Homecoming of American College Women: The Reversal of the College Gender Gap," *Journal of Economic Perspectives* 20(4): 133–56.

Goldin, Claudia, Sari Pekkala Kerr, and Claudia Olivetti. 2020. "Why Firms Offer Paid Parental Leave: An Exploratory Study." NBER Working Paper no. 26617. January. In Isabel Sawhill and Betsey Stevenson, eds., *Paid Leave for Caregiving: Issues and Answers*. Washington, DC: AEI/Brookings Institution.

Goldin, Claudia, Sari Pekkala Kerr, Claudia Olivetti, and Erling Barth. 2017. "The Expanding Gender Earnings Gap: Evidence from the LEHD-2000 Census," *American Economic Review, Papers & Proceedings* 107(5): 110–14.

Goldin, Claudia, and Joshua Mitchell. 2017. "The New Lifecycle of Women's Employment: Disappearing Humps, Sagging Middles, Expanding Tops," *Journal of Economic Perspectives* 31(1): 161–82.

Goldin, Claudia, and Cecilia Rouse. 2000. "Orchestrating Impartiality: The Impact of 'Blind' Auditions on Female Musicians," *American Economic Review* 90(4): 715–41.

Goldin, Claudia, and Maria Shim. 2004. "Making a Name: Women's Surnames at Marriage and Beyond," *Journal of Economic Perspectives* 18(2): 143–60.

Greenwood, Jeremy. 2019. *Evolving Households: The Imprint of Technology on Life*. Cambridge, MA: MIT Press.

Greenwood, Jeremy, Ananth Seshadri, and Mehmet Yorukoglu. 2005. "Engines of Liberation," *Review of Economic Studies* 72(1): 109–33.

Grunwald, Lisa, and Stephen J. Adler, eds. 2005. *Women's Letters: America from the Revolutionary War to the Present*. New York: Dial Press.

Guryan, Jonathan, Erik Hurst, and Melissa Kearney. 2008. "Parental Education and Parental Time with Children," *Journal of Economic Perspectives* 22(3): 23–46.

Handley, Lucy. 2020. "Companies Will Have to 'Seduce' Staff to Go Back to the Office, Real Estate CEO Says." In *Our New Future*, McKinsey and Company report. September 29.

Hegewisch, Ariane, and Heidi Hartmann. 2014. *Occupational Segregation and the Gender Wage Gap: A Job Half Done*. Institute for Women's Policy Research report. January.

HERI CIRP (Astin) Freshman Survey. https://heri.ucla.edu/cirp-freshman-survey/.

Hewlett, Sylvia Ann. 2008. *Off-Ramps and On-Ramps: Keeping Talented Women on the Road to Success*. Cambridge, MA: Harvard Business Press.

Horowitz, Daniel. 1998. *Betty Friedan and the Making of "The Feminine Mystique": The American Left, the Cold War, and Modern Feminism*. Amherst: University of Massachusetts Press.

Hsieh, Chang-Tai, Charles I. Jones, Erik Hurst, and Peter J. Klenow. 2019. "The Allocation of Talent and U.S. Economic Growth," *Econometrica* 87(5): 1439–74

Hwang, Jisoo. 2016. "Housewife, 'Gold Miss,' and Educated: The Evolution of Educated Women's Role in Asia and the U.S.," *Journal of Population Economics* 29(2): 529–70.

Isen, Adam, and Betsey Stevenson. 2010. "Women's Education and Family Behavior Trends in Marriage, Divorce, and Fertility." In J. Shoven, ed., *Demography and the Economy*. Chicago: University of Chicago Press: 107–40.

James, Edward T., Janet Wilson James, and Paul S. Boyer, eds. 1971. *Notable American Women, 1607–1950: A Biographical Dictionary*. Vol. 1–3. Cambridge, MA: Harvard University Press.

Kleven, Henrik, Camille Landais, Johanna Posch, Andreas Steinhauer, and Josef Zweimüller. 2019. "Child Penalties across Countries: Evidence and Explanations," *AEA Papers and Proceedings* 109(May): 122–26.

Kleven, Henrik, Camille Landais, and Jakob Egholt Søgaard. 2019. "Children and Gender Inequality: Evidence from Denmark," *American Economic Journal: Applied Economics* 11(4): 181–209.

Komarovsky, Mirra. 1985. *Women in College: Shaping New Feminine Identities*. New York: Basic Books.

Krentz, Matthew. 2017. "Men Wanted: How Men Can Increase Gender Parity." LinkedIn October. https://www.linkedin.com/pulse/men-wanted-how-can-increase-gender-parity-matt-krentz/.

Ledbetter, Lilly, and Lanier Scott Isom. 2012. *Grace and Grit: My Fight for Equal Pay and Fairness at Goodyear and Beyond*. New York: Three Rivers Press, Crown Publishers.

Lemann, Nicholas. 2000. *The Big Test: The Secret History of the American Meritocracy*. New York: Farrar, Straus, and Giroux.

Lepore, Jill. 2018. "Ruth Bader Ginsburg's Unlikely Path to the Supreme Court." *New Yorker*. October 1.

Lundberg, Shelly, Robert A. Pollak, and Jenna Stearns. 2016. "Family Inequality: Diverging Patterns in Marriage, Cohabitation, and Childbearing," *Journal of Economic Perspectives* 30(2): 79–102.

Manning, Wendy D., Susan L. Brown, and Bart Stykes. 2015. "Trends in Births to Single and Cohabiting Mothers, 1980–2013." Family Profiles FP-15-03, National Center for Family and Marriage Research.

McCarthy, Mary. 1963. *The Group*. New York: Harcourt, Brace & World.

McCracken, Douglas M. 2000. "Winning the Talent War for Women: Sometimes It Takes a Revolution," *Harvard Business Review* (Nov.–Dec.). Reprint R00611.

Medscape. 2018. "Female Physician Compensation Report." https://www.medscape.com/slideshow/2018-compensation-female-physician-6010006#23.

Menken, Jane, James Trussell, and Ulla Larsen. 1986. "Age and Infertility," *Science* 233(4771): 1389–394.

Midwest Pharmacy Workforce Research Consortium. 2000. *Final Report of the National Pharmacist Workforce Survey: 2000*. Alexandria, VA: Pharmacy Manpower Project.

Midwest Pharmacy Workforce Research Consortium. 2005. *Final Report of the 2004 National Sample Survey of the Pharmacist Workforce to Determine Contemporary Demographic and Practice Characteristics*. Alexandria, VA: Pharmacy Manpower Project.

Midwest Pharmacy Workforce Research Consortium. 2010. *Final Report of the 2009 National Pharmacist Workforce Survey to Determine Contemporary Demographic and Practice Characteristics.* Alexandria, VA: Pharmacy Manpower Project.

Molina, V. Sue. 2005. "Changing the Face of Consulting: The Women's Initiative at Deloitte," *Regional Review of the Federal Reserve Bank of Boston* (Q1): 42–43.

National Education Association (NEA). 1928. *Practices Affecting Teacher Personnel.* Research Bulletin of the NEA, VI(4). Washington, DC: NEA. September.

National Education Association (NEA). 1932. *Administrative Practices Affecting Classroom Teachers.* Part I: *The Selection and Appointment of Teachers and Retention, Promotion, and Improvement of Teachers.* Research Bulletin of the NEA, X(1). Washington, DC: NEA. January.

National Education Association (NEA). 1942. *Teacher Personnel Procedures: Selection and Appointment.* Research Bulletin of the NEA, XX(2). Washington, DC: NEA. March.

National Education Association (NEA). 1952. *Teacher Personnel Practices. 1950–51: Appointment and Termination of Service.* Research Bulletin of the NEA, XXX(1). Washington, DC: NEA. February.

Niederle, Muriel, and Lise Vesterlund. 2007. "Do Women Shy Away from Competition? Do Men Compete too Much?" *Quarterly Journal of Economics,* 122(3): 1067–101.

Office of History and Preservation, Office of the Clerk, US House of Representatives. 2006. *Women in Congress: 1917–2006.* Washington, DC: US GPO.

Office of History and Preservation, Office of the Clerk, US House of Representatives. 2008. *Black Americans in Congress: 1870–2007.* Washington, DC: US GPO.

Olivetti, Claudia. 2006. "Changes in Women's Hours of Market Work: The Role of Returns to Experience," *Review of Economic Dynamics* 9(4): 557–87.

Olivetti, Claudia, and Barbara Petrongolo. 2017. "The Economic Consequences of Family Policies: Lessons from a Century of Legislation in High-Income Countries," *Journal of Economic Perspectives* 31(1): 205–30.

O'Neill, June, and Solomon Polachek. 1993. "Why the Gender Gap in Wages Narrowed in the 1980s," *Journal of Labor Economics* 11(1): 205–28.

Pedersen, Sharon. 1987. "Married Women and the Right to Teach in St. Louis, 1941–1948," *Missouri Historical Review* 81(2): 141–58.

Pew Research. 2010. "The Decline of Marriage and Rise of New Families." November 18.

Pew Research. 2012. "Social and Demographic Trends Project, 2012 Gender and Generations Survey." November/December.

Pew Research. 2017. "Gender Discrimination Comes in Many Forms for Today's Working Women." Kim Parker and Cary Funk. July/August.

Pew Research. 2020. "How the Coronavirus Outbreak Has—and Hasn't—Changed the Way Americans Work." Kim Parker, Juliana Horowitz, and Rachel Minkin. December. https://www.pewresearch.org/social-trends/2020/12/09/how-the-coronavirus-outbreak-has-and-hasnt-changed-the-way-americans-work/.

Preston, Samuel H., and Michael R. Haines. 1991. *Fatal Years: Child Mortality in Late Nineteenth-Century America.* Princeton, NJ: Princeton University Press.

Ramey, Garey, and Valerie Ramey. 2010. "The Rug Rat Race," *Brookings Papers on Economic Activity* (Spring): 129–99.

Reid, Margaret G. 1934. *Economics of Household Production.* New York: John Wiley & Sons.

Rotella, Elyce J. 1981. *From Home to Office: U.S. Women at Work, 1870–1930*. Ann Arbor, MI: UMI Research Press.

Rotz, Dana. 2016. "Why Have Divorce Rates Fallen?: The Role of Women's Age at Marriage," *Journal of Human Resources* 51(4): 961–1002.

Rubin, Lillian B. 1994. *Families on the Fault Line: America's Working Class Speaks about the Family, the Economy, Race, and Ethnicity*. New York: Harper Collins.

Seim, David L. 2008. "The Butter-Margarine Controversy and 'Two Cultures' at Iowa State College," *The Annals of Iowa* 67(1): 1–50.

Shinn, Milicent Washburn. 1895. "The Marriage Rate of College Women," *Century Magazine* 50 (1895): 946–48.

Sicherman, Barbara, and Carol Hurd Green, eds. 1980. *Notable American Women: A Biographical Dictionary*. Vol. 4. *The Modern Period*. Cambridge, MA: Belknap Press.

Smith, Daniel Scott, and Michael S. Hindus. 1975. "Premarital Pregnancy in America 1640–1971: An Overview and Interpretation," *Journal of Interdisciplinary History* 5(4): 537–70.

Solomon, Barbara Miller. 1985. *In the Company of Educated Women: A History of Women and Higher Education in America*. New Haven, CT: Yale University Press.

Solomon, Barbara Miller. 1989. "Radcliffe Alumnae Questionnaires of 1928 and 1944." Data archive listing. Henry A. Murray Research Center at Radcliffe.

Steinmann, Marion, and "the Women of the Cornell Class of 1950." 2005. *Women at Work: Demolishing a Myth of the 1950s*. Bloomington, IN: Xlibris Corporation.

Stevenson, Betsey. 2007. "The Impact of Divorce Laws on Marriage-Specific Capital," *Journal of Labor Economics* 25(1): 75–94.

Stevenson, Betsey, and Justin Wolfers. 2007. "Marriage and Divorce: Changes and Their Driving Forces," *Journal of Economic Perspectives* 21(2): 27–52.

US Bureau of the Census. 1904. *1900 Census Special Reports: Occupations at the Twelfth Census*. Washington, DC: US GPO.

US Bureau of the Census. 1933. *1930 Census: Volume 4. Occupations, by States. Reports by States, Giving Statistics for Cities of 25,000 or More*. Washington, DC: US GPO.

US Congress. 1934. *National Income, 1929–32*. 73d Congress, 2d Session. Document No. 124. Washington, DC: US GPO.

US Department of Education, NCES. Various years. *Digest of Education Statistics*. U.S. GPO. See also: https://nces.ed.gov/programs/digest/.

US Department of Labor, Women's Bureau. 1959. "First Jobs of College Women: Report of Women Graduates, Class of 1957," Women's Bureau Bulletin no. 268. Washington, DC: US GPO.

US Department of Labor, Women's Bureau. 1966. "College Women Seven Years after Graduation: Resurvey of Women Graduates—Class of 1957," Women's Bureau Bulletin no. 292. Washington, DC: US GPO.

Ware, Susan, and Stacy Lorraine Braukman, eds. 2004. *Notable American Women: A Biographical Dictionary*. Vol. 5. *Completing the Twentieth Century*. Cambridge, MA: Belknap Press.

Wolfers, Justin. 2006. "Did Unilateral Divorce Laws Raise Divorce Rates? A Reconciliation and New Results," *American Economic Review* 96(5): 1802–20.

Yohalem, Alice M. 1979. *The Careers of Professional Women: Commitment and Conflict*. Montclair, NJ: Allanheld Osmun.

Zimmerman, Seth. 2014. "The Returns to College Admission for Academically Marginal Students," *Journal of Labor Economics* 32(4): 711–54.

INDEX

Note: Page numbers in *italics* refer to figures and tables. End notes are indicated by n and page of original topic discussion following the page number.

of, 98–103, 276nn95,98, 277n101; Class of
1961 survey of, 103–8, 277n103; divorce
in, 29–30, 31, 263nn29,31; drop-out rates
among, 85, 86–87, 274n87; education in,
29–30, 39–45, *41*, 86, 91–92, 95–96, 101–2,
104, 105–6, 112, 124, 274n86, 276n95, 277n101,
278n104; employment rates and experiences
in, 29–30, 38, 39–40, 87, 88–91, 95–96,
98–103, 106–8, 112, 123–24, 141–42, *143*,
145, 233–34, 274n88, 277n103; family then
job in, 29–30, 88, 96, 106, 108, 141–42;
Friedan's critique of, 85–87, 92, 95, 96–97,
101, 108; game plan of, 96–107; gender
earnings gap for, 157, 160; graduation
years of, *24*, 29; lessons from, 25, 31–32,
112, 123–24, 126; marriage in, 29–30, 33–36,
34, 39, 43–44, 86–88, 91–95, 98–99, 103–4,
116, 118, *118*, 233–34, 275n91, 278n104;
overview of, *24*, 29–30; serial lives of, 97;
social norms influencing, 99–100, *100*, 103,
104–5, 108; societal changes for, 92–95;
TV show images of, 84–85, 87–88, 100–101
Group Four (graduating around mid-1960s
to 1970s), 109–32; ambitions and aspirations of, 124–32; birth years of, *24*, 30,
142, 284n139; career then family in, 30–33,
112–13, 115–16; childbearing and childrear-
ing in, 32, 36–38, *37, 39,* 44, 113, 115–16, 119,
121, 132, 138–39, 142, *143,* 279n116, 284nn139,
141; contraception access in, 32, 109–12,
113, 115, 120–23, 236, 278n110; divorce in,
31–32, 115, 118–19, 263n31, 279–80nn118–119;
education in, 30–33, 39–45, *41*, 112–13, 115,
117, 122, 127–30, *129*, 139, 146, 199, 284n139;
employment rates and experiences in,
30–33, 38, 39–40, 107, 112–13, 119–20, 123–27,
125, 130–32, *131*, 142, *143*, 146, 280–81nn124,
126, 282nn130,132; expanded horizons of,
124–32; gender earnings gap for, 132, 157,
160, 224–25; graduation years of, *24*, 30;
Group Three lessons for, 25, 31–32, 112,
123–24, 126; identities in, 119, 121, 131–32;
lessons from, 23, 25, 134–35; marriage in,

30–36, *34, 39,* 44, 113, 115–18, *118*, 121–22,
236, 279nn116–17; names in, 119; overview
of, *24*, 30–33; Quiet Revolution in, 109,
111–12, 119–24, 236; social norm changes
for, 120, 123–32; TV show images of, 109,
111–12, 116, 236
Group Five (graduating around 1980s to
1990s, and beyond), 133–50; age and
career advancement in, 198; ambitions
and aspirations of, 134–35, 234, 283n134;
birth years of, 19, *24*, 33, 284n139, 296n222;
career and family in, 33, 134–35, 147–50,
149, 299n234; childbearing and childrear-
ing in, 33, 36–38, *37, 39*, 133–34, 135–41,
142, *143,* 147–50, *149*, 236, 282–83nn133–134,
284nn139,141; COVID-19 pandemic
effects on, 222–23; Duckworth in, 19, 20,
24; education in, 33, 39–45, *41*, 139, 148–49,
149, 284n139; employment rates and
experiences in, 33, 38, *39–40*, 126, 134–35,
142–50, *143, 149*; gender earnings gap for,
157, 160, *161*, 161–62, 225; graduation years
of, *24*, 33; Group Four lessons for, 23, 25,
134–35; marriage in, 33–36, *34, 39*, 117, *118*,
147, 236, 264n36; overview of, *24*, 33;
success defined by, 141–47, 255–57; TV
and film images of, 133–34, 282n133
GSS (General Social Survey), 100, *100*, 104,
278n104, 299n234

Harris, Kamala, 236
Harvard and Beyond project, 147–50, *149*,
169, 210, 257, 288n164, 293n210
Harvard-Radcliffe. *See* Radcliffe-Harvard
College
Hassan, Maggie Wood, 146
Health and Retirement Study, 256–57
health issues: argument of college leading
to, 58; COVID-19 as (*see* COVID-19
pandemic); employment necessitated by,
58, 91; mortality rates and, 52–53; unsafe
working conditions as, 72
high school movement, 71

A NOTE ON THE TYPE

This book has been composed in Arno, an Old-style serif typeface in the classic Venetian tradition, designed by Robert Slimbach at Adobe.

DISCUSSION QUESTIONS

1. Do you identify with the idea of "greedy work"? Has that brought disparities in your own life—or that of your friends and relatives—into view?

2. Goldin returns again and again to the groups. Did that help you understand the lives of your mother, grandmother, or other members of an older generation and the progress made?

3. In considering the "passing of the baton from one generation to another," what did each do for the next?

4. Describe the role of the Pill for Group 4, and what later marriage and childbearing meant for their careers. What technologies changed across history that had profound impacts on women's economic role?

5. How has the pandemic put into focus disparities between sexes in the workforce?

6. Did you consider flexibility (how many hours, which hours, when the hours are scheduled, whether the hours are predictable) a key aspect of the field you went into, specific jobs, or career paths you have taken? And if you are married, did your spouse?

7. Do you work in a career with a greedy job? And if not, could you speak about your experience of transitioning some of your work to colleagues and then getting back into it after any kind of caretaking leave?

8. Would you advise your daughters or the young adult women in your lives to consider how greedy their occupation might be before they become emotionally invested or pursue education or training?

9. To what extent do you think the book's central message will resonate with men?

10. Do you see the solutions that Goldin proposes as achievable? What aspects of the problem seem more likely to be overcome than others?

11. Has this book changed the way you see career and family, and the so-called balance?